Thomas Hardy and Visual Structures

THOMAS HARDY AND VISUAL STRUCTURES

Framing, Disruption, Process

SHEILA BERGER

New York University Press
New York and London

Copyright © 1990 by New York University
All rights reserved
Manufactured in the United States of America

Library of Congress Cataloging-in-Publication Data

Berger, Sheila, 1935–
Thomas Hardy and visual structures : framing, disruption, process
Sheila Berger.
p. cm.
Includes bibliographical references.
ISBN 0-8147-1142-1 (alk. paper)
1. Hardy, Thomas, 1840–1928—Technique.
2. Visual perception in literature.
3. Description (Rhetoric)
I. Title.
PR4757.T4B47 1990
823'.8—dc20
90-33270
CIP

New York University Press books are printed on
acid free paper, and their binding materials
are chosen for strength and durability.

To my son,
Jamie,
whose delight in words
renews my own

Contents

Acknowledgments ix
Preface xi
Reference Abbreviations xv

Part One: Iconology and Epistemology in Thomas Hardy's Works

1. The Image and the Eye 3

Part Two: Parts of the Picture: Visual Structures

2. Image as Icon 21
3. Framed Images 55
4. Disrupted Images 91
5. Relationships within the Image 133

Part Three: The Whole Picture

6. Metamorphosis 157
7. A Final Frame 188

Notes 193
Bibliography 211
Index 221

Acknowledgments

I am pleased to acknowledge those who have helped to complete this study. Thanks go to my colleagues at the State University of New York at Albany, Walter Knotts, whose intelligent and enthusiastic comments helped to sustain me from start to finish, and Randall Craig, whose response to reading the completed manuscript—a thumbs-up sign and twenty-one pages of notations—were welcome guidelines as I started the manuscript's first revision. My greatest appreciation goes to John Maynard, New York University, my dissertation director and now my colleague, whose wise and perceptive readings and generous support of my work helped bring it to its final form, this book.

I also wish to recognize sources within the State University of New York at Albany that have assisted me—the Department of English with released time to do research and the University with its financial support from the Faculty Research Award Program.

Preface

This book is a study of an imagination massively visual and with a double vision. Studies of Thomas Hardy's picture-making are not wanting. They emphasize his knowledge of painters, paintings, painterly methods, and cinematic methods, and they examine questions of perception generally. Such studies frequently stress his use of visualizations to convey narrative movement, characterization, theme, idea, feeling. My study, however, rather than explain how visual structures are used or what they mean, teaches a new way to see them. Reading Hardy can at times be like walking through a mine field; unlikely shapes will explode through what had seemed to be familiar territory. Even at calmer moments, almost every page is like a magician's crystal ball; a shape will rise to the surface. Using an iconological approach, aided by theories on art and the psychology of perception, I have tried to discover what precisely Hardy's visual structures are: How do they come into being? Are they constructed on any particular system or pattern? Why are they so stunningly effective? Why are they there at all? The critical perspective of this book does not seek to explain the unity of individual works; rather, its aim is to grasp the texture of Hardy's visualizing language as it exists in all his writing.

Hardy is an anti-systemic and deeply skeptical thinker, attracted to the emotional rather than rational aspects in human beings, stressing the human will and the subjectivity with which people learn their "reality." As an empiricist, he stressed the senses—primarily the visual sense—as the basis for knowledge. Sight, however, does not spontaneously mean knowledge. Hardy's epistemology can be summed up as a meeting of the senses, emotions, imagination, human will, and the external world to produce knowledge. Though his prose and poetry are permeated with an extraordinary visual quality, seemingly embedded in concreteness, it is the element of subjective perception—shifting and non-authoritative "impressions of the moment"—that is even more powerful in the knowing of/creation of reality. Human beings find themselves in a world of flux and unknowns. To negotiate with this universe, they tend to enlarge experience into meaning: images become icons as human beings turn objects into metaphors and myths. This creative activity is the process through which Hardy creates aesthetic structures and his characters create their lives. We come to know the characters and they come to know each other and reality through what they see, how they see it, and how they say it.

Chapter 1 begins with the double meaning of a word, "impression": external matter and subjective vision, the image and the eye. This double vision contains the seeds from which my entire study has grown. Several pivotal concepts have emerged in my coming to comprehend the full texture of Hardy's vision: framing, disruption, and process. The fundamental process is the movement of image into icon, a metaphoric construction. This movement develops into a continuing series of visualizations, metaphoric structures of framing and disruption, a metamorphosis of images. By devoting separate chapters to the visual structures by which images are made into icons, images are framed, images are disrupted, and relationships within the image are drawn, I have tried to slow down the process to present—in individual images and in the major formations of the whole movement—the flexible and complex processes of Hardy's poetic thought.

Visual thinking is at the core of Hardy's aesthetics. Seeing for him is not a metaphor for knowing; it is a form of knowing. He saw the essential lines and shapes of everything and tried to let the reader see them, too. The whole world of human concerns seems to have passed through his imagination to become knowledge in the form of visual structures. He knew what he knew by observing the surface of things because his modern perspective of a chaotic universe, without absolute meaning or value, could conceive of no other way to know. If he wished to paint the odor of flesh or the soul outside the body, to make hidden energies visible, it was to pull them forth and make them present in a world of surfaces. Nevertheless, the intensity with which he sees ultimately provides meaning to this world of surfaces only. The existence of external matter as the only reality must exclude any imaginative comprehension; however, an unmediated belief in the value of subjective perception must privilege inner consciousness and vision. Hardy—despite his position as materialist, skeptic, positivist—could not finally be content with cold and lifeless matter; however, neither could he accept the idea of a god in the skies or in the self. The result is an unresolved tension and a dynamic play among images. The image and the eye are not the two parts of a harmonious unity, just as framing and disruption are not two parts of a balanced whole. Rather, these are opposition points of tension, metaphoric of the collision and resulting destabilization from which new metaphors and meanings can emerge.

That oppositions are central to framing meaning is not inappropriate in the irrational world of Thomas Hardy. Indeed, along with visual thinking, a sense of contradiction—unresolved tensions, incongruity, ambiguity, ambivalence—rests at the core of his writing: particularity versus abstraction, belief versus skepticism, mythmaking versus material reality, change versus stasis, imagination versus fact. The sense of contradiction keeps the reader from adopting a single or simple understanding of a text and provides a riveting vitality to the texture of images. In short, intensely realized visualizations placed in the context of intense antagonisms are precisely what produce Hardy's poetic process and reinvest his world of surfaces with a new significance in the creative process itself. One must not look through Hardy's pictures but at them to find meaning. Impressions, unexplained and unsystematized, emerge spontaneously and chaotically; they change, disappear, reappear; the reader is pulled toward their surfaces to create a sense of the relationship among the images: to create reality.

Hardy used so fluid a form in almost everything he wrote, or at least included poetic movement as a somewhat submerged but subversive presence even in his most highly structured works, and confronted the farthest points on his spectrum of oppositions. Such writing hardly presents fatalism or pessimism or any other static and monistic abstraction of the sort too often and simplistically assigned to him. His text displays a mind indeterminate, a sensibility in conflict with itself and unwilling or unable to avoid the conflict; Hardy, too, is in process. It is the vision of his complex imagination that the following pages explore.

Reference Abbreviations

References to the novels are to the New Wessex Edition (paperback) (London: Macmillan, 1974).

UGWT	*Under the Greenwood Tree*
PBE	*A Pair of Blue Eyes*
FFMC	*Far from the Madding Crowd*
RN	*The Return of the Native*
L	*A Laodicean*
MC	*The Mayor of Casterbridge*
W	*The Woodlanders*
TD	*Tess of the d'Urbervilles*
JO	*Jude the Obscure*

Other works by Hardy are cited from the following editions:

CP	*The Complete Poems of Thomas Hardy,* New Wessex Edition, ed. James Gibson (London: Macmillan, 1976)
D	*The Dynasts* (London: Macmillan, 1977)
Life	Florence Emily Hardy, *The Life of Thomas Hardy* (Hamden, Conn.: Archon Books, 1970)

PART ONE

ICONOLOGY AND EPISTEMOLOGY IN THOMAS HARDY'S WORKS

Chapter 1

The Image and the Eye

Thomas Hardy is finally being accepted on his own terms. In *The Life of Thomas Hardy,* the prefaces, and the essays he repeatedly stated that a novel is an "impression, not an argument,"[1] "a series of seemings, or personal impressions";[2] that his poems are "a series of feelings and fancies . . . possess[ing] little cohesion of thought";[3] and that "unadjusted impressions have their values. . . ."[4] And again, in the Preface to his collected works, the Wessex Edition of 1912, he stated that the works should be regarded as "mere impressions of the moment, and not convictions or arguments."[5] Examining two meanings of the single word "impression" will carry one a long way toward following Hardy's advice on how to read fiction: "Catch the vision which the writer has in his eye, and is endeavoring to project upon the paper, even while it half eludes him."[6]

First, Hardy's impressions are personal, subjective, tentative observations—a way of thinking, feeling, and seeing life from a particular perspective and at a particular moment: a surmise. Statements from the life are explicit on this position:

> As, in looking at a carpet, by following one colour a certain pattern is suggested, by following another colour, another; so in life the seer should watch the pattern among general things which his idiosyncrasy moves him to observe, and describe that alone. This is, quite accurately, a going to Nature; yet the result is no mere photograph, but purely the product of the writer's own mind. (*Life*, 153)
>
> Art consists in so depicting the common events of life as to bring out the feature which illustrates the author's idiosyncratic mode of regard. (*Life*, 225)

Hardy's insistence upon the artist's unique vision is matched by his antagonism toward consistency and rationality. He appreciates drama in literature because it "appeal[s] to the emotional reason rather than to the logical reason; for by their emotions men are acted upon, and act upon others."[7] "My own interest," said Hardy, "lies largely in non-rationalistic subjects since non–rationality seems, so far as one can perceive, to be the principle of the Universe" (*Life*, 309). Using the dramatic method he appreciates, Hardy depicts his philosophy as "only a confused heap of impressions, like those of a bewildered child at a conjuring show" (*Life*, 410).

His second vital meaning of "impression" lets us see what the "bewildered child" might see. It is an imprint, an indentation, a stamp; it is the transformation of Hardy's observations into sensory experience, especially visualizations. Hardy's pictures, moving or still, are what a reader remembers: not Sergeant Troy's sentimentality, but water plunging from a gargoyle's jaws; not the character of Bathsheba so much as a figure supremely displayed atop a wagon or terrifyingly etched in air by a flashing sword; not Christminister, but a distant halo or Christminister cakes. We recall a woman's figure rising above a barrow "like a spike from a helmet"; a red man moving across a heath; a scarlet ace of hearts on a white ceiling; a "face, and the God-crust sun, and a tree, / And a pond edged with grayish leaves." Mayor Henchard sits at a formal dinner, wine glasses empty, imaged forever in the frame of an open window. Long after the events of narrative fade, the pictures—and in effect the events—remain,

The Image and the Eye

for the picture is the great event in Thomas Hardy. The ordinary, the bizarre, the grotesque; people, things, experiences, emotions—all issue forth in pictures. The image of Hardy at age sixty-nine on New Year's Eve "crouched by the fire [to hear] in the silence of the night the ringing of the muffled peal down the chimney of his bedroom" (*Life*, 348) is emblematic of his avid quest to sense life. He wanted human experience to be etched on the surface; to be outlined, delineated. His response to snowdrifts—"sculptured, scooped, gouged, pared, trowelled, moulded" (*Life*, 233)—lets us overhear a writer devise ways to see and shape reality with language. His objective was not realism, but impressionism:

> The "simply natural" is interesting no longer. The much decried, mad, late-Turner rendering is now necessary to create my interest. The exact truth as to material fact ceases to be of importance in art—it is a student's style—the style of a period when the mind is serene and unawakened to the tragical mysteries of life; when it does not bring anything to the object that coalesces with and translates the qualities that are already there,—half-hidden, it may be—and the two united are depicted as the All. (*Life*, 185)

In a single word, "impression," and in its double but interrelated meanings, Hardy unites the two major strategies used to convey his art and thought, visual structure and subjective vision: the image and the eye.

That people, including critics, see what they need to see is one of the realities described in Thomas Hardy's works and borne out in their critical reception. However, after two generations have tried to press Hardy into the roles of systematic philosopher and realist, he is now welcomed as a modern expressionist, with critical attention directed toward "catch[ing] the vision which the writer [had] in his eye."[8] Morton Zabel, in the 1940 Centennial issue of *Southern Review*, with acuteness and comprehension caught Hardy's modern outlook and style. He notes that Hardy uses a "poetic method" in fiction through his "tendency toward metaphorical values." Furthermore, he gives appropriate weight to Hardy's assumptions about the validity of subjectivity, both in literature and in life, observing Hardy's resistance to "formulations of a logic of experience or history" and his attraction to the positive aspects of instinct and emotion; his belief that a "reality" can be created through imagination; and his sensitivity to people's need to achieve a consciousness of the relationship between their individuality and the all but incomprehensible universe.[9]

In 1949 Albert Guerard's full-length *Thomas Hardy* further established a new approach, defending Hardy against those who saw him as excessively harsh in outlook and undisciplined in style, redefining him as a "deliberate anti-realist" who used expressionistic means to convey his modern, absurdist perspective.[10] Hardy's modern, absurdist position, more fully described by David DeLaura, is noted in his departure from various forms of Victorian idealism or pessimism or from shallow compromises between religion and rationalism. Rather, he accepted the price that must be paid for the modern view of a world without God: "[P]sychic dislocation and alienation . . . , wandering in an unmapped no-man's land 'between two worlds.' "[11] The characters in his works desire harmony and community but find only fragmentation, the absurd condition.[12] What seemed to an earlier generation to be pessimism now appears to be existential isolation.[13] "Hardy lives in the same world [as his characters]—and he himself created it. He, too, is bruised by circumstance, and he too knows only those things that he can discover for himself in his own intensely personal impressions of existence."[14]

Approaching Hardy's personal impression demands critical examination of his "impressions," his images, and many studies reveal his use and knowledge of art, painterly methods, cinematic methods and acknowledge the pervasiveness throughout his work of visualizations and seeing generally.[15] Overall, his method is accepted as poetic, metaphoric, expressive, a method that allows images—individual objects, people, whole settings and situations —to issue forth as symbols. What had been called a flaw has become a style, a style that demands crossing the line between the visual arts and writing. For example, Hardy often used paintings or a painter's style as models for his scenes[16] or described his writing in terms of the "mad, late-Turner renderings," not only because he was familiar with English and European art[17] but because—more intrinsically—he thought in sensory constructions. He senses the human race as a quivering web (*Life,* 177), sees "the soul outside the body" in Botticelli (*Life,* 217), and smells the "odour of the flesh" in Rubens (*Life,* 217).

One hears echoes of Ruskin's union of character traits, emotions, form, and color: "Affection and discord, fretfulness and quietness, feebleness and firmness, luxury and purity, pride and modesty, and all other such habits, and every conceivable modification and mingling of them, may be illustrated, with mathematical exactness, by conditions of line and colour."[18] Hardy wanted to "regard every object, and every action, as composed, not of this or that material, this or that movement, but of the qualities pleasure and pain in varying proportions" (*Life,* 217); and, on the other hand, to regard qualities—"the heart and inner meaning" of things—as "vividly visible" (*Life,* 177). In short, he wished to bring experience to the surface where feeling, thought, and vision can be imaged as one; through his "idiosyncratic mode of regard" conceptions become perceptions. "The heart and inner meaning" of Thomas Hardy is conceived and perceived through his visualizations: individual visual structures, interactions between those structures, and interactions among the visual structures and the points of view of character, reader, and writer.

In a sensitive exploration of color and movement in *Tess of the d'Urbervilles,* Tony Tanner discusses Hardy's imagery with stunning tactility. However, despite his intensive reflection of the vitality in Hardy's imagery, Tanner sees the major movement in Hardy's best work as a movement toward death. He further notes that to live necessitates action, that "absolute fixity" implies death, yet he adds that "only what moves can crash"[19] and emphasizes the risk of living, the crash: "[T]he vertical returns to the horizontal, motion lapses into stillness, and structure cedes to the unstructured."[20] Finally, in seeking to understand the life of Tess Durbeyfield, he finds neither source nor purpose in structure, movement, life, or death:

> And why should it all happen to [Tess]? You may say. . . , "It was to be." Or you could go through the book and try to work out how Hardy apportions the blame—a bit on Tess, a bit on society,

a bit on religion, a bit on heredity, a bit on the Industrial Revolution, a bit on the men who abuse her, a bit on the sun and the stars, and so on. But Hardy does not work in this way. More than make us judge, Hardy makes us see; and in looking for some explanation of why all this should happen to Tess, our eyes finally settle on that red ribbon marking out the little girl in the white dress, which already foreshadows the red blood stain on the white ceiling. In her beginning is her end.[21]

Tanner invites us to accept the irreducible particular, the isolated image, as the totality of Hardy's vision. It is tempting; in Tanner's analysis the eye is where Hardy wanted it to be, on the image. There is no question as to the centrality of this particular image—red ribbon and white dress—and Tanner's choice of synecdoche, a metaphoric construction, as a self-contained "answer" shows awareness of Hardy's poetic method. Further, the isolated, irreducible particular suggests anxiety—fragmentation, separation, discontinuity—conditions which are part of Hardy's modern outlook. The question is whether or not the irreducible, isolated image is the foundation and totality of Hardy's vision.

In his discussion of *Tess of the d'Urbervilles*, J. Hillis Miller, like Tony Tanner, asks the question, "Why does Tess suffer so?"[22] and also rejects many possible answers. Hardy's stress upon multiple and tentative impressions makes a single or a simple answer unlikely. Accurately perceiving that "Hardy's concept of fate cannot be dissociated from the notion of chance,"[23] Miller concludes that every issue in Tess's life is a matter of chance and accident and that such a sequence of chances can lengthen out and seem to form a pattern.[24] Since Hardy repeatedly used terms such as "sequence" and "series," perhaps there is some pattern that might answer the question, Why does Tess suffer so? But, no. Out of change and chance "a pattern of repetition in differences [emerges] as if by miracle," a chain "with no center, origin, or end."[25] The repetitions are not related, are merely contiguous, leading only to discontinuity.[26] In his emphasis on a decentered text, without origin or end, Miller, like Tanner, locates only one aspect of Hardy's vision.

Hardy's writings are open to Miller's deconstructive analysis: "The bottom drops out, or there is an 'abyssing,' an insight one can almost grasp or recognize . . . but not quite."[27] Ambiguity, indeterminacy, contradiction are givens in the Hardy world, as, for example, in the atmosphere of uncertainty that drifts about the speaker in "The Pedigree." The opening setting is gothic: "I bent in the deep of night" beneath "green-rheumed clouds" and a moon "like a drifting dolphin's eye."[28] The speaker's work late into the night, "half-robed" in the darkened room, "over a pedigree," reveals compulsive behavior, suggesting far more than mere genealogical curiosity. He is closer to one searching for proof of his own existence. The window, opening to possibilities outside himself, converts to a mirror-image, a "dwindling" line of ancestors, "All with the kindred look"; they reflect and embody self-entrapment, "past surmise and reason's reach." He might have seen the long line of ancestors as a significant tradition, a source of identity; instead, he sees himself as "merest mimicker and counterfeit!" As in Miller's reading of Tess, these repetitions are merely contiguous, leading to discontinuity. The poem attests to Hardy's awareness of indeterminacy—in people and in texts.

The terror and insubstantiality of the speaker in "The Pedigree" are also felt in Hardy's *Life,* which is filled with prose-poems[29] whose style and content intensify one's sense of fragility in the human experience. About London he writes, "The fiendish precision or mechanism of town-life is what makes it intolerable to the sick and infirm. Like an acrobat performing on a succession of swinging trapezes, as long as you are at particular points at precise instants, everything glides as if afloat; but if you are not up to time— —" (*Life,* 207). The image of a swaying and fluid movement, the polysyllabic words, and the strong use of assonance and alliteration in the first twenty-six words are mesmerizingly suggestive of life's order and its precariousness; then, "but if you are not up to time— —" pounds with its monosyllabic abruptness the imminence of chaos, of nothingness: "— —" represents the non-verbal, non-rational, unknown. Further, "Footsteps, cabs, etc., are continually passing our lodgings. And every echo, pit-pat, and mumble that makes up the general noise has behind it a motive, a prepossession, a hope, a fear, a fixed thought forward; perhaps more—a joy, a sorrow, a love, a revenge" (*Life,*

206). And in *Jude the Obscure* the boy Jude fears growing older when "all around out there seemed to be something glaring, garish, rattling, and the noises and glares hit upon the little cell called your life and shook it, and warped it" (JU, 38). Not only are things "hit[ting] the little cell called your life," but its very existence might even be in question: "London appears not to *see itself.* Each individual is conscious of *himself,* but nobody conscious of themselves collectively. . . . There is no consciousness here of where anything comes from or goes to—only that it is present" (*Life,* 206, 7).

This decentered world, without origin or end, is described by Robert Kiely. What he observes in *The Mayor of Casterbridge* can be noted about characters in every major Hardy novel: "Though nearly all the main characters are preoccupied with themselves, all . . . do try at some point to see and, by seeing, to know other beings. We learn very early in the novel that if men do not pay attention to one another, each can lapse into a kind of invisibility since there seem to be no heavenly eyes to give substance to his thoughts and actions."[30] This threat of dissolution in Hardy's novels is not far removed from the theory of Harold Rosenberg, one of the brilliant observers of modern art and modern culture, who denied the concepts of universals and absolute identities. For him all appearance is a mask or costume; Rosenberg's conception of our tenuous existence is reflected in Saul Steinberg's observation that "his own personae, buildings, animals can be dripped back into the ink bottle."[31]

Hardy acknowledged this tentativeness and found a way to confront its inevitability. When he states that *Tess of the d'Urbervilles* is "an attempt to give artistic form to a true sequence of things,"[32] he understates the intricate mixture of forces that transforms his "things" into "artistic form." Both Tanner's isolated image and Miller's isolated event omit the energy at the center of Hardy's entire cannon: process.

Energy—the animating power, the thrust into movement—is a thing neither already formed nor definable; it is not a noun. Using Hardy's image of the human race as a quivering web (*Life,*

177), Ian Gregor describes process as an ever-becoming-provisional design defining space.[33] Its creating element is the dynamic interchange between the image and the eye. Hardy's attention to sensory, especially visual, stimulation and response conveys an empiricist's assumption regarding the senses as the basis for human knowledge. Yet while we know only through seeing, seeing does not automatically equal knowing. In Hardy's epistemology, reliance upon the senses combines with the high degree of subjectivity involved in gaining knowledge: our senses plus our emotions and imagination provide both the limitations and the possibilities for knowledge, and all knowledge is mediated by the meaning one desires to give or to withhold. Events are touched with the impassioned imprint of human will. Subjectivity is fully developed in his works through a multiplicity of fallible "seers" and through the human tendency to enlarge personal experience into absolute meaning.

> He deals with the exposure of the individual mind to all the forces and illusions that assault the single, lonely self. . . . [People] are moved or immobilized by the impact of signs which, answering some predisposition, elicit from their innermost nature a feeling evermore intense and consuming. . . . Elective affinities in the structure of Hardy's novels derive from the constructions his characters are prepared to put on all they see and remember.[34]

Hardy understood that people never actually arrive at an "objective reality" because no objective reality is knowable; we are tossed into this "nonchalant universe" (*Life,* 378) of chaos and flux, a world that no one ever made. "It is the on-going—i.e. the 'becoming'—of the world that produces its sadness. If the world stood still at a felicitous moment there would be no sadness in it. The sun and the moon standing still on Ajalon were not a catastrophe for Israel, but a type of Paradise" (*Life,* 202). The accumulation of coincidence in Hardy's works is less a sign of faulty narration or inadequate "realism" than it is a sign of our limited knowledge of the unpredictably changing universe.[35] His writings present this chaotic world and its inhabitants, who yearn to universalize and organize—who try to give meaning to the meaningless and valueless world.

Images become icons as subjects turn objects into metaphors and even into myths. The endless subjective establishment of such metaphors—created and re-created all one's life long—is the process through which Hardy creates aesthetic structures and Hardy's characters create their lives: "[L]ate and soon / Becoming, never being, till / Becoming is being still."[36]

Wallace Stevens, another writer with a thoroughly modern sensibility, describes this yearning for meaning and order as a yearning to see things "exactly as they are."[37] Such a desire must end in impossibility, yet the quest and inevitable failure along the way are not negative. In fact, a searching, creative consciousness is an imperative if one is to survive. The transforming element in the human mind is both an aesthetic and a metaphysical ordering, an "act of finding / What will suffice."[38] To save oneself from delusion, entrapment, even self-destruction, one must learn that it is the process of "finding" itself, not the discovery of any single metaphor, that is the only value of the search: accretion is a pattern of vitality. The highest awareness a Hardy character and reader can reach is that reached by the listeners in Stevens' "The Idea of Order at Key West": they gain the knowledge of the singer who "[k]new that there never was a world for her / Except the one she sang and, singing, made."[39] This calls for a double consciousness, the seeking of signs and the consciousness that one is doing so.

As William E. Buckler states, "The excitement in Hardy's work is generated, not by reconciliation, but by discrepancy, and his 'truth' is that illusion recognized helps us to avoid disillusion by reconciling us only to discrepancy."[40] Hardy repeatedly placed personal and immediate experience in the vital position: *"Let every man make a philosophy for himself out of his own experience"* (*Life*, 310). The final authority is the eye and the I; the final awareness is that metamorphosis and creativity are essential actions of the (modern) mind. This conclusion develops from an iconological study of Hardy's visualizations.

To take Hardy on his own terms, one must return to that crucial word "impression." In that word lie Hardy's rhetorical means for dramatizing action and theme: the ways people gain knowledge and what it is possible for them to know. Buckler's comments on the aesthetic center of *The Dynasts* can—with varying intensity—be applied to Hardy's whole work: "*[The Dynasts]* has an open aesthetic center out of which hundreds of individual poetic structures emerge in an incremental but flexible surfacing of varied and human efforts to systematize reality through or in response to language. These poetic structures in turn become metaphors of human reality."[41] This study will codify these hundreds of individual poetic structures into four patterns to locate Hardy's fundamental visualizing tendencies. The word "pattern" is not meant to suggest a rigid schematization; indeed, Hardy's aversion to systems is borne out in the fluidity and flexibility of his patterns. Also, because parts of a process rarely add up to the process itself, discussion of any pattern will include discussion of its connections to all other patternings, the analysis always being directed toward the protean movement of the whole. While it would be critically unsound to attempt to formulate the essence of such a kaleidoscopic image-maker as Thomas Hardy, one can attempt to glimpse, for a moment, the essence as it moves. This synthesis of principles underlying Hardy's visualizations should lead to an imaginatively informed understanding of his expressive style.

Varied and infinite phenomena are the source of sensory stimulations that invade the isolated human being. However, humanity is not only a receiver; it is both a perceiver and a creator, a duality leading to the first, absolutely fundamental pattern underlying all the other patterns and underlying Hardy's thought and aesthetics—the conversion of image into icon. This pattern includes Hardy's complex narrative voice; the primary part played by subjectivity and will in the acts of seeing and knowing; and the interaction between multiple impressions and fallible, multiple perceivers. Stimulation comes forth and is turned back upon its source through human imagination, infusing the earth with meaning. This study of the interchange between image and eye introduces the reader to Hardy's methods as empiricist and poet, with metaphor as the focal point for experience and meaning. He teaches us to see poetically, "in half and quarter views the whole picture . . . from a few bars the whole tune."[42]

The second pattern is the framed image. The word "framed"

applies to structures framed by both point of view and physical placement. As my description of the first pattern, image into icon, suggests, there is always a viewer of Hardy's structures. From his earliest published novel, *Desperate Remedies,* when three sets of eyes queue up in a melodramatic concatenation to watch Manston reveal his guilt, Hardy never relinquished the seeing eye, though he learned to use it with increased subtlety and variety. Of major importance in this pattern are non-authoritative, fallible viewers, for their limitations and possibilities are an all-encompassing frame for character and reader. Also, analysis of this pattern will address structures formed by the special limitations of a secret watcher; physical framing such as landscapes, doorways, windows, stage settings; and painterly effects, for example, a lighted area at the center of darkness. A frame can hide or reveal knowledge; can determine plot movement; and has an emotive value that heightens experience generally, a useful method for Hardy's expressionistic style. Most encompassingly, framing stands as a metaphor for human subjectivity; it is a formulation of the movement from image to icon.

The variety and complexity of patterning within the structures themselves is embodied in the third pattern, relationships within the image. Relationships can range from a "simple" formulation of a person and her/his clothes or bodily movements to the famous Hardy figure-in-the-landscape to the relationship between people and buildings or between people and people, and to relationships communicated through a series of pictures. Hardy's poetic style allows not only people, places, and objects but also whole scenes and experiences—static or active—to emerge with iconic meaning and dynamism. Here, perhaps, Hardy exhibits the greatest tendency toward visual abstraction. Tableaux are constructed like expressionistic paintings with scenes built through spatial arrangements of line, shape, and color. Meaning appears in the arrangement of the whole. In the sub-patterning within this pattern Hardy displays full control of his irrational subject matter, giving it an expressive, poetic ordering and power.

The last pattern, disrupted images, can be the end of construction; meaning can dissolve into final disillusionment, immobility, death. However, it may also picture forth the simultaneous existence of construction and destruction in a formulation of contradiction. Tensions between external matter and subjective perception, collisions of images within metaphoric constructions, and contradictions between framing and disruption result in a destabilization from which new metaphors and meanings can emerge. Indeed, in the unresolved tension between framing and disruption lies the dynamic force of process. Disruption is not the final description of Hardy's vision. Nor do the patterns, the parts of the picture, simply add up to the whole picture. One must go more than full circle, must move round to and reintroduce the first pattern, image into icon.

This image of a "cycle of renewal" could seem to reflect a cyclical theory of life. Through almost all of Hardy's fiction, the strongly felt presence of Dorset, and of a rural setting in general, tempt one toward theories centered on the tension between country and city, as in the pastoral tradition—toward theories of an ideal organic life as cyclical and harmonious. Nature can appear to provide an analogy for—and even an answer to—human needs and processes. Indeed, the importance of this rural setting has received appropriate attention in Douglas Brown's view that the center of the Wessex novels is the agricultural theme; the "contemporary catastrophe" caused by the urban invasion of the traditional agricultural society.[43] This "catastrophe" is felt keenly in John Holloway's claim that Hardy's characters must live in harmony with nature if they are to survive, all other paths being signs of deracination that must lead to "private self-generated dreams[s]" and destruction.[44] These theories do have their subterranean life in Hardy's world.[45] *Tess* has levels of a "return . . . to the folk, . . . of nature and instinct, the anonymous community."[46] Within Giles Winterborne is the mythic vegetable god of primitive religion,[47] and *Under the Greenwood Tree*, *The Woodlanders*, and *Far from the Madding Crowd* contain elements of the pastoral tradition. But all these pastoral possibilities exist in Hardy's texts only to be undermined. In Hardy is not the recidivism necessary to make such returns possible. Tess is peasant and aristocrat and neither. These labels define irretrievable pasts and, in any case, Tess resists a static definition. She defines herself in the process of making her own, individual choices. Giles lacks the vitality of the traditional nature god and, while he will be remembered, he will not be renewed.[48] The anti–pastoral elements in both *The Woodlanders* and *Far from the Madding Crowd* far outweigh traditions of an ideal green world.[49] Grotesqueries steadily erupt in *Far from the Madding Crowd*'s idyllic setting, making community and unity all but impossible. Traces of pastoral as a means of knowing exist most poignantly in *The Woodlanders;* David Lodge senses the "delicate, precarious balance . . . between the conflicting and logically incompatible value-systems and knowledge systems,"[50] the old cyclical view versus the new evolutionary view of nature. But this is not a tension between equals; pastoral is present to inform us of what we have lost. The sun and the moon will not stand still on Ajalon, nor will their inevitably repeated "risings" and "settings" reflect the patterns of human life.

John Holloway has concluded that Thomas Hardy gave up novel writing because the old rural order could no longer provide the vitality necessary for its continued existence or for his imagination and, furthermore, because Hardy viewed human nature as incapable of renewing the dead land.[51] Tony Tanner's view that Hardy's works move toward death, that action leads to crashes, is noted also by Dorothy Van Ghent and J. Hillis Miller, both of whom suggest that Hardy advocates self-annihilating safety strategies: Van Ghent's "return to folk instincts of concealment and anonymity"[52] and Miller's modern detachment, which "lies in passivity, in secrecy, in self-effacement, in reticence, in the refusal of . . . involvement."[53] It is a mistake, however, to place loss as the pivotal point for Hardy's aesthetics. On the contrary, his works stress willed creation and self-definition as imperatives for human survival. Tess's "blighted planet" is less a pessimistic definition of the "contemporary catastrophe" than a prod to the question Hardy's works seek to answer: how shall we live on such a planet? The answer is neither in returns nor in detachment but in process, the process of creation, disruption, and re-creation —of metamorphosis. "Nothing but the illusion of truth can permanently please, and when the old illusions begin to be penetrated, a more natural magic has to be supplied."[54] The old illusions have faded and Hardy's "more natural magic" is found in a linear and evolutionary view of history in which subject and object meet in metaphor.

The outreachings of the irreducible particular to a never-ending process of destruction and re-creation insists on a return to metaphor—the particular, experiential, personal exchange between the image and the eye. No matter how far one seems to travel from Hardy's "impressions," the return is inevitable. Process is seeing. To establish process, with its original separation of subject and object, its non-rationality, Hardy hides himself. Tony Tanner has observed that things in Hardy appear to be "watched in their otherness, something perceived but not made over . . . something seen . . . something there; it is an effect on the retina, it is a configuration of matter."[55] This simultaneity of sensory presence and authorial absence distances Hardy from the subject matter to achieve his non-authoritative and multi-perspective point of view. Even more important, by placing endless objects—things, scenes, actions, personae—between himself and the reader, Hardy pulls the reader into the work, giving her or him a view of life to some extent analogous to the way life is experienced by characters. We are all, characters and reader, forced to create meaning and metaphor through the interaction of the image and the eye. We must all bear the possibility and anxiety of self-evolution.

For a moment Hardy seems invisible, outside the scene, dispassionately observing pictures that pass before his eyes. For a moment his art may seem to be "at once a reaction to the external world, and a protection against it . . . , a transformation of the reaction into a shape which imitates it at a distance."[56] But no, ultimately he is part of the picture, intimately involved, revealed, and vulnerable; we are witnessing an imagination. He has made his choices; he too is in process. Poetic structures—as he was fully and painfully aware—are one of the myths by which he willed to live his life:

> I do not think that there will be any permanent revival of the old transcendental ideals; but I think that there may gradually be developed an Idealism of Fancy; that is, an idealism in which fancy is no longer tricked out and made to masquerade as belief, but is

frankly and honestly accepted as an imaginative solace in the lack of any substantial solace to be found in life. (*Life*, 310)

"The poem of the mind is the act of finding / What will suffice."[57] Visual structures become a continuum along which character, reader, and writer seek and create meaning.

PART TWO

PARTS OF THE PICTURE: VISUAL STRUCTURES

Chapter 2

Image as Icon

The term "icon" is used today by semiotic writers to refer to a verbal sign which somehow shares the properties of, or resembles, the object which it denotes. The same term in its more usual meaning refers to a visual image and especially to one which is a religious symbol. The verbal image which most fully realizes its verbal capacities is that which is not merely a bright picture (in the usual modern meaning of the word image) but also an interpretation of reality in its metaphoric and symbolic dimensions. Thus: "The Verbal Icon."[1]

In this clarification of his book's title, W. K. Wimsatt helps to explain the word "icon" in terms that are useful to this study of Thomas Hardy, which explores the outreachings of an image to its iconic interpretation of reality. This topic is further explained and explored in Erwin Panofsky's *Studies in Iconology: Humanistic Themes in the Art of the Renaissance*. That Panofsky's approach to the study of Renaissance art should apply readily to the study of modern literature is not extraordinary. Much recent criticism on imagery has crossed the line between historical periods and disciplines.

> [Recent studies examine] rules for encoding and deciphering imagery in the various arts and in the structure of perception and consciousness. They investigate the ways we interpret imagery, from representational or illusionistic picturing to abstract patterning . . . from imagery in the literal sense (graphic or plastic artifacts . . .) to the various metaphoric extensions of the concept of imagery in literature, music, and psychology. They are also concerned with the ways imagery interprets us, in the sense that our attempts to understand the world and our own creations are organized by tacit images, sublimated structures by which we represent to ourselves the orders of time, space, and language.[2]

Panofsky's methodological approach moves from an examination of individual images to all the images in a painting and, beyond that, to the images as they exist in a series of paintings. He moves from analysis to synthesis; however, far from reaching any fixed or final conclusions about "reality," his major assumption is that "what we see"—our structures of perceptions and consciousness—is controlled by the historical-cultural conditions in which we live. Under these conditions, an iconological study can reveal the "essential tendencies of the human mind" as expressed symbolically.[3]

That images do express reality, that reality is known through subjective perception, and that cultural assumptions contribute to what and how we see are all major principles on which this Hardy study is based. However, while the term "icon" is appropriate and useful, its traditional religious meaning is not applicable. Nor does its use invest images with a special meaning as symbols for the "new religion"—a Romantic idealism of the imagination—for our modern age. Indeed, this iconic reading of Hardy, like the traditional images that surface in Hardy, stands as an ironic commentary on the unavailability of religious beliefs to supply absolute value in the modern world. Nevertheless, the term is illuminating, for it is by the characters' enlargements of images into icons—myths, metaphors, meanings—that Hardy uses character to establish the essential tendencies of the modern mind and to reveal his view of the historical-cultural conditions in which we live.

On the surface one might see a crucial difference between

approaching subjective enlargement of unique experience into metaphors that carry symbolic value in Hardy's fictions and approaching the received allegorical figures, frequently religious icons, that carry symbolic value in the Renaissance art works addressed by Panofsky. However, these Renaissance figures are not stable and static in meaning; one image may emerge with varied meanings in different contexts, derived from different sources. Still, meanings are less subjectively assigned than they are in Hardy's world. Nevertheless it is the inclusion of the elements of non-rationality and process in Panofsky's iconological approach that helps define and inform the present study.

First, Panofsky's insistence that the art historian must take a final intuitive leap to unify and understand the whole picture is analagous to the final intuitive leap the critic must take to understand Hardy's visualizing process. Intuition is essential because it is impossible to comprehend the whole merely by analyzing and defining its parts. Similar to the critic, pulled into Hardy's works and forced to create meaning, the art historian must inevitably enter the art work subjectively to arrive at meaning. Second, Panofsky orders his study into three separate methods for interpreting his materials, but he cautions that, although these categories "seem to indicate three independent spheres of meaning, [they] refer in reality to aspects of one phenomenon, namely, the work of art as a whole. So that, in actual work, the methods of approach which here appear as three unrelated operations of research merge with each other into one organic and indivisible process."[4] Similarly, Hardy's text will not be understood merely by examining the four patterns of visualizations but by seeing their interrelationships and the process of metamorphosis. Finally, these very aspects of synthesis—of non-rational leaps and organic and indivisible processes—must constantly be balanced in a fruitful tension with analysis of the fundamental categories and patterns.

Before analyzing the first pattern, image into icon, however, one must learn how to read Hardy's visualized texts. In discussing John Ruskin, Elizabeth K. Helsinger notes that description in *Modern Painters I* is meant not only to give knowledge about the physical behavior of nature but also to sensitize readers to a new way of seeing. She notes of a particular descriptive passage, "What is being conveyed is not, of course, 'the' truth of a bank of foliage in sunshine, but one kind of painterly vision, a way of seeing that can be learned and will then influence the way other scenes—real, painted, or described—are perceived."[5] In like manner, Hardy's text and this study guide readers to a new kind of seeing.

Teaching the Reader to See

Thomas Hardy uses a vocabulary of seeing, presenting things as sights or views or scenes or pictures, and he frequently alludes to paintings.[6] He presents a world of images at which readers are asked to look, and to look from a variety of perspectives. Christminster is seen as the abstract and ideal heavenly Jerusalem, a blaze of flame, an over-arching halo, an ancient pile of stones, even as gingerbread cakes to be bought and eaten at a fair. There are bird's-eye view scenes, like the narrator's comparison of the two valleys in *Tess of the d'Urbervilles:*

> The world was drawn to a larger pattern here. The enclosures numbered fifty acres instead of ten, the farmsteads were more extended, the groups of cattle formed tribes hereabout; there only families. These myriads of cows stretching under her eyes from the far east to the far west outnumbered any she had ever seen at one glance before. The green lea was speckled as thickly with them as a canvas by Van Alsloot or Sallaert with burghers. The ripe hues of the red and dun kine absorbed the evening sunlight, which the white-coated animals returned to the eye in rays almost dazzling, even at the distant elevation on which she stood. (TD, 139)

When Tess reaches the valley floor, it is—unexpectedly, from the long view—large enough to be a verdant flatland in which she appears as a figure in the landscape "like a fly on a billiard-table of indefinite length, and of no more consequence to the surroundings than that fly" (TD, 142). But the simile and the philosophical statement are replaced as Tess enters the scene, causing a movement from the former distant view of the cows as "burghers" and abstract colors to the sensuous immediacy of cows moving along at milking-time, "their great bags of milk swinging under them as they walked"; "[A]s each animal lingered for her turn to arrive the milk oozed forth and fell in drops to the ground" (TD, 142–43).

This process of displacement of one perspective by another introduces the reader to Casterbridge, initially viewed from about a mile away, "shut in by a square wall of trees . . . as compact as a box of dominoes." Then we soar like a bird to see colors and shades, and Casterbridge becomes "a mosaic-work of subdued reds, browns, greys, and crystals, held together by a rectangular frame of deep green." Then we land: "[T]o the level eye of humanity it stood as an indistinct mass behind a dense stockade of limes and chestnuts, set in the midst of miles of rotund down and concave field. The mass became gradually dissected by the vision into towers, gables, chimneys, and casements. . . ." (MC, 59). Our eye moves as with a camera—aerial shots, long shots, close-up, wide angle, telephoto.

And Hardy's text pictures more than material reality. He visualizes all experience—aspects of society, human emotions, psychological states. The fullness of the cows' "great bags of milk," which "oozed forth," pictures the lushness of Talbothays and the sexual attractions that will ripen there. The change of Casterbridge from a neat and compact square to multiple and varied shapes pictures the confusing social complexity that exists there. At times an image is inscribed with psychological stress, as in Gabriel Oak's response to his flock's sudden death:

> Oak raised his head, and wondering what he could do, listlessly surveyed the scene. By the outer margin of the pit was an oval pond, and over it hung the attenuated skeleton of a chrome-yellow moon, which had only a few days to last—the morning star dogging her on the left hand. The pool glittered like a dead man's eye, and as the world awoke a breeze blew, shaking and elongating the reflection of the moon without breaking it, and turning the image of the star to a phosphoric streak upon the water. All this Oak saw and remembered. (FFMC, 73)

In "Wessex Heights" tormented memory surfaces in a series of images, and the speaker in "Neutral Tones" recalls an experience from the past by precisely such an emphatic imprint as Oak's: "Your face, and the God-curst sun, and a tree, / And a pond edged with grayish leaves" (CP, 12). Cosmic depression is stamped upon landscape when its "sharp features seemed to be / The Century's Corpse outleant" (CP, 150). And the view of misery on a rainy day can effect the lens on a lifetime: "Though thirty years of blur and blot / Have slid since I beheld that spot" (CP, 315).

Hardy is teaching several things: to see, that seeing is subjective, and that one view is not the only view. And fundamental to all this teaching is that "experience *un*teaches—(what one at first thinks to be the rule in events)" (*Life,* 175). While his works teach one to see and look and watch, he also notes "[t]he Hypocrisy of things. Nature is an arch-dissembler. A child is deceived completely; the older members of society more or less according to their penetration; though even they seldom get to realize that *nothing* is as it appears" (*Life,* 176). Nor is he only speaking of the "meaning" of things; for Hardy, seeing and meaning are one. And so he deliberately shows changing views of things, even contradictory views. Early in *Tess of the d'Urbervilles* the May-Day dancers' dresses are described twice. First, "The banded ones were all dressed in white gowns." Second, "Ideal and real clashed slightly as the sun lit up their figures against the green hedges and creeper-laced house-fronts; for, though the whole troop wore white garments, no two whites were alike among them. Some approached pure blanching; some had a bluish pallor; some worn by the older characters . . . inclined to a cadaverous tint." (TD, 40, 41). The white suggests Tess's purity, provides the irony of Angel meeting and leaving her at this "white" time, presents a realistic picture of a dying rural tradition, and starts one half of the red and white color motif that runs through the novel. But encompassing all the whiteness, the second description instructs the reader to see that nothing is as it seems.

Early in *The Return of the Native,* the reader is given conflicting views of the heath and of human beings in relations to the heath and to the universe in general. First the heath is presented as sublime and absolute, as the inevitable, cosmic, amoral universal. It seems to be The Truth, The Reality. However, the surface of the heath is actually confusing: it can convey night while the sky conveys day, and readers are caught in a tension as the burden of reaching accurate perceptions falls upon them. Similarly, we first meet Eustacia as a form upon a barrow. From a distant view she "rose from the semi-globular mound like a spike from a helmet," timelessly recalling the ancient Celts. "There the form stood, motionless as the hill beneath. Above the plain rose the hill, above the hill rose the barrow, and above the barrow rose the figure. Above the figure was nothing that could be mapped elsewhere than on a celestial globe" (RN, 41). All time, all space, are all one:

> The scene was strangely homogenous, in that the vale, the upland, the barrow, and the figure above it amounted only to unity. Looking at this or that member of the group was not observing a complete thing, but a fraction of a thing. . . . Immobility being the chief characteristic of that whole which the person formed portion of, the discontinuance of immobility in any quarter suggested confusion. (RN, 41)

But the figure does move: "[I]t descended on the right side of the barrow, with the glide of a waterdrop down a bud, and then vanished" (RN, 41). Stillness and unity disintegrate into movement and fragmentation; experience unteaches.

At times the narrator's voice gives information and assumes the tone of authority; at other times, the voice seems to see and know no more than the reader and is capable of seeing inaccurately. For example, impressions of the human form's harmonious relationship to the heath are incorrect. Eustacia hates the heath and feels her whole life to be a misery and a frustration because of it. Her telescope and hourglass show involvement with particularity and measurable time, not with the monolithic and cosmic scene. Also, the smooth and easy image, "with the glide of a waterdrop down a bud," is the distant view, merely; she has been motivated to move against her will. In part, the image of movement and, therefore, confusion does visually prefigure what the reader will soon be told about Eustacia. However, "the glide of a waterdrop" does not depict her massive discomfort. One learns the limits of narrative voice and the limits of vision itself. Indeed, scenes and images exist to be undermined, teaching the reader that meanings are not fixed and static in Hardy; rather, meaning is achieved through process. In "At a Lunar Eclipse" the speaker sees earth's shadow steal "[i]n even monochrome and curving line / Of imperturbable serenity." The image, combined with the alliterative and lyrical language that describes it, creates a harmony disrupted by both the content and sound that follow: "How shall I link such suncast symmetry / With the torn troubled form I know as thine" (CP, 116). Experience unteaches, but it is not meaningless.

Things and people, despite their emphatic presence in Hardy, are kept at a distance and give the effect of being autonomous, not quite graspable, because of the changing perspective and because there is always an uncertain and/or subjective pair of eyes between the reader the object. Spying and voyeurism play important roles both in highlighting the act of watching and in suggesting obstacles and uncertainty. Readers and characters frequently peer through doors and windows, holes in fences, across a heath, between the trees. Even an honest figure like Gabriel Oak spies on Bathsheba and her aunt through a hole in a roof one night, and spies on Bathsheba doing horseback-riding tricks through the loophole of his hut the next morning. Eustacia spies with her telescope on Wildeve; Diggory Venn spies on Eustacia and Wildeve and on everyone else as well. Captain de Stancy secretly ogles Paula as she performs an "optical poem" in her gymnasium while Dare and Havill deviously observe de Stancy's watching. Elizabeth-Jane and Lucetta search for their secret objects of desire while looking down at the marketplace from the window of High-Place Hall. As with the May-Day dance in *Tess,* Hardy uses a country tradition for his own visualizing purpose in the early window scene in *The Mayor of the Casterbridge:* the shutters of the King's Arms bow window are purposely left open so that the uninvited village people can glimpse the elegance at a great public dinner. In *Jude* Jude first gazes at Sue in a photograph, proceeds to watch her in his imagination, and—for some time after he sees her in person—seeks her out not to meet her but to watch her secretly. While much of the poetry has less to do with a spectator watching an other than with the self-expression of a speaker, in many of the poems—for example in *Satires of Circumstance*—there are specific watchers: the pupil in "In Church" or the particular speakers in "At a Watering-Place," "In the Cemetery," "Outside the Window." Other poems in this series give a clear sense of some unseen person—the reader—seeing scenes and overhearing conversations. These variations of spectatorship place the spotlight not only on the thing seen but also on the seer, in an act of reaching for experience, of reaching out to know.

Hardy is "attuning his reader's response" to visualizations, and he is certainly doing so, as Norman Page states, to achieve an "effective narrative device." He is forcing the reader "to grasp some of the essential elements in the story which narrative summary could only have rendered less strikingly."[7] Because narrative is rendered more strikingly and with assumptions far different from those present in narrative summary, Hardy is, in fact, "deliberately renouncing some of the freedom of representation and report traditionally afforded by the verbal medium" in favor of "imag[ing] and represent[ing] his materials in primarily visual terms."[8] David Lodge, like Page, notes that Hardy's visual effects are not used merely "for effect" but are "part of some larger aesthetic and thematic pattern." For example, in *The Woodlanders*, "the recurrent motif . . . of the illuminated figure inside, observed by an unobserved observer outside, symbolizes the imperfect . . . communication . . . between the main characters in the novel."[9] However, I suggest that the most encompassing aspect in this example of Hardy's cinematic method is not the revelation of theme but the revelation of method itself: the authoritative narrative voice replaced by endless subjective observers—including the reader—who know what they know by observing the surface of things.[10]

Hardy's methodology operates on both characters and reader; we are all presented with the options and limitations provided by the surface of things. Seeing in Hardy is not merely a metaphor for knowing; it is a form of knowing. The visualizing method has foundations in his empiricism; with the senses as the basis for human knowledge, Hardy joins subjectivity, imagination, and will to arrive at our fullest possibilities for knowledge. The method is further illuminated by recent studies in the psychology of perception, in which two related aspects are stressed: (1) seeing is a process of learning, and (2) seeing (and therefore learning and knowing) is a subjective, a creative process. Rudolf Arnheim, in *Visual Thinking,* states,

> My contention is that the cognitive operations called thinking are not the privilege of mental processes above and beyond perception but the essential ingredients of perception itself. I am referring to such operations as active explorations, selection, grasping of essentials, amplification, abstraction, analysis and synthesis, completion, correction, comparison, problem solving, as well as combining, separating, putting in context. These operations are not the prerogative of any one mental function; they are the manner in which the minds of both man and animal treat cognitive material at any level. There is no basic difference in this respect between what happens when a person looks at the world directly and when he sits with his eyes closed and "thinks." . . . I must extend the meaning of the terms "cognitive" and "cognition" to include perception. Similarly, I see no way of withholding the name of "thinking" from what goes on in perception. No thought processes seem to exist that cannot be found to operate, at least in principle, in perception. Visual perception is visual thinking.[11]

Furthermore, influenced by studies in gestalt psychology, Arnheim notes the

> active striving for unity and order manifest in the simple pattern of lines. Far from being a mechanical recording of sensory elements, vision proved to be a truly creative apprehension of reality—imaginative, inventive, shrewd, and beautiful. It became apparent that the qualities that dignify the thinker and the artist distinguish all performances of the mind. Psychologists also began to see that this fact was no coincidence: the same principles apply to all the various mental capacities because the mind always functions as a whole. All perceiving is also thinking, all reasoning is also intuition, all observation is also invention.[12]

E. H. Gombrich also rejects a split between sense data and thought processes in his works on the psychology of pictorial representation. Gombrich stresses the vital factor of subjectivity, what he calls "the beholder's share," as influencing how to paint and how to see. Sense data and thought processes interact in the "activity of the living organism that never ceases probing and testing its environment."[13]

Alan Spiegel echoes Arnheim and Gombrich in a discussion of cinematic novelists when he notes that a new type of audience is needed for a new type of novel, a novel whose author is not an active presence; this new audience must be

> active rather than passive, an audience that must now learn to move toward, seek out, and grapple with the remote and autonomous narrative form. . . . Flaubert's reader must not only accustom himself to read works that refer continually to things that he can see, but he must now make an added effort, just as he would in life, to grasp the meaning expressed by the things themselves. . . . He must learn to read a verbal language that embodies a seemingly unmediated visual language.[14]

This new way to read is the process and the problem to be explored by this critical study, as well as what—ultimately—Hardy teaches the reader to see. Now we can explore more fully the presence of Hardy's images and the theoretical assumptions that inform the patterning of image into icon.

The Reality of Half and Quarter Views

Virginia Woolf, in her essay on Thomas Hardy, notes an essential doubleness in his novels. Discussing *Desperate Remedies,* she says,

> He was "feeling his way to a method," he said himself; as if he were conscious that he possessed all sorts of gifts, yet did not know their nature, or how to use them to advantage. To read that first novel is to share in the perplexity of the author. . . . There is a feeling that Hardy's genius was obstinate and perverse; first one gift would have its way with him and then another. They would not consent to run together easily in harness. Such indeed was likely to be the fate of a writer who was at once poet and realist.[15]

There are two strains in Hardy, and he knew the risk of not being understood because of the division:

> The reader will almost invariably discover that, however numerous the writer's excellencies, he is what is called unequal; he has a specialty. This special gift being discovered, he fixes his regard more particularly thereupon. It is frequently not the feature . . . which common repute has given him credit for. . . . [Rather it] lurk[s] like a violet in the shade of the more obvious, possibly more vulgar, talent.[16]

The two strains in Hardy are what I call the storyteller (Woolf's "realist") and the poet. His "speciality"—what at other times he called his "idiosyncratic mode of regard"—was that of the poet, expressionist, visualist. But he frustrated his readers with this "specialty" because they had learned to expect his more obvious talent, that of a popular, traditional storyteller. First let us look at the storyteller.

There is no doubt that Hardy loved narrative. In addition to his plot-filled novels and his ballads, the autobiography is liberally sprinkled with glimpses of short narrative. He is even fascinated by the potentiality for story:

> That girl in the omnibus had one of those faces of marvelous beauty which are seen casually in the streets but never among one's friends. It was perfect in its softened classicality—a Greek face translated into English. Moreover she was fair, and her hair pale chestnut. Where do these women come from? Who marries them? Who knows them? (*Life*, 220)

> Was told a story of a handsome country-girl. Her lover, though on the point of matrimony with her, would not perform it because of the temper shown by her when they went to buy the corner-cupboard and tea things, her insistence on a different pattern, and so on. Their child was born illegitimate. Leaving the child at home she went to Jersey, for this reason, that a fellow village girl had gone there, married, and died; and the other thought that by going and introducing herself to the widower as his late wife's playmate and friend from childhood he would be interested in her and marry her too. She carried this out, and he did marry her. But her temper was so bad that he would not live with her; and she went on the streets. On her voyage home she died of disease she had contracted and was thrown into the sea—some say before she was quite dead. Query: What became of the baby? (*Life*, 247)

A man I met in the train says in a tone of bitter regret that he wore
out seven sets of horseshoes in riding from Sturminster Newton to
Weymouth when courting a young woman at the latter place. He
did not say whether he won and married her, or not; but I fancy
he did. (*Life,* 184)

While not always as cynical about marriage as the above example
suggests, he was drawn to bizarre stories related to marriage:

Mary L., a handsome wench, had come to Bockhampton, leaving
a lover at Askerswell, her native parish. William K. fell in love
with her at the new place. The old lover, who was a shoemaker,
smelling a rat, came anxiously to see her, with a present of a dainty
pair of shoes he had made. He met her by chance by the pathway
stile, but alas, on the arm of the other lover. In the rage of love the
two men fought for her till they were out of breath, she looking
on and holding both their hats the while; till William, wiping his
face, said: "Now, Polly, which of we two do you love best? Say it
out straight!" She would not state then, but said she would consider (the hussy!). The young man to whom she had been fickle
left her indignantly—throwing the shoes at her and her new lover
as he went. She never saw or heard of him again, and accepted the
other. *But she kept the shoes, and was married in them.* I knew her
well as an old woman. (*Life,* 217–18)

Am told a singularly creepy story—absolutely true, I am assured
—of a village girl near here who was about to be married. A watch
had been given her by a former lover, his own watch, just before
their marriage was prevented by his unexpected death of consump-
tion. She heard it *going* in her box at waking on the morning of the
wedding with the second lover, though it had not been touched
for years. (*Life,* 297)

Hardy can even manage a miniature story within a story:

In December Hardy was told a story by a Mrs. Cross, a very old
country-woman he met, of a girl she had known who had been
betrayed and deserted by a lover. She kept her child by her own
exertions, and lived bravely and throve. After a time the man
returned poorer than she, and wanted to marry her; but she refused. He ultimately went into the Union workhouse. The young
woman's conduct in not caring to be "made respectable" won the
novelist-poet's admiration, and he wished to know her name; but

the old narrator said, "Oh, never mind their names! They be dead and rotted by now." (*Life*, 157)

Hardy's stories operate within the tradition of conventional storytelling not because the events and characters are ordinary and familiar and expected. Though many are, his novels and poems are also saturated with bizarre situations and settings, extraordinary characters and coincidences. However, events are usually governed by customary conventions of narrative, such as the selection of events for the story; the significant relatedness of a series of events; a chronological framework in which events occur; an assumption of structure and order; a human interest invested in the sequence of events.[17] Indeed, his novels are often highly schematized, perhaps—as Guerard and other critics have mentioned—to a fault: "One of his greatest weaknesses is his tendency to shape and plan his novels according to some obvious architectural principle and his failure to conceal the blueprint."[18]

No, he did not conceal the blueprint, for his aim was not the art of hiding narrative structure but the art of revealing poetic structuring, a pattern of verbal pictures that moves beneath or alongside the plot, submerged, perhaps, but not hidden. It is more like the effigy of Henchard, thrown into the river at an unknown source but rising to great effect at a chance moment. And when that moment comes, we are reading Hardy the poet. In addition to describing Hardy as both realist and poet, Woolf understands him as an unconscious writer, one who

> seem[s] suddenly and without [his] own consent to be lifted up and swept onwards. . . . His own word, "moments of vision," exactly describes those passages of astonishing beauty and force. . . . We see, as if it existed alone and for all time, the wagon with Fanny's dead body inside travelling along the road under the dripping trees; we see the bloated sheep struggling among the clover; we see Troy flashing his sword round Bathsheba where she stands motionless. . . . Vivid to the eye, but not to the eye alone, for every sense participates, such scenes dawn upon us and their splendour remains. But the power goes as it comes. The moment of vision is succeeded by long stretches of plain daylight, nor can we believe that any craft or skill could have caught the wild power and turned it to a better use. The novels therefore are full of

inequalities; they are lumpish and dull and inexpressive; but they are never arid; there is always about them a little blur of unconsciousness, that halo of freshness and margin of the unexpressed which often produce the most profound sense of satisfaction. It is as if Hardy himself were not quite aware of what he did, as if his consciousness held more than he could produce, and he left it for his readers to make out his full meaning and to supplement it from their own experience. . . . For these reasons Hardy's genius was uncertain in development, uneven in accomplishment, but, when the moment came, magnificent in achievement.[19]

According to Woolf's examples, when the moment came, he achieved magnificent sensory, especially visual, structures; she is reading Hardy the poet.

Hardy was aware of the problems of writing fiction and recognized the part played by the reader and the unconscious in its creation. In "The Profitable Reading of Fiction," after noting the scarcity of perfect novels and the mere two hundred years in which the novel has had to develop, he advised the reader to "see what the author is aiming at, and by affording full scope to his own insight, catch the vision which the writer has in his eye, and is endeavoring to project upon the paper even while it half eludes him."[20] He discourages belief in a consciously finished product either in the imagination or on the page. Hardy's submerged, even subversive, patterning is a series of visual structures—spontaneous and chaotic—ever-changing, disappearing, reemerging through the novels and poems, not like an architect's blueprint but like Coleridge's "Kubla Kahn." He explains his creative process in "The Science of Fiction": "To see in half and quarter views the whole picture, to catch from a few bars the whole tune, is the intuitive power that supplies the would-be storyteller with the scientific basis for his pursuit."[21]

Hardy's science of fiction, his aesthetics, invokes a storyteller who can tell the truth only partially, demands the reader's subjective view to construct a whole truth, reveals in fact that there is no one truth, no *vérité vraie*. The tension between storyteller and poet is productive in that Hardy's traditional narratives, despite the blueprint showing, cannot create a final answer because they are questioned by visualizations. Indeed, it is the pictures that readers remember. "Despite his rather stylized, conventional plots, Hardy manages to create . . . clear, precise pictures which can later epitomize a whole work in a single memory. . . . One 'sees' what one is reading; the words paint . . . [an] image in the mind."[22] In Hardy's chaotic universe, story is one more "half [or] quarter view," an icon of explanation. Even the brief narrative sketches from the *Life* provoke responses other than to the stories themselves. The image of the face in the omnibus lingers with the reader beyond Hardy's questionings. It seems disembodied and haunting, like Pound's "[t]he apparition of these faces in the crowd; / Petals on a wet, black bough."[23] "What became of the baby?" amusingly jolts the reader out of her or his preoccupation with the eventful sketch that preceded it. And from the other stories, visual objects remain in the mind: horseshoes and wedding shoes, a ticking watch, dead and rotting bodies.

Summaries of *Tess* sound like soap operas, melodramas about the trials and tribulations of the innocent maiden repeatedly wronged by the various evils of mankind. Combinations of bad luck, coincidence, and calculated misuse directed at Tess could appear to be simplistic, overly schematized. But that is not what lasts in the reader's mind. One sees Tess splashed with Prince's blood, Tess ceaselessly feeding the Satanic machine, the blood-red ace of hearts, Tess and Angel among the stone pillars of Stonehenge. Or one could summarize the story of Bathsheba Everdene as that of an overly prideful, high-spirited young woman who—incident by incident—is made a wiser and more mature woman. But the grotesqueness of incident and image refutes bland summation. Oak's revising the coffin lid's "Fanny Robin and child" to read "Fanny Robin" is again revised when Bathsheba stands facing the bodies of Fanny and baby framed in their coffin. Troy's macabre kissing of the corpse, Boldwood's frenzied entreaties, Troy's shrouded entrance to the party—all contribute to a realization not of a character's progressive improvement but of the terrifying, unexpected, irrational nature of our lives.

Also, a narrator's voice can serve to bring events to an ordered closing. Toward the end of *Far from the Madding Crowd,* the narrator speaks of Bathsheba's and Gabriel's perfect union as a rational consequence of all the troubles preceding it. However, the picture of Bathsheba framed within the porch, smiling "(for she never laughed readily now)" (FFMC, 424), suggests a deep sadness, even horror, that will not be pulled into the happy ending. And there may be few more incomplete cause-effect summaries in Hardy than "the President of the Immortals . . . had ended his sport with Tess" (TD, 449). How does this encompass the rhetoric of a "scarlet . . . ace of hearts" on an "oblong white ceiling" (TD, 433)? Or compare the narrator's summary of Elizabeth-Jane's views, which state the wisdom arrived at from the experiences with the novel, with Henchard's final words. She speaks unemotionally of a wise passivity, limited objectives, and limited expectations. The summary is weighted with polysyllabic words and convoluted sentence structure. She had discovered the secret

> of making limited opportunities endurable; which she deemed to consist in the cunning enlargement, by a species of microscopic treatment, of those minute forms of satisfaction that offer themselves to everybody not in positive pain; which, thus handled, have much of the same inspiriting effect upon life as wider interests cursorily embraced. (MC, 354)

As a contrast, Henchard's will leaps out of the page, a picture of the will he had embodied his whole life:

'MICHAEL HENCHARD'S WILL

'That Elizabeth-Jane Farfrae be not told of my death, or made to grieve on account of me.

'& that I be not bury'd in consecrated ground.
'& that no sexton be asked to toll the bell.
'& that nobody is wished to see my dead body.
'& that no murners walk behind me at my funeral.
'& that no flours be planted on my grave.
'& that no man remember me.
'To this I put my name.
                    'MICHAEL HENCHARD'

Each line is simple, balanced, emphatic, negative; nevertheless, his command that he be erased from memory is contradicted with the final words: "Michael Henchard" (MC, 353). His will does not resolve problems, it questions them, and contradicts the view that unimpassioned reason can tell the whole story.

George Levine's study of realism and the nineteenth-century English novel, *The Realistic Imagination,* places Hardy firmly within a tradition of experimentation that embodies contradiction:

> Resisting forms, it explores reality to find them; denying excess, it deserts the commonplace self-consciously asserted as its subject. Positing the reality of an external world, it self-consciously examines its own fictionality. . . . The realistic novel persistently drives itself to question not only the nature of artificially imposed social relations, but the nature of nature, and the nature of the novel.[24]

This study makes no attempt to resolve the tension between storytelling and poetry; rather, it attempts to grasp the fullest implications of just such oppositions in the production of Hardy's text. Neither story nor image tells the whole story, but these "one half and quarter views" are the center from which one reaches out to grasp "the whole picture."

Mind, Matter, Metaphor

Early in *Jude the Obscure,* Jude is tossed into chaos, his world thrown out of focus. As punishment for feeding the "dear little birdies," Farmer Troutham swings him round and round, a "whirling child, as helpless under the centrifugal tendency of his person as a hooked fish swinging to land, and beholding the hill, the rick, the plantation, the path, and the rocks going round and round him in an amazing circular race."[25] Later on that day he senses his own "shuddering" from life as "all around you there seemed to be something glaring, garish, rattling, and the noises and glares hit upon the little cell called your life, and shook it, and warped it" (JO, 38). The annihilating objectification that Jude notes here is, however, only part of his experience. He feels matter hurtling past him and at him but he, like most other Hardy characters, tries to stop it; he reaches out a hand, an eye, a word; he touches, sees, names; and creation has begun.

In discussing the hidden view of Christminster, a worker notes that he has seen it "when the sun is going down in a blaze of flame, and it looks like I don't know what." "The heavenly Jerusalem," suggests Jude. "Ay—though I should never ha' thought of it myself," answers the workman (JO, 40). The investment of external matter with internally generated meaning is apparent, first with the sunset as a "blaze of flame," next with Jude's "heavenly Jerusalem." That the meaning is private, subjective, is also apparent when the workman notes the foreignness of Jude's image to him. Creation of meaning proceeds when Jude finally does get a view of the city at night: "What he saw was not the lamps in rows, . . . only a halo . . . over-arching the place against the black heavens behind it. . . ." And as he departs he throws a "last adoring look at the distant halo" (JO, 42, 44). The seemingly passive and battered Jude, affected by reverence for Phillotson, has managed to transform a misty haze into a glory. This exchange between Jude's mind and external matter introduces us to the way in which empiricism is dealt with in Hardy's narrative technique. Before proceeding further, it will be fruitful to examine briefly two other writers influenced by empiricism, Virginia Woolf and Walter Pater.

Woolf moves "from narration through a limited subjectivity to a more 'elementaristic' presentation. . . . [She] began to develop a style in which subjectivity is dissolved and 'world' and 'self' are reduced to a loosely associated bundle of elements—a style in which things and sensations have equal valency within the entire complex."[26] As the idea of "self" is merely a pragmatically convenient category of thought, Woolf wished to eliminate this observing "self" but not the act of observing. Even as early as *Mrs. Dalloway,* the opening shows an indifference to shifts in point of view:

Mrs. Dalloway said she would buy flowers herself.
   For Lucy had her work cut out for her. The doors would be taken off the hinges; Rumpelmayer's men were coming. And then, thought Clarissa Dalloway, what a morning—fresh as if issued to children on a bench.

> What a lark! What a plunge! For so it had always seemed to her when . . .[27]

The text moves from a narrator close at hand, hearing Mrs. Dalloway talk, to—after three unassigned lines—the information that we have been and are in Mrs. Dalloway's mind, to two exclamations which may be spoken by Mrs. Dalloway or by a narrator, to an all-knowing narrator ("so it had always seemed"), who may or may not be identical to the first narrator. There are thoughts and sensations, but their source does not seem to be important.

To the Lighthouse, Between the Acts, and *The Waves* present a narrative voice that moves in and out of minds and places, back and forth in time, deemphasizing separations and never assuming complete knowledge of anything or anyone. *To the Lighthouse* moves away from the "I, I, I"[28] of Mr. Tansley's ego to the intermingling of self and stimulus, as when Mrs. Ramsey becomes the things she sees, the lighthouse light or the waves and ocean floor: the light "silvered the rough waves a little more brightly, as daylight faded, and the blue went out of the sea and it rolled in waves of pure lemon which curved and swelled and broke upon the beach and the ecstasy burst in her eyes and the waves of pure delight raced over the floor of her mind."[29] Here, metaphor is used to close the gap between the self and the thing, to make two things one. This intermingling of stimuli and response is felt throughout *Between the Acts,* like bubbles of thoughts and feeling and objects colliding, merging, developed, forgotten. The novel is made up of fragments of action, character, dialogue, scene—suggesting the random nature of life. Neither plot nor a single consciousness (except the author's) controls the content. "Objective events are shown to have the same texture as internal monologues, so that everything, inside and out, in this person and that, combines to make what Mrs. Ramsay called a 'single stream.' "[30] It is Woolf's attempt to convey what she would call real life:

> Examine for a moment an ordinary mind on an ordinary day. The mind receives a myriad of impressions—trivial, fantastic, evanescent, or engraved with the sharpness of steel. From all sides they

come, an incessant shower of innumerable atoms; as they fall, as they shape themselves into the life of Monday or Tuesday, the accent falls differently from of old; the moment of importance came not here but there. . . . Life is not a series of gig lamps symmetrically arranged; but a luminous halo, a semi-transparent envelope surrounding us from beginning of consciousness to the end.[31]

Hardy would not disagree with this statement.

Pater seems at first moment to be a contrast both to Woolf and to Hardy's Jude. He celebrates both the fullest possible individual consciousness, Woolf's shunned "I," and the fullest possible response to sensory experience, Jude's glares and rattles. The "Conclusion" to *The Renaissance* explains:

Every moment some form grows perfect in hand or face; some tone on the hills or the sea is choicer than the rest; some mood of passion or insight or intellectual excitement is irresistibly real and attractive to us,—for that moment only. Not the fruit of experience, but experience itself, is the end. A counted number of pulses only is given to us of a variegated, dramatic life. How may we see in them all that is to be seen in them by the finest senses? How shall we pass most swiftly from point to point, and be present always at the focus where the greatest number of vital forces unite in their purest energy?

To burn always with this hard, gemlike flame, to maintain this ecstasy, is success in life.[32]

Pater's *Marius the Epicurian* also concentrates on the moment, on process, on a constant state of change. "Both the individual and his moment are in states of motion, of death and resurrection, of *being* only through *becoming.*"[33]

All three empiricists, however, exist in contradiction. Jude must turn a glare into a halo, and neither Pater nor Woolf can omit some grim aspects in their embracing a world that is nothing beyond individual consciousness and sensory experience. Mrs. Ramsay's "wedge-shaped core of darkness"[34] is visionary but frightening, too, in its isolation. Part 2 of *To the Lighthouse* contains death and war; lack of communication and the presence of war hover over *Between the Acts. Mrs. Dalloway* is interwoven with madness, suicide, and isolation. *The Waves* calls into question the existence of both subject and object; "all that remains is the act of perception itself."[35] And Pater's magnificent moments of experience are the impressions of the isolated individual and have within them their immediate death. Carol T. Christ, in *The Finer Optic,* comments upon the Victorians' observation of minute particulars as "signify[ing] both the solipsism the Victorians feared and their last attempt to discover order in the world of things."[36] In such attempts desperation often arises "from the tension between subjectivism and objectivism . . . [from] the fragmentation of the Romantic understanding of a world we half perceive and half create into a frantic search for the reality of objects and a growingly burdensome conviction of the isolating subjectivity of all experience."[37]

Nevertheless, and despite differences in subject matter, preoccupations, and style, all three empiricists—Woolf, Pater, and Hardy—manage to construct something positive out of this desperation. Though death, war, time passing, and isolation are motifs from which she is not free, Woolf is able to take the risk of eliminating the concept of self. She shares with Pater his "exhortation to enjoy the 'flamelike' moments of life." Mrs. Ramsay and Bernard have moments in which they can go anywhere, see anything; "The very unity in which self and world appear lost can also be perceived in a positive light, as a vital 'moment of being.'"[38] Pater, though both the "Conclusion" and *Marius* are surrounded with death and solitariness, "does not spend time regretting the new relativist spirit of modern thought, but welcomes it and immediately turns his energy toward forming new values that will free our sensibilities to appreciate the details experience presents us."[39] Hardy, too, accepts the relativist spirit, and he is willing to confront it, both its anguish and its possibilities. Most of his characters, however, are less accepting and less conscious of the nature of their lives. Hardy sees the dilemma in the modern world and presents the survival strategies human beings use to structure the chaos.

Examining Hardy's use of individual works of art, artists, and schools of art to help describe his aesthetics gives insight into his empirical methodology and narrative technique. He felt Turner's question "in his maddest and greatest days: 'What pictorial drug can I dose man with, which shall affect his eyes somewhat in the manner of this reality which I cannot carry to him?' " (*Life*, 216). Hardy, too, could not carry "reality" to his readers because empiricism had taught him that there is no objective reality. He rejects merely "optical effects," the "simply natural" in favor of the "mad, late-Turner rendering," a style that brings something "to the object that coalesces with and translates the qualities that are already there, —half hidden, it may be—and the two united are depicted as the all" (*Life*, 185). What he brings to the object is a multiplicity of perspectives that undercuts the very notion of a single reality. When Hardy notes that Turner paints chiefly *"lights as modified by objects"* (*Life*, 216), he suggests a fundamental element—the "light"—in his own works: the subjectivity of all perception. Innumerable atoms "may hit upon this little cell called your life" but ever more forcefully the human mind—perception, imagination, will—projects onto a world of matter a world of meaning: image into icon.

The "boundary line" at which mind and matter meet takes on a shape in metaphor, a term which itself can take on iconic meaning. R. N. Furbank, in *Reflections on the Word 'Image,'* speaks of the inadequacy of speaking of our world as if it were a "whole" or "unity." Rather, it is all there is. "It hasn't 'a' structure, it has an infinity of structures."[40] It is this modern understanding of the world, one without a Platonic or Christian or any ideal form, that leads Furbank to the general distrust of any dualism, including metaphors. Since dualisms imply ideals, a word whose meaning died in the nineteenth century, he prefers to think in terms of the unique, monistic, particular, concrete—in terms of images—thereby "cut[ting] through the whole issue of duality raised by metaphor."[41] The usefulness of metaphor to this study, however, is supported by a different understanding of metaphor. C. D. Lewis notes not so much dualisms or similarities in metaphor, but that "we find poetic truth struck out by the collision of images."[42] "Recent discussions have often insisted," observes Karsten Harries, "that, in poetry at least, metaphor joins dissimilars not so much to let us perceive in them some previously hidden similarity but to create something altogether new."[43] And

Paul Ricoeur sees in metaphor "the projection of new possibilities of redescribing the world . . . of 'remak[ing]' reality."[44] It is precisely because a lack of ideals, of dualisms, of God exists alongside a will to make meaning that metaphor is the operative visual structure in Hardy.

Earlier we observed the narrator of *The Return of the Native* describe the heath's barrow in several different ways. It became a spiked helmet used by ancient Celts; part of an abstraction, unity; and a bud along whose side a waterdrop slid. What we witness here is the narrator's seeing eye, wandering in the world of sensory stimulation and emerging with vehicles of meaning. Indeed, the narrator may be getting carried away with her or his own rhetoric; almost all of Hardy's voices do, to some degree or another, use rhetoric to make their subjective projections "real." For example, we meet a Boldwood consumed by the valentine anonymously sent by Bathsheba.

> Here the bachelor's gaze was continually fastening itself, till the large red seal became as a blot of blood on the retina of his eye; and as he ate and drank he still read in fancy the words thereon, although they were too remote for his sight—
> MARRY ME.
>
> (FFMC, 132)

The letter takes on added meaning from the grave setting of Boldwood's home, the words now carrying a "deep solemnity." Further, the words seem to take on a will: "Boldwood looked, as he had a hundred times the preceding day, at the insistent red seal" (FFMC, 132, 133). In fact, the seal is not insistent; Boldwood has created its insistence.

The valentine is a neutral agent that, as it travels from hand to hand, takes on meaning. From Liddy and Bathsheba it is a vehicle of amusement, mischief, mildly piqued pride, chance, indifference. Above all, it is sent on its way off-handedly, unreflectively. The narrative movement that follows travels much like a camera, moving from shot to shot, focusing on surfaces and omitting explicit interpretation. Chapter 13 ends with

MARRY ME.

Then the camera moves back as the letter is mailed and sorted in the post office. A narrative voice does come through in a brief, general reflection; however, with the first sentence of Chapter 14, we move to Boldwood at his dinner, to the valentine on the mantel shelf, back to Boldwood with the "blot of blood on the retina of his eye," and once again to

> MARRY ME.

It is quite simple to summarize the plot of Chapters 13 and 14: an amusing if slightly irresponsible prank is received with far greater seriousness than intended. But less simple to grasp are the varied perspectives, visual structures, and the ambiguity of meaning that finally emerges.

The casualness of Chapter 13 is somewhat undercut by the MARRY ME so emphatically set off on the page itself and set off again as Boldwood stares at the message in Chapter 14. The narrator's tone of explanation in Chapter 14 is pompous and reserved with its polysyllabic words and, as the paragraph moves along, its removal of all proper names and even personal pronouns:

> The letter must have had an origin and a motive. That the letter was of the smallest magnitude compatible with its existence at all, Boldwood, of course, did not know. And such an explanation did not strike him as a possibility even. It is foreign to a mystified condition of mind to realize of the mystifier that the processes of approving a course suggested by circumstance, and of striking out a course from inner impulse, would look the same in the results. The vast difference between starting a train of events, and directing into a particular groove a series already started, is rarely apparent to the person confounded by the issue. (FFMC, 132)

As a contrast is Boldwood's involved imagination working on this "origin" and "motive," this "mystifier" with an "inner impulse:

> Somebody's—some *woman's*—hand had travelled softly over the paper bearing his name; her unrevealed eyes had watched every curve as she formed it; her brain had seen him in imagination the while. Why should she have imagined him? Her mouth—were the

lips red or pale, plump or creased?—had curved itself to a certain expression as the pen went on—the corners had moved with all their natural tremulousness: what had been the expression? (FFMC, 133)

The language is informal, personal pronouns—male and female—are coupled repeatedly, and additional emotive language is used in words such as "curve," "lips," "red," "plump."

The reader is left in some degree of confusion, for while the narrator's distant analysis does seem to be correct, the "MARRY ME" stands apart from the text in both chapters and the "blot of blood on the retina of his eye" is also the narrator's word choice and a far leap from detachment. Nor is this strong image hyperbolic, ultimately, for Boldwood has named the small red seal with a passion that will claim two lives and from which he will never escape. The disinterested view is, in fact, only another metaphoric construction, another view, the voice of abstract reasoning. Readers cannot see with Boldwood's eyes but neither can they distance the incident into abstraction. What meaning does come through the varied layers of discourse—impersonally abstract, sensuous, metaphoric, visual, metalinguistic—is neither the narrator's nor Boldwood's view but something new all together: process. These multiple perspectives and efforts to name the world emblemize the dialectical relationship between the ambiguity, chance, and uncertainty of "reality" and the desperate human will to negotiate with the unknown, through rhetoric, to make it known.

Will

The conflict between the inevitably ambiguous world, always in flux, and the human will to make it clear and still is the major collision in much of Hardy's work. Since characters do, to some degree or other, fail in their quests, the question arises—exactly what is humanity's appropriate relationship to will? J. Hillis Miller—seeing the noise, glare, and violence that young Jude saw—claims that only by a character's "remain[ing] self-contained, sealed off from everything, can he escape this violation. Hardy's fundamental spiritual movement is . . . the will not to will."[45] Indeed, to will is to act self-destructively, to become a puppet to a universal will: "As soon as [one] engages himself in life he joins a vast streaming movement urging him on toward death and the failure of his desire."[46] Miller sees Hardy's narrators as detached, as viewing events from a distance, and he sees this "detachment of consciousness" as essential to Hardy's perspective, allowing "him and his spokesmen to see reality as it is."[47] "Reality as it is" is the reality of human beings trapped in their consciousness, isolated, forever separate from all others and from all their desires.

Or, as Lawrence O. Jones sees it, "reality as it is" may be the reality of those

> who seem more in touch with the objective world. For example, Thomasin in the storm on Egdon Heath is contrasted to Eustacia: "To her there were not, as to Eustacia, demons in the air, and malice in every bush and bough. The drops which lashed her face were not scorpions, but prosy rain; Egdon in the mass was no monster whatsoever, but impersonal open ground. Her fears of the place were rational, her dislikes of its worst moods reasonable."

Gabriel Oak, too, is noted as someone whose "more general vision is seen by Bathsheba to be superior to her limited personal vision: '. . . Oak meditatively looked upon the horizon of circumstances without any special regard to his own standpoint in the midst.'"[48] And finally, Jones sees the novels' narrators as omniscient viewers, able to see beyond their own subjectivity. Although Jones and Miller do not see "reality as it really is" in the same way—Jones believing that characters and narrators can see beyond their own subjectivity and Miller believing that they cannot see beyond their isolated consciousnesses—each believes that Hardy's narrators and spokespersons do convey a particular Hardyan version of reality.

In fact, the works as a whole do convey a particular vision, but it is not a vision of detachment or omniscience. Far more frequently, character and narrator are involved and limited, seeing no more than the reader and forcing readers to become involved in the novel's or poem's process. The above description of Oak is an excellent example; his superiority is described to us by the "limited personal vision" of Bathsheba. The reader must make some judgment about the validity of that vision. As to Thomasin's "prosy views," perhaps Eustacia's view comes closer to the truth of life as lived on Egdon Heath when one considers that before the novel's end, three people die violently, the deaths caused to some degree by the heath's life as embodied in a stream and an adder; that two characters throw dice on the heath to gamble with their own and others' lives, surrounded by the dark of night and the light of glowworms; and that a red man stalks the heath, in one instance moving toward and spying on Eustacia while hidden beneath turves. Malice may indeed be in every bush and bough. Robert Kiely's observation about *The Mayor of Casterbridge* can be applied to most of Hardy's works:

> Hardy cannot deal with his crowd of fictional characters any better than they can deal with one another unless he assumes a point of departure from which they can be seen and at least tentatively judged. Yet, as the narrative moves us from one vantage point to another, though we always find reason to sympathize, we cannot give full assent to the apprehension of any single character. We are constantly confronted . . . with the limitation of human vision.[49]

Thomasin's objective view or Gabriel's distant view or some other models such as the views of prudent Elizabeth-Jane and Farfare or passive Giles and Marty are inadequate for the multiplicity of experiences and events in the novels. A Hardy work distances itself from rational structures and abstractions, tending rather toward contradictions and combinations of the seemingly incompatible. Kiely places individual structures and perspectives into a larger picture:

> Henchard's illusions and sufferings demand a larger scope than prudence provides. . . . Hardy's sudden shifts in standpoint challenge the complacency and narrowness of one vision. . . . Thus, while it is true that Hardy provides the sensible models who keep the novel from ending in total confusion and despair, he also supplies the overtones of doubt and mockery which give the best of human models an uneasy footing in his universe.[50]

Ultimately, through the townspeople and through physical nature, Hardy makes nature the novel's most reliable commentator, the one that encompasses the immutability of change and demands that characters accept or anticipate the effects of process. One may look for a "point of departure," but one must do so with the "melancholy recognition that in a universe of perpetual change one never gets it right for very long."[51]

Miller's idea of uninvolvement as a strategy for safety is also questionable. For one thing, seemingly uninvolved characters such as Elizabeth-Jane and Gabriel do suffer, at times terribly. They are recipients of circumstance and cannot will themselves not to feel pain. Elizabeth-Jane is exhausted and very near total despair by the end of her "uninvolved" ordeals. She has not used detachment as protection; rather, she is finally uninvolved because experience has made her too depressed to feel life. She recalls two sets of characters from Dickens' land of despair, the cheerful eccentrics and the ideal couples. Captain Cuttle, Mr. Toots, Wemmick—all lead one-half lives, warped and stunted, in order to survive their worlds. Pip and Estella, Joe and Biddy, Florence and Walter, Amy and Clellam are drained of vitality and, like Alice Carker (or Elizabeth-Jane), withdraw to the side of the road. Giles "passively" dies for the woman he loves and poor Diggory Venn is found unfit for loving as long as he refuses to participate in life.[52] Withdrawal and passivity often mean death, not safety. As noted earlier, Tony Tanner sees the major movement in Hardy as a movement toward death and observes that "only what moves can crash"; however, he also notes that absolute fixity implies death: "to be human is to be animated, is to move. . . . All the confusions that make up Hardy's plots are the result of people who perceptibly give up their fixity. To say that this is the very condition of life itself is only to point to the elemental nature of Hardy's art."[53] Miller's ideal of detachment as safety is one more myth, one more point of departure, none of which "gets it right for very long."

Will operates within a complexity of cultural and pyschological influences. A character such as Donald Farfrae may not appear to have desires and intentions, but his seeming objectivity is actually a perfect meshing of his aggressions and the culture around him.

He sings nostalgic songs about the past, but he is in fact the man of the future—of science, machines, progress—who can adapt easily to the mechanism, commercialism, and viciousness of Casterbridge. Donald's individual desire has disappeared into a system of desire. Hardy frequently uses place and setting metaphorically to create social and/or psychic states within which characters must respond.

In *The Woodlanders* the woodlands are felt as emphatically as the heath is in *The Return of the Native*. The surroundings seem to enclose and press against any movement forward, and willed responses are often obstructed, turned inward, or muted. The woodlands, enclosed geographically and atmospherically, plus the historical moment, a transition point between past and future, create a convergence of time and place that stymies the will. George Fayen describes Hardy characters as "moved or immobilized by the impact of signs,"[54] and Hardy seems to be experimenting with varieties of immobilization and movement. Both Marty and Giles blend into the woods and the past, all their desires turned inward. Early in the novel Giles, "fixed to the spot by his apple-tree, could not advance to meet [Grace]" (W, 68), and in his death he "dissolves into the wood by imperceptible degrees."[55] Grace is not without will but is locked into a semi-paralyzing irresolution by conflicting tendencies toward both past and future. Fitzpiers displays multiple wills that act simultaneously, canceling out each other in a self-consuming, modern ennui. On the other hand, Egdon Heath, that "vast tract of unenclosed wild" (RN, 33), gives the illusion of limitless possibility. Fires seen across distances and telescopes contracting distance provoke the imaginative reaching out to control space, to recreate external reality. Even Diggory Venn, despite the mask of uninvolvement, acts out an obsessive will—the will toward perfecting the universe for Thomasin. The atmosphere of unimpeded time and space encourages dreams to proceed into actions. Characters mistake the heath for a "vast arena" or a "battlefield" when it is actually a "little flat stone" where dreams are brutally circumscribed.

To deny our subjectivity or our mythmaking is to deny our humanity. Will operates as an internal force, interacting with external change to produce process—"a series of seemings," of collisions, of metaphors—which are the inevitably evolving becomings of a lifetime. However, will can be a negative or a positive force. It can be negative when human beings lack the consciousness of their own willed involvement in the creation of meaning or when human beings cannot or will not learn that life is a process of becoming that neither ends nor gives a final answer, merely answers that are only "[f]or a moment final."[56] Metaphors translate not into final meaning but into new metaphors, enacting the process of metamorphosis. Will can be positive when it embodies an awareness of involvement, an acceptance of change, and a willingness to confront and act in a world of subjective creation, of self-creation. Action can be terrifying in its combination of responsibility and powerlessness, godliness and godlessness. But unawareness and denial of change may be equally terrifying, as Boldwood's entrapment in his rigid delusion bears witness; without consciousness, our creations may more easily create us.

"What a fresh and virginal daughter of nature that milkmaid is" (TD, 158), says Angel, and with the barest shred of evidence places upon Tess a label that will lead to his own self-centered disillusionment. Angel is most impressed with Tess when she becomes "a visionary essence of woman—a whole sex condensed onto one typical form. He called her Artemis, Demeter" (TD, 170), indulging his own imagination and denying the concrete milkmaid before his eyes. Tess, too, plays a part in the coming destruction. Though she is more inclined to the practical and concrete, she does create a mythic angel, a god, the object of her unquestioning devotion and worship. Her inflexible idealization of Angel helps devastate Tess when her self-created god rejects her self. Unfortunately for them, most Hardy characters do to some extent resist confronting the facts of self-creation and process.

Characters often erect ideals when in fact ideology is functioning or demand reification when only tentative generalizations exist. The speaker's trauma in "At Waking" (CP, 224) grows out of the belief that love is objective and everlasting, coherent, perfect. The disruption of belief leads to complete depression, projected onto the drifting clouds, "Dead-white as a corpse outlaid," but the speaker resists the truth of his experience:

> An insight that would not die
> Killed her old endowment,
> . . . .
> I covered my eyes
> As to cover the thought,
> And unrecognize
> What the morn had taught.

Finally, a tone of hysteria creeps into the concluding lines of resistance and realization:

> Off: it is not true;
> For it cannot be
> That the prize I drew
> Is a blank to me!

Hardy's novels and poems are filled with the topic of love and disillusionment. Miller's understanding of this theme as paradigmatic of the human situation generally is borne out in the lover's desire for structures and absolutes in conflict with the reality of subjectivity and change. In "At Waking" the loved woman had been "the one believed-in thing"; when it fails, so fails "all to which hope can cling." An imprisoned consciousness had created a false structure and is now left with blankness.[57] However, Hardy does not always choose to show the vast gap between desire and reality.

"On the Departure Platform" (CP, 221) presents a perception of the loved object from a different angle. While the lover has positive images of his loved one, "We kissed" is followed by "at the barrier"; "And she who was more than my life to me" is followed by "[h]ad vanished quite"; new plans and her future reappearance "[p]erhaps in the same soft white array" are followed with "[b]ut never as then!" The poem is a series of diminishments—"smaller and smaller," "but a spot," "diminishing platform"; of obstacles—"barriers," "under," "behind"; and of endings—"Departure," "She left me," "apart," "She would disappear," "Had vanished quite." However, the speaker is not disillusioned but is reconciled to the knowledge that "nought happens twice thus; / Why, I cannot tell." The poem interweaves two categories of images in a paralleled construction—love's presence and future alongside love's presence and disappearance into flux and loss. While Miller notes, "The only happy love relationship for Hardy is one which is not union but the lovers' acceptance of the gap between them,"[58] Hardy displays more possibility than this arrangement permits. The poem is, indeed, weighted with persistent images of loss. Nevertheless, instead of recognizing a gap, the speaker has a confrontation with anguish. The persona's immersion in this emotion is unlike Keats's "empathy with the particular that enabled him to experience all the existential possibilities of the universe."[59] It is the confrontation of anguish not as an idealizatioin of experience itself but as a way of negotiating with that incomprehensible universe. The speaker manages involvement, confrontation, acceptance of change—but not without pain. Or, to see yet another angle, there is Stevens' "After the final no there comes a yes."[60]

This reversal is not inappropriate for Thomas Hardy. The movement must be forward and back because the parts do not add up to the whole; it is the imprint of one part upon the others, seen in relation to others, that culminates in vision as process. While in one sense there is an enormous experience of anguish and loss, in another sense nothing is ever lost:

> For Hardy's world is a yearning world. It exists within a perpetually changing universe in which the sensitive observer is always looking backward and forward; nothing that happens is ever over and done with, as each event goes on to be an object of eternal questioning in space and time. The purpose of man's existence in this world is to feel the suffering involved in the processes of life . . . which are past understanding. In the modern universe cosmic agony is overwhelmed by cosmic energy.[61]

The visual structure, image into icon, is the fundamental and essential groundwork in this iconological study of Hardy. This groundwork has been laid with a broad exploration of many texts—early and late, novels and poems—to establish this visual structure's far-reaching presence in Hardy's writings. It explains and exemplifies his iconology as based in subjective responses to an ambiguous reality; in multiple, varied, and ever-changing perceptions of reality; in self-creation of reality. This structure embodies Hardy's empiricist assumptions, joining the individual's response to the external world with her or his imaginative and emphatically creative projections upon that external universe. To see is neither a passive activity nor mere trope; it is an imperative act of involvement if one is to live a life. The act of moving image into icon also reveals the tension within Hardy's art between plot and picture and the vital role of visualization in his text. The following chapters on framed images, disrupted images, relationships within the image, and metamorphosis will further reveal the manner in which poetic form and poetic process emerge from chronological narrative. The transformation of image into icon, of external matter into subjective meaning, defines and establishes Hardy's view of the "essential tendencies of the human [modern] mind"[62] and provides the source from which all other structures spring and develop.

Chapter 3

Framed Images

What does it mean to have a framed image? A fairer quesstion might be, how can literature exist without framing? A book, in itself, is an image bounded by its own rectangular frame. Titles, also, are frames, at times multiple frames. The title *Far from the Madding Crowd* suggests a place of tranquility, harmony, and—with its literary antecedent—tradition; simultaneously and unknown to the uninitiated reader, its ironic intention identifies a place of physical, economic, and psychological upheaval. What the informed reader gets are three frames: idyllic world, chaotic world, and an ironic tone that connotes the changing perspective. The critical question is not whether or not frames are present in Hardy's writing. Explicit or oblique, the frames are everywhere —scene and setting, doorways and windows, cliffs and lightning; changing perspectives, multiple perspectives, subjective perception. And they have their practical functions. They fulfill the demands of narrative by limiting or providing knowledge, intensifying the emotive content of subject matter, carrying themes. Also, the explicit frames, such as doorways and windows, enable Hardy to distance himself further from the text, adding to the multiple and subjective voices another, concrete layer of separation between text and artist and thereby deepening one's sense of an autonomous text.

In addition to the density of frames, and encompassing Hardy's entire text, are not only frames but framing, an act, which images forth subjective will seeking to overcome the dichotomy between the external world and human desire. This study does not question the presence and overall usefulness of frames; rather, it argues that the central concern in Hardy's world is process and that therefore the importance of frames is felt most in the vital process of framing. Paradigmatic of the transformation of image into icon, framing is a fictional enactment of Hardy's empiricism and his aesthetics, the exchange between external stimuli and creating perception, the image and the eye. To anatomize this process with a disciplined eye, let us first isolate a number of the familiar Hardyan frames.

Frames

Probably no writer is as closely connected with a particular territory than Thomas Hardy is with Wessex. He is, of course, one of the great literary landscape painters, in prose and in poetry. Landscape can be used to shape the very conditions of life for the world of the novel; it may seem passive, static, indifferent—yet it is within this frame, this limit, that human beings must survive. In *The Woodlanders,* setting seems to circle impenetrably around one:

> At one place . . . the leaves lie so thick in autumn as to completely bury the track. The spot is lonely and when days are darkening the many gay charioteers now perished who have rolled along the way, the blistered soles that have trodden it, and the tears that have wetted it, return upon the mind of the loiterer. (W, 35)

When Grace and Mr. Melbury walk through the woods, it is as if emphatic traceries had been formed, multi-layered and abundant, outlining the texture and path of movement:

> They went noiselessly over mats of starry moss, rustled through interspersed tracts of leaves, skirted trunks with spreading roots whose mossed rinds made them like hands wearing green gloves;

> elbowed old elms and ashes with great forks, in which stood pools of water that overflowed on rainy days and ran down their stems in green cascades. . . . They dived amid beeches under which nothing grew, the younger boughs still retaining their hectic leaves, that rustled in the breeze like a sound almost metallic, like the sheet-iron foliage of the fabled Jarnvid wood. (W, 83)

The weight of this world is felt not only in metal but also in human anatomy, not only in growth but also in decay: "On older trees . . . huge lobes of fungi grew like lungs. . . . The leaf was deformed, the curve was crippled, the taper was interrupted; the lichen ate the vigour of the stalk; the ivy slowly strangled to death the promising sapling" (W, 83).

Noting an early description of Little Hintock as "one of those sequestered spots outside the gates of the world" (W, 38), David Lodge takes exception to this description: "The effect of the novel is rather to think of the world as being outside the leafy, rooted 'gates' of the woodland."[1] And so, for the most part, it is. People are defined and define themselves and their relationships to one another within this heavy-gated frame. The novel's opening is like layers of framing; from the frame of landscape to the window frame of Marty's house to Mr. Percomb's subjective framing of Marty's hair, the reader is led into the intricate design of the novel, the woods, and subjectivity. Little Hintock is a place of "meditation," "listlessness," "narrow premises," and "inferences wildly imaginative"; a place where "dramas of a grandeur and unity truly Sophoclean are enacted in the real, by virtue of the concentrated passion and closely knit interdependence of the lives therein" (W, 38) within the "leafy, rooted 'gates' of the woodlands."

The Return of the Native opens:

> A Saturday afternoon in November was approaching the time of twilight, and the vast tract of unenclosed wild known as Egdon Heath embrowned itself moment by moment. Overhead the hollow stretch of whitish cloud shutting out the sky was as a tent which had the whole heath for its floor. (RN, 33)

The unenclosed heath is transformed into an enclosure: tent and floor. Later in Chapter 1 we are "in the central valley of Egdon

... where the eye could reach nothing of the world outside the summits and shoulders of heathland which filled the whole circumferences of its glance" (RN, 36), and later still we meet highway and barrow, the bottom and top frames of a novel and a world. Nor are they presented as minor figures. At the end of Chapter 1 the highway crosses the lower part of Egdon "from one horizon to another" (RN, 36) and, despite growing darkness, "the white surface of the road remained almost as clear as ever" (RN, 36). This clarity is underlined soon after Chapter 2 opens: the highway, "long, laborious, dry, empty, and white . . . bisected that vast dark surface like the parting-line on a head of black hair, diminishing and bending away on the furthest horizon" (RN, 37). Setting is not only the outer frame—tent and floor, bottom and top, circumference and horizon—but also the very center of the thing framed: the barrow "formed the pole and axis of this heathery world" (RN, 41).

Woods and heath, as frames, function metaphorically as the conditions under which life is lived. *The Woodlanders* takes place at a particular historical moment and the woodlands do, literally, grow beneath one's feet and above one's head closing in everywhere so that one might expect to feel entrapped within this time and this place. On the other hand, the heath is static and open, seeming to permit free movement upon it, less suggestive of particularity than of the ahistorical, general, abstract, cosmic. However, the narrator's rhetoric emphasizes the stopping points of distances and the absolute lines of shape and structure, limitations that seem to be true not only for individuals in history but for the human condition itself. Such an ambiguous frame may produce a world even more gated in than Little Hintock.

While landscape does not always shape the moods and experiences of an entire novel, it frequently outlines experiences and states of being in individual scenes. As Knight clutches the escarpment, in the stunning cliff-hanging scene of *A Pair of Blue Eyes*, he notes the boundaries of the moment:

> From the fact that the cliff formed the inner face of the segment of a hollow cylinder, having the sky for a top and the sea for a

bottom, which enclosed the bay to the extent of nearly a semicircle, he could see the vertical face curving round on each side of him. He looked far down the facade, and realized more thoroughly how it threatened him. Grimness was in every feature, and to its very bowels the inimical shape was desolation. (PBE, 239–40)

Gabriel Oak saw and remembered a scene—pond, moon, morning star—in his moment of despair, and the depressed speaker in "Neutral Tones" recalled face, sun, tree, pond, leaves. Similarly do the sky above, the sea below, and—primarily—the cylindrical form curving round Knight forever shape the reader's memory of Knight's desperate situation.

Hardy ventures into cosmic landscape in the wildly sublime storm in *Far from the Madding Crowd*. First the lightning outlines earthly matters; then the outline explodes into a picture:

> On the slope in front of [Gabriel] appeared two human shapes, black as jet. . . . It had been the sixth flash which had come from the east behind him, and the two dark forms on the slope had been the shadows of himself and Bathsheba. . . . [Then] there was more light, and he saw as it were a copy of the tall poplar tree on the hill drawn in black on the wall of the barn. . . . Heaven opened then, indeed. The flash . . . sprang from east, west, north, south, and was a perfect dance of death. The forms of skeletons appeared in the air, shaped with blue fire for bones—dancing, leaping, striding, racing round, and mingling altogether in unparalleled confusion. (FFMC, 279)

Of course, just as there is no final, single view in Hardy, so there is no final, single frame or picture. Immediately after the narrator's summary of human life as "trifling in . . . an infuriated universe," Gabriel's gaze fixes upon "how strangely the red feather of [Bathsheba's] hat shone in the light" (FFMC, 280). Perhaps it is not a large philosophical lesson but a red feather framed in lightning that Gabriel and the reader will remember.

Not infrequently, landscape scenes suggest the relationship between nature and human nature. Alienation surrounds Tess and Marion as they work on the swede-field at Flintcomb-Ash farm. The expressionless landscape spreads out into a frame that isolates and overwhelms the picture:

> The whole field was in colour a desolate drab; it was a complexion without features, as if a face, from chin to brow, should be only an expanse of skin. The sky wore, in another colour, the same likeness; a white vacuity of countenance with the lineaments gone. So these two upper and nether visages confronted each other all day long, the white face looking down on the brown face, and the brown face looking up at the white face, without anything standing between them but the two girls crawling . . . like flies. (TD, 331)

The grotesqueness of the featureless faces injects a note of terror; objectifying anonymity presses from above and below, mutely acknowledging the dehumanization of the life lived between them. Again, however, the frame depends on the framer; earlier in the novel female workers in the corn fields are found to be more interesting than male workers

> by reason of the charm which is acquired by woman when she becomes part and parcel of outdoor nature, and is not merely an object set down therein as at ordinary times. A field-man is a personality afield; a field-woman is a portion of the field; she has somehow lost her own margin, imbibed the essence of her surrounding, and assimilated herself with it. (TD, 123)

From grotesque obliteration to charmed harmony, Hardy's Wessex is not a place but a tone, a feeling, a point of view.

Clym seems to eliminate the margin between himself and the heath: "He was a brown spot in the midst of olive-green gorse, and nothing more. . . . His familiars were creeping and winged things, and they seemed to enroll him in their band" (RN, 273). Bees, butterflies, grasshoppers, flies, snakes—in their humming, tugging, quivering, leaping, falling, flirting, buzzing, gliding, sunbathing—in their colors of amber, emerald-green, brilliant blue and yellow, blood-red—permit their full vulnerability to show: "none of them feared him" (RN, 274). But Eustacia does. His comfort in obscurity is an obstacle to all her desire and a humiliation to her pride. Unable to be at one with a "brown spot . . . and nothing more," she enters the scene and disrupts the harmony.

Moments of brief, harmonious mergings recall Hardy's words on the sun and moon standing still on Ajalon: the event was "not a catastrophe for Israel, but a type of Paradise" (*Life,* 202). But in the momentary quality of this jointure lies the actual truth: between nature and human nature lies a vast difference. Robert Kiely's observation that nature, encompassing the immutability of change, is the most reliable commentator in Hardy[2] is different from the idea that characters can or will be absorbed into this assumption of process. They rarely are. More often they wish to make the process stand still or change its pattern; they wish to order it. One can see this difference between human nature and nature in Wallace Stevens' "Anecdote of the Jar":[3]

> I placed a jar in Tennessee,
> And round it was, upon a hill.
> It made the slovenly wilderness surround that hill.

The human product's entrance upon the scene orders, objectifies landscape into a frame for human action just as Eustacia's entrance reorders the furze-cutting scene. But the jar is not of nature—"it did not give of bird or bush, / Like nothing else in Tennessee"—any more than Eustacia or Clym are of nature. Clym's disappearance into nature is a form of stasis, unlike the natural life that moves around him. Human beings, who may—according to Kiely—find wisdom in accepting inevitable change and process as it is exemplified in nature, can never be nature.

Many of Hardy's poems give the sense of a figure defining the landscape. In "Why Did I Sketch" (CP, 477), the speaker feels bitterly mocked because he sketched an "upland green" with the figure "of a woman's silhouette," a woman he has since lost. He advises other painters to paint "no soft curves," but to "show the escarpments stark and stiff / As in utter solitude." The picture with soft curves is painful, but without them, it is harsh. "The Figure in the Scene" (CP, 476) tells of painting a picture of a woman sitting "where the cragged slope was green." Because it began to rain, the painting was stained, leaving only an outline of the woman; "Yet her rainy form is the genius still of the spot, / Immutable." In "The Phantom Horsewoman" (CP, 353) a man appears:

> He comes and stands
> In a careworn craze,

> And looks at the sands
> And the seaward haze
> With moveless hands
> And face and gaze,
> Then turns to go . . .
> And what does he see when he gazes so?

He sees a vision he carries everywhere, "A phantom of his own figuring":

> A ghost-girl-rider. And though, toil-tried,
> He withers daily,
> Time touches her not,
> But she still rides gaily
> In his rapt thought
> On that shagged and shaly
> Atlantic spot,
> And as when first eyed
> Draws rein and sings to the swing of the tide.

Neither death nor rain, which are nature's processes, can upset the figure's presence in the landscape of imagination and memory, which are human processes. Further, it is the poet's creative imagination that unites the two kinds of processes with a rhythmic language that "sings to the swing of the tide."

In *The Return of the Native,* at the end of Chapter 1 the empty white road is described with insistence: despite coming darkness, "the white surface of the road remained almost as clear as ever" (RN, 36). Chapter 2 opens: "Along the road walked an old man," yet the road persists in remaining empty—"dry, empty, and white"—until the man "discerned, a long distance in front of him, a moving spot" (RN, 37). The man and the "spot," Diggory Venn and his van, meet, talk, obliquely introduce Thomasin's dilemma, and then part; Diggory turns his horses and van off the road, watching the old man's "form as it diminished to a speck on the road and became absorbed in the thickening films of night" (RN, 40). The relationship between humanity and nature is reflected in the titles of Chapters 1 and 2: "A Face on which Time makes but Little Impression" and "Humanity appears upon the Scene, Hand in Hand with Trouble." Repeatedly, Hardy novels open with landscapes in which there is a road—*Tess of the d'Urbervilles, Return of the Native, Far from the Madding Crowd, The Woodlanders, The Mayor of Casterbridge.* Repeatedly, though the form will vary slightly, characters appear, meet, exchange words, and introduce "trouble." Time itself might not upset the scene, but human beings will.

Throughout Hardy's works there is a constant and repeated awareness of figure and landscape and the changing relationship between them. Often, before our eyes, landscape moves from being the picture to becoming the frame for a figure. Recall from *Tess of the d'Urbervilles* the overwhelming quality of the sky: "a white vacuity of countenance with the lineaments gone." The figures that look like flies are there as part of the picture, but barely. At the end of the novel, Angel turns back to observe the road he has just traveled away from Tess: "The tape-like surface of the road diminished in his rear as far as he could see, and as he gazed a moving spot intruded on the white vacuity of its perspective" (TD, 435). A moving spot turns road into frame and in a moment the new picture, Tess, floods out of the frame altogether. This constant interchange between landscape and figure is itself a figure—a trope—for the inevitable element of change; simultaneously, it is an interchange that places figure in the primary position. A character's entrance into a scene restructures or redefines the scene; this activity, metaphorically, enacts the characters' efforts to order their lives. If at moments there seems to be a merging or if nature seems to be the subject, such moments will pass and landscape will pass from picture to frame. The figure in the landscape, including the figure of the voice describing it, not the landscape itself, is Thomas Hardy's topic. "An object or mark raised or made by man on a scene is worth ten times any such formed by unconscious Nature. Hence clouds, mists, and mountains are unimportant beside the wear on a threshold, or the print of a hand" (*Life,* 116). Wessex is Hardy's "partly real, partly dream-country";[4] the final frame is not the scene but the seeing. A woodlands or a heath may contain the seeds of ontological significance, but it is character in process, on the move, that gives the last and lasting view; ontology, ultimately, is not in the scene but in the eye.

Concrete and conventionally recognized frames abound throughout Hardy's works. The regularity of voyeurism, discussed in Chapter 2, introduces such frames with doors, windows, a telescope, a hole in a fence. Images can frame, as Tess is framed as a fly on a billiard-table and Casterbridge is framed as a box of dominoes. Mirrors reflect the texture of new influences in Grace Melbury's life. Her excited absorption in the upcoming meeting with Mrs. Charmond is brilliantly reflected in candlelight the preceding evening as she poses "before a cheval glass that her father had lately bought expressly for her use; she was bonneted, cloaked, and gloved, and glanced into the mirror, estimating her aspect" (W, 87). But her hopes—and much future happiness—are damaged when vanity is again mirrored forth. Both women "pause before a mirror which reflected their faces in immediate juxtaposition. . . . Both looked attractive as glassed back by the faithful reflecter; but Grace's countenance had the effect of making Mrs. Charmond appear more than her full age" (W, 92). The effect, ruthlessly abrasive to Mrs. Charmond's image, is found unforgivable by Mrs. Charmond's vanity. The mirror's frame becomes Mrs. Charmond's framing. The second new influence is also framed in a mirror when Grace happens upon a sleeping Fitzpiers:

> Approaching the chimney her back was to Fitzpiers, but she could see him in the glass. An indescribable thrill passed through her as she perceived that the eyes of the reflected image were open gazing wonderingly at her. Under the curious unexpectedness of the sight she became as if spell-bound, almost powerless to turn her head and regard the original. However, by an effort she did turn, when there he lay asleep the same as before. (W, 157–58)

The strangeness of this "introduction," to Grace and to Fitzpiers, helps to mesmerize them both and to prefigure the indirect path their future connection will take.

Mirrors are further used as metaphors of self-reflection and self-revelation. In "The Pedigree" (CP, 460), the mirror frames the personal, subjective experience of anxiety as the speaker sees in a line of mirrored images just like himself not a meaningful tradition or mere background but "merest mimicker and counterfeit!"—a self without identity or meaning. "Moments of Vision" (CP, 352) presents an anxious moment as the speaker confronts her or his inner self: "Who holds that mirror / And bids us such a breast-bare spectacle see / Or you and me?" The poem is crowded with stressful questions about what is seen, about why such "tincts" surface at all, about the unpredictable source of self-revelation, and about the fear of self-revelation: who else might see what the mirror sees, "Glassing it—where?" This question is literally and uncomfortably answered in "In Church" (CP, 416) when a preacher's adoring pupil looks through an open door and a mirror —and an illusion—to see

> her idol stand with a satisfied smile
> and re-enact at the vestry-glass
> Each pulpit gesture in deft dumb-show
> That had moved the congregation so.

At times a window, too, can act as the vehicle of a "breast-bare spectacle": "Outside the Window" (CP, 419) shows a beloved woman seen from outside a window "rating her mother with eyes aglare." Her lover, " 'behold[ing] her soul undraped!' " quietly creeps away. Framed images can turn narratives in new directions.

Doorways, both small and large, are used for character development, presentation of theme, plot movement. Through Johnny Nunsuch's eyes and the open door of Diggory's van, the reader sees oppositions in Diggory Venn, hellish mystery and earthbound domesticity: "By a little stove inside the van sat a figure red from head to heels. . . . He was darning a stocking, which was red like the rest of him. Moreover, as he darned he smoked a pipe, the stem and bowl of which were red also" (RN, 101). Great barn door openings can frame scenes as traditional and stable as the sheep-shearing scene in *Far from the Madding Crowd* or as dramatic and disturbing as Alex d'Urberville's preaching. In both scenes, however, Hardy dramatizes the openings and their importance in the two novels' development as proscenium frames for a stage with the sun as spotlight on the central activity:

> Today the large side doors were thrown open towards the sun to admit a bountiful light to the immediate spot of the shearers' operations. . . . Here the shearers knelt, the sun slanting in upon

their bleached shirts, tanned arms, and the polished shears they flourished, causing these to bristle with a thousand rays strong enough to blind a weak-eyed man. (FFMC, 177)

The low sun beamed directly upon the great double-doored enrance on this side; one of the doors being open, so that the rays stretched far in over the threshing-floor to the preacher and his audience. . . . But her attention was given to the central figure, who stood upon some sacks of corn, facing the people and the door. The three o'clock sun shone full upon him. (TD, 349)

Windows are ubiquitous in Thomas Hardy's world. When Grace Melbury appraises herself in the mirror, she is seen from outside as Giles looks up to her window. Indeed, this scene of the illuminated figure inside glimpsed by an unobserved watcher outside is repeated so frequently that David Lodge uses it to support what he sees as a theme of non-communication in *The Woodlanders*,[5] and Alistair Smart notes it as a major pictorial method used in the service of narrative strategy. Hardy often used such scenes "consciously to mark some definite stage in the development of his drama, holding up for our contemplation a static picture in front of which we pause before the next scene unfolds."[6] A variation of this sort of concentration is used when Paula Power is introduced to the reader and to Somerset in a dramatic window scene. The window's limited view provides strangeness, mystery, and emotional intensity. Somerset at first cannot find anyone in the room to be the subject for the baptism. Then, from the vestry, "a woman came out clothed in an ample robe of flowing white which descended to her feet. Somerset was unfortunate in his position; he could not see her face." (L 46). When he does see her face, the description continues for over half a page: her beauty, her age, her hair, her features, her sophistication, her morality, her experience, her stress. What makes his extraordinary insight other than ridiculously improbable is the drama of the situation itself. Somerset is a secret watcher, his view is limited, he is expecting to see an unusual religious ritual, he does see a public disruption of expectation, and he knews absolutely nothing about Paula Power, not even her name. All of this is calculated to provoke the imagination of both Somerset and the reader, and as he takes a stroll afterward, "The stranger's girlish form stamped itself deeply on Somerset's soul" (L 50).

While two hidden eyes observing Paula's unfulfilled ritual are led into mystery, the many eyes observing a Casterbridge ritual produce information. The King's Arms bow-window reveals sights and sounds of a public dinner party. Outside, Susan and Elizabeth-Jane (and the reader) watch and listen. While a fellow listener does explain that Henchard is the mayor, an important businessman, and a non-drinker, the explanations are not actually needed. One can see Henchard in the principal position, "at the end of the table"; can see his unfilled wine glasses; and can see his attire: "[A]n expanse of frilled shirt. . . , jewelled studs, and a heavy gold chain." When the question of bad bread arises, "Henchard's face darkened," showing the temper that had helped him lose a wife. The scene provides exposition and characterization, and it opens the way to future events as Elizabeth-Jane and Susan learn about Henchard and "a stranger—a young man of remarkably pleasant aspect" sends in his note on how to turn bad wheat to good (MC, 63–69).

In *Jude the Obscure* Sue's response to entrapping situations is depicted with the help of windows. She escapes through a casement window from the Melchester Normal School and escapes through a window again, in terror, from the in fact harmless Phillotson: "In a moment he heard her flinging up the sash. . . . She had mounted upon the sill and leapt out" (JO, 247). She keeps Jude at a distance by showing her emotions only when she has a windowsill between them. At Shaston she strokes his forehead with the "high window-sill . . . between them, so that he could not get at her" (JO, 226). And at Marygreen this scene is repeated:

> In a moment of impulse she bent over the sill, and laid her face upon his hair, weeping, and then imprinting a scarcely perceptible little kiss upon the top of his head, withdrawing quickly, so that he could not put his arms around her, as otherwise he unquestionably would have done. She shut the casement, and he returned to his cottage. (JO, 236)

Windows can frame complex feeling and action.

On occasion the seeing eyes are inside the window, looking out. Elizabeth-Jane looks down from a window as Henchard and Farfrae walk down High Street together the morning after the King's Arms bow-window scene. She continues in this lofty view from her room in Henchard's house, overlooking the hay-stores and granaries, and continues still from the best lookout post in Casterbridge, Lucetta's High-Place Hall. In addition to placing Elizabeth-Jane in accurate relationship to a willed involvement with life, this distant view provides opportunity for plot development and tone. Elizabeth-Jane and Lucetta sit in their superior windowed positions, above the town's marketplace, keeping their eyes out for Henchard and Farfrae. This setting lends an extra layer of irony when these two women peer again from a high perch, the balcony of Donald's house, onto the effigy of Henchard and Lucetta. But for the moment they are high and safe and playful. When Lucetta meets Donald for the first time, she tells him that watching the fairs and markets from her window interests her. "How many things I think of while I watch from here!" "Do you look out often?" Donald asked. "Yes, very often." "Do you look for anyone you know?" "I look as at a picture merely," she answers with a pretended disinterestedness. "But . . . I may do so now—I may look for you" (MC, 185). Lucetta lies when she says, "I look as at a picture merely," but more than reveal a deception, the statement begs a question: How does one "look as at a picture merely"?

Lucetta's words suggest an uninvolvement contrary to her actual situation and contrary to the situations of all other Hardy characters as well. To answer the question it is necessary to examine the overwhelming quality of pictures in Hardy's works. He is known not only as a painter of landscapes but also as a painter of paintings, and his frequent visits to museums from 1862, when he moved to London, through all the years that followed show him to be one of the most knowledgeable British novelists in the visual arts.[7] Often his works make reference to particular paintings or artists or painting techniques. He may mention "Sallaert, Van Alsloot, and others of that school" to describe a character's perception (RN, 2) or "a Wouvermans eccentricity" to help describe a landscape (W, 235) or "Düreresque vigour and dash" (RN, 45) to describe the heath people by bonfire light. Angel Clare and 'Liza-Lu walk along a highway, "the drooping of their heads being that of Giotto's 'Two Apostles' " (TD, 448), and earlier, Angel's shocking appearance when he returns home is described as "match[ing] Crivelli's 'Christus' " (TD, 417). He names schools of painting or a much-used style, describing Miss Templeman's placement on the sofa as "somewhat in the pose of a well-known conception of Titian's" (MC, 178) or Mrs. Charmond's eyes as "almond eyes—those long eyes so common to the angelic legions of early Italian art—" (W, 90). We are shown the female profiles of Correggio (L, 57), the skin color and texture of a Terbury or a Gerald Douw (FFMC, 107), and the dark beauties in paintings of the Spanish school (JO, 150). At times descriptions are directly derived from the style of a particular artist or school of art. For example, the Rembrandt device of a highlighted figure surrounded by darkness is used again and again.[8] We have already seen this technique in the illuminated figure in a window and in the long shafts of light that fall on Alex d'Urberville in his role as preacher. Rembrandt's name is at times mentioned in connection with this device:

> A face showed itself with marked distinctness against the dark-tanned wood of the upper part [of the settle]. . . . The spectacle constituted an area of two feet in Rembrandt's intensest manner. . . . Though his whole figure was visible, the observer's eye was only aware of his face. (RN, 161–62)

And an effect like that in Impressionist paintings is seen in examples such as Mr. Percomb's spying on Marty South's coveted hair:

> In her present beholder's mind, the scene formed by the girlish spar-maker composed itself into an impression-picture of extremest type, wherein the girl's hair alone, as the focus of observation, was depicted with intensity and distinctness, while her face,

shoulders, hands, and figure in general, were a blurred mass of unimportant details, lost in haze and obscurity. (W, 41)

Both Joan Grundy and Alistair Smart provide the scholar with an abundance of examples, suggestive of how full Hardy's works are not only of visual descriptions generally but of a multi-faceted allusiveness to art. Smart notes:

> So vivid are Hardy's evocations of the scenes which he is describing that one is tempted to suspect some recollection of a picture even where no painting or painter is mentioned. This impression is often reinforced by his emphatic use of terms like "highlight," "foreshortening," "middle distance," "plane," and "outline," and by the precision and subtlety of his notations of color.[9]

And even when a specific artist, picture, or style is not suspected, Grundy describes him as a painter

> using words as his medium instead of paint. He makes no attempt to disguise or camouflage this fact; on the contrary, he draws attention to it by his use of the technical language of the painter: "foreground," "middle distance," "perspective," "plane," "line," "curve," "tone," "chromatic effect." The effect of the introduction of such technicalities is to distance the action or scene for us . . . so that the style itself might be said in this respect to provide a frame for the picture, an over-all frame additional to the particular ones supplied by such things as windows . . . or doors.[10]

Joan Grundy is certainly correct when she says that complaints about Hardy's pictorialism, such as Lloyd Fernando's "Thomas Hardy's Rhetoric of Painting," "wish Hardy other than he is."[11] Fernando sees Hardy's painter's habits merely as unfortunate embellishments, which often freeze character and plot and detract from realism.[12] Nevertheless, it is ironic that Fernando comes close to perceiving exactly what Hardy is doing: "His pictures are less pictures of reality than pictures of pictures. . . ; they are, after Plato, thrice removed from reality. . . . The writing . . . is . . . self-enclosing. . . ; [it] draw[s] its inspiration from a species of personal emotion . . . not sufficiently disciplined by the ordinary realistic demands of the novel."[13] Fernando's perceptive notations on pictorialism, self-enclosure, and subjectivity are unfortunately lost to his inadequate assumptions about realism. The subjective nature of reality in Hardy renders concepts of idealism meaningless.

Hardy's eyes are riveted to things. Though, as Grundy notes, we are aware of looking at pictures,

> the effect . . . is to heighten rather than to diminish our sense of reality. The pictures are so vivid that they have life, as actual pictures . . . have it. Their effect is simultaneously to idealize and to reify. The pictures have such finish and perfection *as* pictures that we seem to see the scenes and objects depicted with an almost hallucinatory clarity.[14]

This comes much closer to the Hardy who is actually on the page —to the Hardy who wanted to see and write so that "the heart and inner meaning is made vividly visible" (*Life,* 177). Grundy is describing an expressionistic style—"hallucinatory clarity" catches it nicely. However, one must be wary. The very pictures that seem to "reify" and "idealize" carry with them the framework of subjective experience. If at times Hardy seems to be holding "reality" in his hands, far more often he protects himself from this naïveté, and from his own desires, with the skepticism implied by multiple, non-authoritative, subjective viewers. He does not reify things so much as inner states of being. When the lightning storm in *Far from the Madding Crowd* leaves Gabriel observing "how strangely the red feather of her hat shone in the light" (FFMC, 280), and when the narrator in *Under the Greenwood Tree* sees that "a curl of woodsmoke came from the chimney and drooped over the roof like a blue feather in a lady's hat" (UGT, 110), we are seeing private, highly subjective, even unconscious realities. Hardy gives the fullest possible rein to the reality of things only to pull them back into the frame of subjective perception.

To return for a moment to Lucetta's speaking with Donald, there is a special irony in her thinking any scene is "a picture merely." She frames herself with a painter's art and, blatantly, with words and body. Immediately before Farfrae's arrival, she had arranged herself "picturesquely in the chair; first this way and then that; next so that the light fell on her head. Next she flung herself on the couch in the cyma-recta curve which so became her, and with her arm over her brow looked toward the door" (MC, 183). And in their conversation, her first response to the scene outside the window—"a picture merely"—pictures her as the aloof lady, indifferently looking at the surface of things; her second response—"I may look for you"—pictures her as a flattering coquette, involved with turning the marketplace into a frame for Donald. More seriously and devastatingly, social condemnation conveyed in a moving picture—the effigy of her and Henchard—kills her.

Therefore, how does one—in Lucetta's words—"look as at a picture merely"? One does not. It is merely a convention to believe that one looks at pictures or at life with total disinterestedness, without partaking in the beholder's share. Such a convention has its place in the history of art. A theory, introduced in the nineteenth century, proposed that an artist's reality consists only of surfaces—of lines, shapes, and colors—not of what the surfaces represent. The viewer should not look as through a frame but directly at the canvas itself, at "flat patches of color."[15] However, only a trained eye can develop this "innocence of the eye."[16] Hardy people have neither the training nor the innocence. Their seeing lies within the Renaissance tradition, in which pictures are windows onto reality;[17] Hardy's use of frames has a long history.

Settings, doorways, windows, stages, mirrors, pictures—all call attention unrelentingly to the framed nature of reality and of language. These concrete forms are the most explicit visual signs of Hardy's empiricism and the persistent human tendency to frame others and/or oneself in meaning.. They form an overarching subjective framework for every word in his books. Just as the spaces on a page give frames to the signpainter's words in *Tess of the d'Urbervilles:*

> THY, DAMNATION, SLUMBERETH, NOT
> 2 Pet. II 3
> (TD, 114),

or

> THOU, SHALT, NOT, COMMIT—
> (TD, 115),

or the valentine's words in *Far from the Madding Crowd:*

'Marry Me'

(FFMC, 32),

so every word has a frame. Paintings were probably immensely serviceable to Hardy. While he obviously had a sharply developed visual imagination, he needed varied modes of discourse, of imaginations, for all the speakers in his works, who arrive at versions of reality by what they see, how they see it, and how they say it.[18] Jude sees the distant Christminster with adoration and calls it the "heavenly Jerusalem," on which words the narrator comments, "Though there was perhaps more of the painter's imagination and less of the diamond merchant's in his dreams thereof than in those of the Apocalyptic writer" (JO, 40–43). Language, like everything else, has its private frame; no single metaphor or imagination tells the whole story.

Framing

"Active selectivity is a basic trait of vision," Arnheim informs us,[19] and such selectivity is a framing. Far more goes on, much of it unconscious, in the process of seeing than merely the projection of an image on the retina. The eye can rapidly move to make innumerable selections, all striking the viewer as a single stream similar to what one sees on a moving picture screen: "Each photograph presents a set spatial configuration composed in terms of the frame, yet the film projects, as it moves from reel to reel, a fluid, developing space; it is constantly alluding to the space outside the frame."[20] Furthermore, either perceiver or object may change, thereby changing what is seen.[21] Finally, "to see means to see in relation";[22] all seeing, except for that of the most highly trained eye, is done in a context of what the eye sees and what the mind knows.[23] Just as seeing a single image is a process we cannot without training isolate as a physical activity of the eye, so too is the process of seeing one that cannot be isolated from mediating factors extraneous to the physical activity of the eye but central to the project of knowing. Imagination, subjectivity, will, emotions, ideology, all play their roles in formulating—in framing—that final "reality," the thing seen: the thing known. Looking at the world, we select an image of ourselves; projecting ourselves, we select with a multitude of influences that have already selected us.

Now that Hardy's frames and the implications of their presence in his iconology have been analyzed, this section on framing will locate individual framings and their interrelationships, which form the movement of a text. Discussion will concentrate on this process as it enacts itself in two texts. First, examination of the mummers play event in *The Return of the Native* will reveal the subtleties of framing and self-framing as they are activated by the heart and mind of Eustacia Vye. Secondly, by tracing the large, framed structures that picture the experience of Bathsheba Everdene in *Far from the Madding Crowd,* my analysis will demonstrate the process by which these structures function to form a character's experience and a novel's poetic movement.

Eustacia the Knight: Framing Fictions Multiple layers of framing are not unusual in Hardy, nor is it rare for one layer to be that of ritual; the reader glimpses action through the lens of tradition. Traditions can be witnessed in the Fifth of November bonfires, in Book 1 of *The Return of the Native,* which are united to a series of mythologies—British, Scandanavian, Celtic, Greek; in the May-Day dance in Chapter 2 of *Tess of the d'Urbervilles;* in the King's Arms bow-window scene early in *The Mayor of Casterbridge;* and in the mummers play in *The Return of the Native.* In all these cases, the frame of general tradition is superseded or overturned by present and particular meanings. Eustacia's fire is actually a framed message sent to Wildeve; she protests, "Why shouldn't I have a bonfire on the Fifth of November, like the other denizens of the heath?" Wildeve accurately replies, "I know it was meant for me" (RN, 88). The May-Day ritual is changed before it begins, as the custom is almost extinct, yet in Marlott this group activity for women is still intact. However, the group is soon distracted by John Durbeyfield, drunk and singing about his noble ancestors, and by Tess's pained response. The scene closes when Angel looks back—as he will again toward the novel's close—to see a single figure: while the other white figures whirl about on the green grass, one "white shape stood apart by the hedge alone" (TD, 45). The window scene onto Henchard, a traditional division between different social classes, becomes an immediate source of current information and a clue to future events. Mumming, while not yet extinct, is somewhat of a dead tradition, "carried on with a stolidity and absence of stir which sets one wondering why a thing done so perfunctorily should be kept up at all" (RN, 147). Progressing within this toned down tradition will appear the vibrant framings of Eustacia Vye.

The introduction of an emotional structure to disrupt the traditional structure takes place even before Eustacia enters the scene and is a playful prologue to the later intensity. Sisters and sweethearts who helped to make the costumes

> could never be brought to respect tradition in designing and decorating the armour; they insisted on attaching loops and bows of silk and velvet in any situation pleasing to their taste. Gorget, gusset, basinet, cuirass, gauntlet, sleeve, all alike in the view of these feminine eyes were practicable spaces whereon to sew scraps of fluttering colour. (RN, 147)

The women, in competing with one another to create the most elaborate costume for their brothers or beaus, overlook the character's role entirely: if one "added ribbon tufts to the shoulder pieces . . . [another] would affix bows and rosettes everywhere" (RN, 148). The result is a melding of identities, of good and evil, and of sexes.

From the moment Eustacia conceives the idea of playing the Turkish Knight, she starts framing herself to manipulate people and events. First, to get Charley's role, she agrees to let him hold her hand, playing the role of idolized woman. At the end of the first handholding, when Charley opts to save a few minutes for another time, she becomes absolutely businesslike; "As you like. . . . But it must be over in a week" (RN, 152). When the minutes are finally consumed, the femme fatale creates another self: "Hand and person she then withdrew to a distance of several feet, and recovered some of her old dignity. The contract completed, she raised between them a barrier impenetrable as a wall" (RN, 153). A further strategy is her choice to be the Turkish Knight. The other characters took direct falls, "not an elegant or decorous part for a girl. But it was easy to die like a Turk, by a dogged decline" (RN, 160). That this is not a heroic movement does not distress her. When the Turkish Knight is finally killed, Eustacia manages not only to die by gradual degrees but also to arrange her body in a graduated position, her head high enough to survey the room. Now she can observe the audience, and soon a part of the room "riveted her gaze" (RN, 160). A face stands out against the dark wood of the settle: "The spectacle constituted an area of two feet in Rembrandt's intensest manner. A strange power in the lounger's appearance lay in the fact that, though his whole figure was visible, the observer's eye was only aware of his face" (RN, 161–62). The Rembrandt style mentioned earlier is put to excellent use. Not only is Rembrandt's manner intense; the emotions in Eustacia are intense. And the layers of picture upon picture help convey this intensity visually to the reader. A picture in Rembrandt's style is a picture of the effect of Clym upon Eustacia is a picture of Eustacia's "extraordinary pitch of excitement" (RN, 163) as she views him. The framing Eustacia is framed in a troubling response she is only too eager to grasp. And she is framed in more than one way.

The Turkish Knight's head piece of course serves the purpose of concealing Eustacia's identity. However, the barred visor is also representative of her own "barred" vision, a frame placed around her vision of Clym that existed even before she saw him and that continues to shape him long after Clym's counter-vision of himself asserts itself. Ironically, Eustacia's frame is broken before it is built. She knows—and even tells Clym—that love does not last as her love of Wildeve did not last; from the first time she hears Clym speak, she hears the voice of a man who "saw friendliness and geniality in these shaggy hills" (RN, 141), the hills she hates; and she has her extravagant, brilliant, wondrous, fantastic dream that ends when the silvery-armored figure with his visor closed "fell into fragments like a pack of cards" (RN, 143). The colorful bars of ribbon are metaphors of Eustacia's limited awareness of her own desperate will to give meaning to her life, a desperation that produces enclosing and destructive dreams. She understands Clym and her own self with as limited a view as Clym has when he sees the Turkish Knight, "only the sparkle of her eyes being visible between the ribbons which covered her face" (RN, 166).

Indeed, Clym's initial contact with Eustacia is as enticing as is her first contact with him. She falls in love with a fantasy, a means of escape from Egdon to the cosmopolitan world; he, too, falls in love with a fantasy, a mystery: the sparkle of eyes, a confusing suggestiveness emanating from a Turkish Knight, and —finally—a few words exchanged under the repeatedly referred to moonlight. That Clym is able to know nothing about this person except his own feeling of astonishment that she is a woman disguised as a mummer/man is both restrictive and fascinating. What the eye does not see the mind's eye may still develop at length. Here is another function of the Knight's costume, now aided by moonlight. Her presentation of herself in ambiguity and unfamiliarity here on the heath that is so absolutely "known" to Clym deflects any wariness of the unusual and places her as a stimulus to dreams. The chapter title, "The Two Stand Face to Face," implying a picture of openness and revelation, reverberates with irony. The ideal is "to see in half and quarter views the whole picture"[24] but, unfortunately, dreams permit Eustacia and Clym to avoid the whole picture, avoid confronting the part of each that is dangerously antagonistic to the other, and to replace it with an illusion.[25]

An earlier chapter, "Queen of Night," is an absurdly aggrandizing commentary upon Eustacia, a narrator's wild dreams, but dreams that do exist.[26]

> Her presence brought memories of such things as Bourbon roses, rubies, and tropical midnights; her moods recalled lotus-eaters and the march in "Athalie": her motions, the ebb and flow of the sea, her voice, the viola. In a dim light, and with a slight rearrangement of her hair, her general figure might have stood for that of either of the higher female deities. The new moon behind her head, an old helmet upon it, a diadem of accidental dewdrops around her brow, would have been adjuncts sufficient to strike the note of Artemis, Athena, or Hera respectively, with as close an approximation to the antique as that which passes muster on many respected canvases. (RN, 94)

And in her first moments of success at attracting Clym, while still hidden by her disguise, she again recalls the narrator to imagery of gods, goddesses, heroes, drama: "When the disguised Queen of Love appeared before Aeneas a preternatural perfume accompanied her presence and betrayed her quality. If such a mysterious emanation ever was projected by the emotions of an earthly woman upon their object, it must have signified Eustacia's presence to Yeobright now" (RN, 166). What is a mere woman on mere Egdon to do with such trappings? She does what her culture and her personality have taught her to do: she lives through others by falling in love with love, the only adventure possible for a young woman on Egdon Heath. She may be merely a Turkish Knight, anti-heroic and doomed to die, but at least she is a knight, and off on a quest.

However, there is another level of imagery more closely embedded in the novel's external reality, the white palings near Blooms-End. At times these palings are mentioned so frequently as to seem ubiquitous, to frame the novel and Eustacia. Derwent May, in an introduction to the novel, discusses these images as barriers to Eustacia's quest. Just before her first glimpse of Clym, near his house, she sees

> the "row of white palings, which marked the verge of the heath in this latitude. They showed upon the dusky scene that they bordered as distinctly as white lace on velvet." Those white palings glimmer through the whole novel. We have to associate them with such things as the white road that leads across Egdon, and away from it. But the palings are the perfectly expressive detail. For they are like Clym; luring her with the promise of escape from Egdon, and proving in the end to bar her way out of it. This is a sign we cannot expect her to notice, any more than the other warning that seems hinted at in Clym's first conversation with her in full knowledge of her identity. She—all fire, as the imagery of the book reminds us again and again, under the "curse of inflammability" as Wildeve says of himself—what is she offered by Clym at that first meeting? Water, from the house called Blooms-End. And so she goes to her fate.[27]

Those palings and Clym lure her, but even more strongly she lures herself. She seems to set out with the mummers to see and to know Clym, but this is a deception and a self-deception. It is the will of self masquerading as a will to know others. Her will, central to the act of framing self and others, is the will toward an absolute; she cannot be without a teleology. Eustacia is a creator of myriad frames, but her framing—while a process—is not a process of metamorphosis. She lacks the self-awareness necessary for change, remaining within her own closed visor, her barred perception, her illusion.

Bathsheba Everdene: Shaping Experience Viewed from a great distance, the experience of Bathsheba Everdene in *Far from the Madding Crowd* might be seen as a series of visual shapes: triangle, kaleidoscopic movement, square, outlined female form, triangle, rectangle, a second rectangle. Moving a bit closer, one could see the abstract forms becoming detailed pictures. We see a spring wagon, carrying household goods, plants, animals, and, "on the apex of the whole, . . . on the summit of the load" (FMCC, 43), a young woman. The next day we see the same woman performing acrobatics on a moving horse. Soon afterwards we peer through the four-hundred-year-old doorway frame of the great barn to witness Farmer Bathsheba Everdene directing everything. A short time later—in a hollow surrounded by ferns, further enclosed in light and sound, opposite a soldier—stands "a mould of Bathsheba's figure" (FFMC, 216). In the next scene, atop the ricks, surrounded with lightning, alongside a shepherd/farmer, works Bathsheba. The final two pictures are of Bathsheba, face to face with Fanny and baby, within their uncovered coffin; and of Bathsheba, as Gabriel's wife, within the farmhouse porch. The above series is what Thomas Hardy called "a series of seemings,"[28] impressions of the moment."[29] While he rejected any systematic philosophy, there is a consistency in the presence of seemings, impressioins, momentary visions throughout his works. We know Hardy's novels and characters by observing the seemings and impressions—the intensely realized visual structures—and the way in which these "seemings" and "impressions" accumulate into a "series," a continuing process.

Ian Gregor, whose book *The Great Web* places process at the center of Hardy's aesthetics, observes that in Hardy's world, "We cannot understand what we know unless we know how we know it."[30] Therefore, it is essential to realize that we know Hardy not from a single or total view or pattern but from an open-ended unfolding process and from our sense of this process as it unfolds in our own process of reading.[31] The impressions are not merged but presented more like images in a poem—unexplained; meaning will emerge in the reader's sense of relationships between and among the images. Analogous to Hardy's characters who must reach out to frame meanings, the reader must enter the text and become involved with framing meaning. The way one writes, the way one reads may also be the way one knows reality; the above series of scenes is the result of one reader's involved process of framing the reality of Bathsheba Everdene in bold outline.

The first scene of Bathsheba atop her wagon is a celebration of life in its varied forms. Joan Grundy has noted its multiple sources in genre paintings: "the out-door, wagon-with-pretty-girl picture; the indoor, cottage-kitchen one; the young-lady-at-her-mirror one."[32] After Bathsheba's mirror-looking, the narrator tries to cut down the bright force of the scene as one might cut the opposition's position in a debate. Recognizing the novelty of an indoor scene out of doors, the speaker proceeds to observe that the novelty was merely superficial and continues in an ironic tone, "Women's prescriptive infirmity had stalked into the sunlight, which had clothed it in the freshness of an originality" (FFMC, 44). Even Gabriel regards the scene cynically, we are told, and, after the young lady ignores him, is provoked into naming the "prescriptive infirmity": "Vanity" (FFMC, 45). At this point we are back to no point of view at all on the scene except our own. For one thing, Gabriel's words are suspect, a product of his own wounded vanity; for another, his direct language about the greatest fault of a pretty woman—"What it is always . . . Vanity" (FFMC, 45)—certainly disrupts the narrator's pedantic and avoiding language. The opposition is not defeated; the scene is original and not merely because of the unfamiliar yoking of two places.

Hardy has made of the three genre types his own new form. The page glitters with the wagon, "painted yellow and gaily marked," and the sun "light[ing] up to a scarlet glow the crimson jacket she wore" (FFMC, 44). Besides the repetition of "scarlet" and "crimson," Hardy repeats the list of plants on the wagon, the second time after she smiles in the mirror, and this time to the list is added their freshness and greenness: "[A]t such a leafless season they invested the whole concern of horses, wagon, furniture, and girl with a peculiar vernal charm" (FFMC, 44). Nature, domesticity, humanity are brought to one of their momentary mergings.

Further, this scene of young-lady-at-her-mirror, in its specific detail here, is an original. For one thing, there is a watcher within the picture itself, and the reader sees both watcher and lady. As Gabriel secretly watches, Bathsheba smiles in the mirror; then, "She blushed at herself, and seeing her reflection blush, blushed the more" (FFMC, 44). J. Hillis Miller, talking about the beginnings of Gabriel's love, brings this scene to a point, and the point is not "vanity."

> An extraordinary text! It shows Hardy's great insight into the nuance of interpersonal relations and also his ability to embody these relationships in concrete gestures which objectify them. So objectified, they are comprehensible to the reader without commentary or analysis. Bathsheba's charming vanity, smiling at herself, blushing at the smile, and blushing more at her perception of the blush, in echoing self-reflection, brings into the open the hidden intimacy of her relationship to herself. . . . Bathsheba plays the role of both lover and beloved, seer and seen . . . Gabriel has been stealing from her that sovereignty over herself she thought she has been enjoying in secrecy and security.[33]

From the start we meet both the woman and the problem that will be further unfolded to us in the course of the novel. Bathsheba possesses some vanity, yes, but—as the unfolding process will reveal—she also possesses a self-confidence and an appreciation of her abilities that are fully merited. Having some knowledge of herself, she is a person in whom subject and object meet; a person who exhibits an exhilarating control over her own life; the woman who will want to manage her own farm and will not be overly eager to marry. It is this, in Miller's words, "sovereignty over herself" that is traumatically violated by her experiences with Boldwood and with Troy; and, in this indeed original scene, Gabriel, a passive watcher without fault or blame, inadvertently starts that violation. And here, too, starts the novel's problem: the degree to which characters are subjects or objects of the changing events of their lives.

Gabriel's future moves are neither so faultless nor so blameless; hereafter, he seeks and finds ways to approach Bathsheba and to watch her in secret. His spying through the roof that very evening is mere preface to the far more rewarding scene the next day when he watches through the focusing intensity of his loophole. Riding a horse and needing to pass under some low branches, Bathsheba checks to be sure no one is watching her; then she

> dexterously dropped backwards flat upon the pony's back, her head over its tail, her feet against its shoulders, and her eyes to the sky. The rapidity of her glide into this position was that of a kingfisher—its noiselessness that of a hawk. Gabriel's eyes had scarcely been able to follow her. . . . She had no side-saddle, and it was very apparent that a firm seat upon the smooth leather beneath her was unattainable sideways. Springing to her accustomed perpendicular like a bowed sapling, and satisfying herself that nobody was in sight, she seated herself in the manner demanded by the saddle, though hardly expected of the woman. (FFMC, 53–54)

This scene exhibits the vitality in the movement of Bathsheba's body plus the independence of her will as she seats herself not to convention but to her own needs. The pictures thus far depict Bathsheba at the apex of a picture and in kaleidoscopic movement, subject and creator of scenes.[34] She is in command of Oak, of her horse, of her body, and soon she will inherit property, putting her in command of even more. She seems to be in continual process; not only does she inherit a farm but she also plans to manage it herself. Announcing this plan to her men, not without swagger, she sets her own challenge: "I shall be up before you are awake; I shall be afield before you are up; and I shall have breakfasted before you are afield. In short, I shall astonish you all" (FFMC, 117).

Her promise is kept in one of the most fully realized idyllic rural scenes in Hardy's works, the sheep-shearing scene in the great barn. The large doors are open, sunlight shines in, order and harmony are contained for a moment in a "frame of four hundred years ago" (FFMC, 177), and "[b]ehind all was Bathsheba, carefully watching the men. . . . Gabriel . . . flitted and hovered under her bright eyes like a moth. . . . Bathsheba . . . throw[s] a glance here, a caution there. . . . Poor Gabriel's soul was fed with a luxury of content by having her over him, her eyes critically regarding his skilful shears" (FFMC, 178). Bathsheba's eyes are everywhere; she is the subject, the creator of the activity and the scene. Her position is central in the first two scenes but is mediated in part by a secret observer who objectifies her. In this scene she is acknowledged in a new way. She is the observer—the accepted, public observer and evaluator of a community that assumes her knowledge of a traditional and productive activity. Her stamp is on the scene as clearly as "B. E." is stamped upon the flock's shorn skin. However, tradition is never the final frame in Hardy; the personal relationship between Bathsheba and Gabriel is always kept in the reader's mind, and a more disruptive element arrives with Boldwood's entrance. He not only disrupts Gabriel's joy and the workers' talking; he also disrupts Bathsheba's "sovereignty over herself":

> He spoke to her in low tones, and she instinctively modulated her own to the same pitch, and her voice ultimately caught the inflection of his. She was far from having a wish to appear mysteriously connected with him; but woman at the impressionable age gravitates to the larger body not only in her choice of words, which is apparent every day, but even in her shades of tone and humour when the influence is great. (FFMC, 180)

This subtle scene is the merest indication of the ways in which our creations may create us. Bathsheba's valentine has created a doting (and eventually mad) Boldwood. Here she is suppressing herself as a result of his attentions, and soon he will be rejecting her words, her reality, in a violent form of verbal oppression. However, Bathsheba's chief objectification is the result of a major passion within herself that changes her from the subject who creates events to an object at the mercy of them.

From their first meeting in the fir plantation, Bathsheba's relationship to Troy was that of someone pinned down, imprisoned by Troy's spur and words. In the sword-exercise scene our horsewoman, whose body's motion "could hardly be followed by Gabriel's eyes," whose body springs "like a bowed sapling," is told to "stand as still as a statue":

> In an instant the atmosphere was transformed to Bathsheba's eyes. Beams of light caught from the low sun's rays, above, around, in front of her, well-nigh shut out earth and heaven—all emitted in the marvelous evolutions of Troy's reflecting blade, which seemed everywhere at once, and yet nowhere specially. These circling gleams were accompanied by a keen rush that was almost a whistling—also sprang from all sides of her at once. In short, she was inclosed in a firmament of light, and of sharp hisses, resembling a sky-full of meteors close at hand. . . . It may safely be asserted with respect to the closeness of his cuts, that had it been possible for the edge of the sword to leave in the air a permanent substance wherever it flew past, the space left untouched would have been almost a mould of Bathsheba's figure. (FFMC, 216)

The disciplined body and industry of Bathsheba confront an unanticipated element, passion, that results in a paralysis of her will: "She felt powerless to withstand or deny him. He was altogether too much for her, and Bathsheba seemed as one who, facing a reviving wind, finds it blow so strongly that it stops the breath" (FFMC, 218). She was master in the great barn, but Troy is master now.

The text in every way presents Troy as irresponsible, unstable, deceitful. At the most obvious level, he lies constantly; even Bathsheba can hear that, but she cannot see the many images that the reader can see. Her first view of Troy in the lantern light affects her like a "fairy transformation," but to the eyes of the reader the light also sends "over half the plantation gigantic shadows of both man and woman, each dusky shape becoming distorted and mangled upon the tree-trunks till it wasted to nothing" (FFMC, 193). The magical couple first surfaces into grotesqueries, then disintegrates into nothing, a process that demystifies the reader's view of Troy but does not demystify Bathsheba's view. The sword, also, transforms the atmosphere; its movement resembles meteors, and his arm "spread[s] in a scarlet haze" (FFMC,

216). He has the discipline of a swordsman but the flash of a carnival man: grotesque images, phony meteors, an unclear picture, and magic achieved with lighting effects. Other figures are framed in doorways, windows, landscapes, mirrors; Bathsheba is framed in neon. From this point in the novel Bathsheba is repeatedly objectified by chaotic events, events over which she has, or seems to herself to have, little control.

However, paralysis briefly converts to dynamic energy in the depiction of Bathsheba and Gabriel working desperately to save the ricks. The contrast between this scene and the sword scene comments on character development and on the nature of Bathsheba's reality. Because she does not know the reality of sexual experience, Troy's sword and his "meteors" are more dangerous to her than is lightning, which can literally kill her. Troy says the sword is blunt when actually it is as sharp as a razor. Passion within herself and sexual control by another is a construct Bathsheba has not known before. But she does know the reality of a farm and the financial disaster that can follow if the harvest is destroyed. Her powerlessness vis à vis Troy does not render her absolutely powerless. Unlike Eustacia and Clym and Boldwood, she can face reality, withstand change, and even change herself. Side by side, atop the rick, she and Gabriel are lifted almost to a picture of sublimity by limitless light or impenetrable darkness, and their forms are reflected with clear and absolute lines. In the lightning, "every knot in every straw was visible. On the slope in front of him appeared two human shapes, black as jet. The rick lost its sheen—the shapes vanished. . . . [T]he two dark forms on the slope had been the shadows of [Gabriel] and Bathsheba" (MC, 278–79). And then the atmosphere is actually transformed:

> [The lightning] sprang from east, west, north, south, and was a perfect dance of death. The forms of skeletons appeared in the air, shaped with blue fire for bones—dancing, leaping, striding, racing around, and mingling altogether in unparalleled confusion. With these were intertwined undulating snakes of green. (FFMC, 279)

Like one frame superimposed over another, this scene of Bathsheba and Gabriel saving the ricks is played against reader's and character's consciousness of the great barn, now filled with the results of Troy's drunken revelry. Bathsheba must go one step further to take in the full reality of her marriage to Troy; she must face Fanny Robin and child.

However, first I would like to return to the opening of this discussion of framed structures in *Far from the Madding Crowd,* to the description of narrative movement as abstract shapes. These shapes are important to show something of the visualized aspects of metaphoric movement: "In the perception of shape lie the beginnings of concept formation."[35] Visual shapes are visual thoughts, and a sequence of shapes is a process of visual thinking and knowing. The two triangle scenes, wagon and rick, are related; both have Bathsheba, the central actor, at the top of the picture, and both connect nature, humanity, and domesticity. Furthermore, the second triangle carries out what was mirrored in that earlier scene, Bathsheba's self-confidence. Gabriel's reference to Bathsheba as "the only venturesome woman in the parish" (FFMC, 278) is surely hyperbolic, but not notably inaccurate. Her courage is fully realized and her self-confidence justified as she rises above the ricks despite the chaos of lightning. The similarity of shape and content also bring out differences. The independent woman at the "apex" of her wagon has been molded and married by Troy and is striving to save the idyllic world of the great barn from Troy's destructive irresponsibility. The kaleidoscopic movement and the moulded female form stand as the extreme points on a continuum along which all the action is placed: Bathsheba, the subject of her own life, spontaneous, perpetually open to possibility and process; and Bathsheba, objectified and defined by others, by events, and by her own irrationality. Though the great barn scene, in its union of nature and humanity and its depiction of Bathsheba in full possession of herself, overlaps with the content of triangles and of motion, the square form does stand out as separate and rare, the idyllic pastoral with everyone functioning to perfection in an ordered community. Much of the rest of the novel disrupts this ideal. "Experience *unteaches*" (*Life,* 176), Hardy said, but it is not meaningless. Characters live through a changing reality that tells them that it changes, and no character in Hardy lives only in a single frame. It is necessary for readers to move forward and back among the images to catch the developing process. And now let us move forward to the two rectangles, which are related to each other and to the whole series of scenes.

Bathsheba's confrontation with the dead Fanny and her baby demonstrates the will that has been the force behind her accomplishments and her integrity. Will can be harmful; Boldwood's will to materialize a dream leads to madness. But Bathsheba's is the constructive will to avoid self-deception. She is not greatly influenced by illusions. After a brief try at thinking well of Troy, she gives up, knowing what he is and loving him anyway. Unable to will order in the world, she is willing to confront the chaos. That was evident in the lightning scene and may have been part of her desire to confront Troy's sword-exercise: the desire to confront her own passion. Now she yearns to know the true connection between Fanny and Troy: " 'If I could only look in upon you for one little minute, I should know all!' A few minutes passed, and she adds slowly, *'And I will'* " (FFMC, 323). Bathsheba's actions are not entirely conscious; she is consumed with the need to know the truth of her life with Troy, and as "one in an extravagant dream" (FFMC, 323), she moves toward that truth. Bathsheba is framed by the rectangular coffin, even taken into it, so completely and unalterably does this knowledge of Troy's life change her perspective on her own life. After actively opening the coffin, Bathsheba is struck still, and stiller yet when for a moment she acts out a resistance to this new knowledge. She begs Troy to kiss her, to undo what he has done and said and what she has seen, to stop movement. Even Troy finds "something so abnormal and startling in the childlike pain and simplicity of this appeal from a woman of Bathsheba's calibre and independence, that [he] . . . looked at her in bewilderment" (FFMC, 326).

The final shape, the porch rectangle, on one level tries to package the novel into a tidy ending, an effort that will be discussed more fully in Chapter 4, on disrupted images. To some degree problems have been resolved, traumas have been survived, and a customary ending, marriage, has taken place. However, this marriage, like Bathsheba's marriage to Troy, has secretiveness around it and takes place off stage. Marriage had never been Bathsheba's final objective and, as a final frame, it is a confinement, a containment of energy and process. Furthermore, the view of Bathsheba looking like her youthful self on the yellow wagon, Gabriel's "fascinating dream" (FFMC, 423), is not impossible, physically, but it is desperately sad considering the concatenation of horrors in her life since that time. She can never be a former self after entering the frame of Fanny's coffin. Not porch and triangle but the rectangular porch and coffin are parallels; one stopped her movement, the other contains her stillness. The porch/rectangle, however, is closely intertwined with other forms; never could it seem so limiting without the contrasting triangles and motion that preceded it. There is an appalling discordance between that crimson girl atop the gaily decorated yellow wagon, that courageous woman upon the lightning-brightened corn ricks, and the present, ironically understated aside about Bathsheba: "(for she never laughed readily now)" (FFMC, 424) as she stands within the farmhouse porch, framed in a final position. As already noted (see notes 33 and 34), Bathsheba's independence, even at her highest moments, has been compromised by Gabriel's watching her when she believes she is alone, by Gabriel's helping on several occasions to save her farm from destruction, by Boldwood's and Troy's successful oppression of her will, and by Hardy's history of repeatedly destroying his energetic heroines. However, this last item wins back Bathsheba's bright energy. Hardy seems to have had some ambivalence in the creation of several of his heroines, giving them the brains, energy, and power to be independent women—along with a poetic language to make their strength convincing—yet denying them their independence and often their lives by the novel's end. However, he is too successful with his series of vital visualizations for these characters to be fully contained in a muted conclusion. Though Bathsheba ends in a static structure, Hardy's insistence upon seemings, impressions, momentary and tentative images—connected poetically, emotively, not chronologically—permits the reader to travel back and forth, seeing not only the final structure but the process of movement among the structures.

This is the process of metaphoric construction, framings, in many Hardy poems. "The Place on the Map" (CP, 321) frames memory and contradiction in a map. Looking at the map becomes looking into the map as the speaker sees his own history in "a jutting height / Coloured purple, with a margin of blue sea." However, past images of love in their turn frame disruption: his lover's words, which "wore a torrid tragic light / Under order-keeping's rigorous control." The map itself contains both the purple of passion and the control of "order-keeping," for if it is a metaphor of the entrance to joyous memory, "a jutting height / Coloured purple," it is also a metaphor of precision and measurement, "lined in varnished artistry" "the charted coast stares bright." The map revives possibility and restraint, a linkage that produces a now-silent frustration; the "episode comes back in pantomime." This final state of mind and feeling is not a conclusion—it is only the last item in a series that could have been longer or shorter. Traveling through the metamorphosis of metaphors is the closest we will get to another's exact, subjective, changing experience. The speaker himself has a double view of the multiple images: one is the memory his mind creates, the map as a window onto meaning; the other is the concrete, external reality of the map, like flat patches of color on a canvas, without meaning beyond the literal lines themselves. As well as being a poem of memory and loss, its process talks about ways of seeing and knowing.

The scenes discussed from *Far from the Madding Crowd* do not add up to a complete picture of the novel's content. Their sum is not even a complete picture of Bathsheba Everdene. The list could be longer: Troy and Fanny outside All Saints', Bathsheba and Troy in the fir plantation, Fanny's coffin's lonely journey through fog, Troy's gravesite garden and the gargoyle's destruction, the shearing supper, the harvest feast and drunken revel, Boldwood's valentine and party, Gabriel's eye on everything. But a "complete" list is irrelevant to Hardy's art because nothing is ever completed. The final scene is more provocative than it is conclusive. Gregor observes that Thomas Hardy's "seemings" do not "constitute the shape of a life. They are true to consciousness heightened in moments of vision."[36] The quality of a heightened consciousness is greater than the summary of parts; it includes aspects of vision and aspects of relationship, an imaginative grasp of reality as process. What the scenes discussed do bear out, in their metaphoric and interrelated meanings, is the triple vision projected in the title's words, "far from the madding crowd": an implied though possibility illusory stable rural world, violent disruptions of this illusion/stability, and an ironic tone that connotes the changing perspective. Bathsheba's series of experiences —seemings, impressions, frames—place in continuing process the novel's central problem: the unanticipated and possibly horrifying nature of change, which is at all times the potential condition of reality.

    Hardy's frames can be massive or minute, monstrous or subtle. He frames entire novels with woods or heath and presents settings within cliffs, storms, fields, doors, windows, telescopes, holes, mirrors, doorways, painterly styles. Not only are the frames themselves varied, but they are subject to further variations as frames and framed exist in a potentially changing relationship. The ultimate frame is subjective perception and the ultimate framer the writer whose creative vision halts its process only by reaching the first frame mentioned in this chapter, a rectangular shape. The interaction within and between framings is analogous to the interactions among Hardy's primary visual structures. The pattern of image into icon underlies all, and all framings are iconographic, embodying metaphoric outreachings of meanings for characters and readers. Because all framings are liable to disruption and, as seen in this chapter on framed images, because disruption is frequently realized, disrupted images are integral to the fact of framing. As Chapter 4 will discuss in detail, disruption need not mean destruction; it means change. In a vision of process, nothing is ever final and nothing is ever separate. Since one must create meaning out of chaos, creation and disruption form an unpredictable but inevitable intermingling.

Chapter 4

Disrupted Images

Images of framing and disruption are found in our, and Hardy's, culture in many and varied visual/conceptual signs. It is from such signs that one begins to see Hardy's iconology, like Panofsky's, as reflecting "essential tendencies of the human [modern] mind" expressed symbolically.[1] Observing people's unresponsiveness to the presence of a nuclear power plant near their homes, a journalist refers to

> mentalit[ies] that require a frame around any experience in order to recognize it—the frame around a shopping mall, or around a miniature golf course, or, at the very least, an idea of what a given place is and what one is supposed to do there. . . . [Experiences] exist only as a kind of interior, in much the same way that spas and shopping malls are places that seem to be primarily interiors, unrelated to what lies around them. . . . For such people, . . . the . . . [nuclear power] plant is unreal because it exists outside all recognized frames.[2]

Even people who take trips to exotic places can be framebound, constructing their entertainments "to preserve fantasies about what the world is like rather than to yield knowledge of the world, expeditions of escape rather than of discovery."[3] In a cartoon frame, a seated man is placed sideways, looking straight ahead toward the left of the cartoon square, toward a framed and curtained window. In the background, to his right, stands a TV set with a blank screen. In the background to his left stands his wife, framed in the kitchen doorway, holding a stirring utensil, wearing an apron, and asking, "Nothing on?" Everything in the cartoon's frame—and in the man's life—is framed. A slightly more ominous and startling cartoon depicts two moving men carrying a chest of drawers down stairs. No other people are in sight. However, atop the chest is attached a circular mirror reflecting a man, from the waist up, caught in the moment of tying his tie—caught like all the above people in packaged and static lives.

Frames not only exist, however; they also exist to be broken. A five-by-seven–inch newspaper advertisement for reptile belts has within its outside frame a smaller frame of four-by-six inches. A woman is sketched in a dress, occupying about a two-inch width running diagonally from top to bottom of the inner frame. But the reptile belt, instead of circling the dress, circles the entire inner frame, encompassing the dress in a greatly over-sized image, its buckle alone covering the female figure's waist and hips combined. The disproportionate size of the belt, plus its movement outside the advertisement's inner border, gives a unique effect of two pictures, one incomplete—dress without belt—and one unfamiliar—frame with belt. Frame and expectation have been broken, and we have been forced to see anew. In a series of advertisements for women's boots, again we see two borders, inner and outer. Within the inner border is a woman whose legs are positioned so that either heel or toe of the advertised boot "kicks through" the inner frame. The boot cannot move, but the broken line imaginatively conveys an image of energy through unexpected disruption.

P. N. Furbank notes an "abolishing the frame" in many areas, such as typography's freedom from ornamentation; informal photoportraits of people in spontaneous activity; dramatic interactions between actors and audience; visual interaction between the plastic arts and the environment. The history of picture framing itself reveals ideological disruption. The gilded picture frame introduced in the Renaissance was a sign that carried some notion of a separate level of reality, an ideal. As a contrast, the Impressionists' plain, white-framed—and even unframed—canvases were a revolt against ornament and the notion of any ideal. Furbank sees this "abolishing the frame" ultimately as "the recognition not only that traditional standards of reference have to be abandoned, but that there is something wrong with the whole *idea* of standards of reference," of any reference assumed or anterior or abstract or absolute.[4]

The tension between frames and disruptions is being felt also in contemporary literary theory. Deconstructive criticism approaches literature from a "tradition of 'difference' ":

> All similarities are produced out of difference. Thus difference is constitutive of resemblances, repetitions, and similarities. To say, for instance, that two birds resemble each other is to affirm their initial difference. . . . The relationships between entities, therefore, are not based on unity and continuity but rather are composed as differential and decentered formations. . . . The force of difference undermines the traditional concerns of origin and unity.[5]

Here, too, there is the rejection of any idea of standards of reference, of any reference. Deconstruction does not only disrupt references to the external world, traditional or otherwise; it eliminates them: "Language is from the start fictive, illusory, displaced from any reference to things as they are."[6] On the one hand, this makes all language framed—all is artifice; on the other hand, however, nothing is already framed, already known, essentially.

In *The Madwoman in the Attic,* Sandra Gilbert and Susan Gubar approach literature through a feminist criticism that describes nineteenth-century women artists as framed by patriarchal definitions of life and of art. Gilbert and Gubar discover

> a distinctive female literary tradition. . . . Images of enclosure and escape, fantasies in which maddened doubles functioned as asocial surrogates for docile selves. . . . [A] striking coherence . . . in literature by women could be explained by a common, female

impulse to struggle free from social and literary confinement through strategic redefinitions of self, art, and society.⁷

The study attempts to constitute a new ideology and a new way to read and write texts.

Related to Gilbert's and Gubar's "madwoman in the attic" trying to struggle free is George Levine's "monster." In *The Realistic Imagination* Levine notes the connection between the two studies, only he changes the "madwoman" to a "monster" and argues that the " 'monstrous' is an aspect of all realistic literature, that the repression of it is part of the strategy of realism, not exclusively or even primarily of women's literature."⁸ He explains this fundamental strategy of realism:

> Nineteenth century realistic fiction tends to be concerned with the possibility of accommodation to established power, and yet, given its inevitable interest in character, it explores with at least equal intensity the possibility of resistance as well: The "madwoman in the attic" . . . has her male counterpart. . . . Female resistance to the patriarch is echoed in a general Victorian resistance to the tyranny of society, of convention, of the majority.⁹

This tradition of conflict and contradiction is manifested not only in content but in form. While realism is framed by formal narrative conventions, it also disrupts these conventions; while it writes with the assumption of empiricism, it always includes a doubt about language's connection to the world outside the text. A resistance to this very doubt may be what prompts Hardy to his strong statements of intention to write so that "the heart and inner meaning [of things] is made vividly visible" (*Life,* 177); to make "abstract thoughts . . . [become] visible essences" (*Life,* 177); to translate material facts and their hidden qualities, with imagination, into a creation of "the All" (*Life,* 185). Victorian realists, Hardy among them, question "the conventions of order they inherit but struggle to construct a world out of a world deconstructing."¹⁰

This chapter's opening examples of framings and disruptions in social commentary, cartoons, and advertisements are serviceable metaphors for Hardy's way of working within a contradiction. Two things must be noted: (1) when the frames are broken, they remain present, not eliminated; (2) when the frames are not actually broken—the shopping mall, the TV set, the mirror—they are disrupted through exposure. In the first instance, the frames—prior structure and meaning—do not disappear from human consciousness; in the second instance, the frames—unrecognized or unconscious—are revealed as frames to human consciousness. That people package their lives in spas or TV screens or housewife roles or lose their lives completely to an image of themselves is a fact, but a fact usually unconscious or consciously avoided. Without its former carapace, experience is defamiliarized and, thereby, rediscovered. It is unexpected revelation that makes the cartoons funny or, more precisely, funny and frightening—grotesque. Hardy's interrogation of frames, then, works through two forms of disruption: upsetting, but not eliminating, prior frames and unmasking unacknowledged frames.

For example, Chapter 2 mentioned criticism of Hardy's excessively schematized plots, shaped "according to some obvious architectural principle and his failure to conceal the blueprint."[11] As Chapter 2 makes clear, he did not conceal the blueprint of his narrative structuring because he is disrupting its validity and vitality with a poetic structuring that comes closer to actual human experience; furthermore, the pattern's blatancy undoes its own effectiveness. He rebels against the established pattern by questioning the architecture as he builds it. Superprecision of structure uncovers the calculated artistry that shaped it, turning the reader to the emotive—even if irrational and improbable—content as more "real." However, the blueprint should not be viewed as present merely to be destroyed.

Hardy is not reaching final conclusions; he is looking forward and back and asking hard questions. Both in "In Tenebris II," in 1895, and in the "Apology" introducing *Late Lyrics and Earlier,* in 1922, he states, "If way to the Better there be, it exacts a full look at the worst."[12] Hardy was writing at a time when old and new values, meanings, forms are present simultaneously. This doubleness exists in a dialectical relationship whereby oppositions become metaphors of collisions that, by their very state of disorientation, make possible the evolution of new forms.[13] Hardy's works must be understood as Levine wishes to make the label "realism" understood, as a formulation "unstably in process."[14] In revealing, upsetting, reorganizing cultural and narrative expectations, Hardy's iconology is a process of discovery, enacting the "essential tendencies of the human [modern] mind" expressed symbolically.[15] The following discussion will examine the disruptive element in Hardy's iconology as it is signified in narrative voice, genre formation, plot resolution, and the grotesque style. These general and inclusive sections will be followed by a close look at the disruptive qualities in a single text, *The Dynasts*.

The Translucent Mask of Authority

Disruption seeps into every aspect of Hardy's writings. While it is often presented in the form of visual structures, it is present in other ways as well, for example in multiple and contradictory narrative voices and in the opposition between a voice and a vision. However, these ambiguities and tensions are not always apparent; his novels and poems can give the sense of having a single, authoritative narrative voice, which is quoted in book reviews and in scholarly articles as being the voice of and carrying the value of a particular Hardy novel or the novelist himself. At the end of *The Mayor of Casterbridge,* Elizabeth-Jane's views, expressed through the narrator's words and voice, seem to be so conclusive, so quotable: her youth has taught her "that happiness was but the occasional episode in a general drama of pain" (MC, 54). We hear Hardy's well-known pessimism. *Tess of the d'Urbervilles* ends with " 'Justice' was done, and the President of the Immortals, in Aeschylean phrase, had ended his sport with Tess" (TD, 449). We hear Hardy's well-known fatalism. *The Woodlanders'* narrator analyzes the environment:

> Here, as everywhere, the Unfulfilled Intention, which makes life what it is, was as obvious as it could be among the depraved crowds of a city slum. The leaf was deformed, the curve was crippled, the taper was interrupted; the lichen ate the vigour of the stalk; the ivy slowly strangled to death the promising sapling. (W, 83)

Disrupted Images

Fatalism and pessimism. When not presenting themes, the speaker often shows an omniscient knowledge of character. The reader learns that "Tess was trying to lead a repressed life, but she little divined the strength of her own vitality" (TD, 164) and that Angel was "more spiritual than animal; . . . singularly free from grossness. . . . [He] could love desperately, but with a love more especially inclined to the imaginative and ethereal" (TD, 234).

Furthermore, the narrator frequently sums up the past, makes time pass, directs the reader to the next season, the next event. About Tess's seduction by Alec d'Urberville, the narrator looks to past and future:

> One may, indeed, admit the possibility of a retribution lurking in the present catastrophe. Doubtless some of Tess d'Urberville's mailed ancestors rollicking home from a fray had dealt the same measure even more ruthlessly toward peasant girls of their time. . . . An immeasurable social chasm was to divide our heroine's personality hereafter from that previous self of hers who stepped from her mother's door to try her fortune at Trantridge poultry-farm. (TD, 108)

The second part of *Jude the Obscure*, "At Christminster," begins by bringing the reader up to date:

> The next noteworthy move in Jude's life was that in which he appeared sliding steadily onward through a dusky landscape of some three years' later leafage than had graced his courtship of Arabella, and the disruption of his coarse conjugal life with her. . . .
> He had at last found himself clear of Marygreen and Alfredston: he was out of his apprenticeship, and with his tools at his back seemed to be in the way of making a new start—the start to which, barring the interruption involved in his intimacy and married experience with Arabella, he had been looking forward for about ten years. (JO, 96)

Often concrete observation moves toward large conclusions: a description of Egdon Heath—a plain, a hill, a barrow, and a figure—becomes the abstraction "unity," absolutely dependent upon one characteristic, "immobility," the discontinuance of which would inevitably lead to one result, "confusion" (RN, 41, 42).

However, as noted earlier about the grand description of the figure on the hill, this description is told not by an all-knowing authority but by a very limited viewer; he knows what he sees but does not know the limits of seeing. Far from being part of a unified vision of Egdon Heath, Eustacia spends the entire novel and her very life trying to leave it. Also, the simple generalizations about life made by Elizabeth-Jane or the narrators of *Tess* and *The Woodlanders* must compete with other characters, conclusions, events, and visual structures that compel far more complex and uncertain conclusions. Nevertheless, these voices of authority are present in the texts; and a number of the observations about Tess, Angel, and Jude are appropriate and accurate. At still other times the narrator sees surfaces, nothing more, as with the figure on the barrow, but he pretends to nothing more than the ability to see surfaces. This latter way of looking is what leads Norman Page to describe the narrator—at the opening of *The Mayor of Casterbridge*—as an "interested but ignorant observer":[16]

> What was really peculiar, however, in this couple's progress, and would have attracted the attention of any casual observer otherwise disposed to overlook them, was the perfect silence they preserved. They walked side by side in such a way as to suggest afar off the low, easy, confidential chat of people full of reciprocity; but on closer view it could be discerned that the man was reading, or pretending to read, a ballad sheet which he kept before his eyes with some difficulty by the hand that was passed through the basket strap. Whether this apparent cause were the real cause, or whether it were an assumed one to escape an intercourse that would have been irksome to him, nobody but himself could have said precisely. . . . [The woman] . . . seemed to have no idea of taking his arm, or he of offering it; and far from exhibiting surprise at his ignoring silence she appeared to receive it as a natural thing. (MC, 35, 36)

The narrator is attracted to concrete details and is a careful watcher; conclusions are drawn from the specific scene only and are likened to those that could be drawn by anyone—"any casual observer"—fastening them even more closely to what is actually seen. Furthermore, the speaker has a mind open to the scene, easily admitting alternate possibilities—"the man was reading, or pretending to read"—and his own ignorance—"nobody but himself could have said." This restriction to the observable, what David Lodge calls Hardy's cinematic method,[17] is absolutely resistant to the privileges of an all-knowing, authoritative narrator. Yet Hardy's novels contain both.

The poetry, also, has a voice that believes in authority and systems, most often the framed and programmatic pessimism and fatalism. "Hap" begs for a conscious, vengeful God but knows all is brief because

> Crass Casualty obstructs the sun and rain,
> And dicing Time for gladness casts a moan. . . .
> These purblind Doomsters had as readily strown
> Blisses about my pilgrimage as pain.
>
> (CP, 9)

In "The convergence of the Twain," ship and iceberg, "Pride of Life" and "A Shape of Ice," are mated by "The Immanent Will that stirs and urges everything." Each one grows and moves

> Till the Spinner of the Years
> Said "Now!" And each one hears,
> And consummation comes, and jars two hemispheres.
>
> (CP, 307)

"The God-Forgotten" presents a "Lord Most High" (CP, 123) who has no remembrance of creating earth and promises messengers of help who never arrive. In "New Year's Eve" god—when asked about earth's creation, "And what's the good of it?"—answers that his labors were and are "logicless / . . . Without a guess / That I evolved a Consciousness / To ask for reasons why" (CP, 278). "Doom and She" presents "a mighty pair" (CP, 118), the creator of all things and her servant. The former is blind; the latter is numb. Again we hear the so-called Hardyan voice of doom, not only in content but also frequently in emphatic rhythmic beats and repeated sounds.

Yet, as discussed in Chapter 1, Hardy stressed that his works are a "series of seemings or personal impressions";[18] "a series of feelings and fancies . . . possess[ing] little cohesion of thought";[19] "mere impressions of the moment, and not convictions or arguments."[20] He repeatedly emphasized in the prefaces to his poems that they were "dramatic or impersonative: even where not explicitly so."[21] The poems are not meant to contain authoritative speakers or ultimate answers, but tentative impressions of highly individualized voices; and even without the prefaces' explicit statements of intention, this is what the poems are. Frequently they have at their core tensions between competing epistemologies: essentialism, generalization, abstraction—framed and static forms of knowing—are placed against subjectivity, imagery, particularity, ambiguity, change—knowledge as process and discovery.

Far from expressing a singleness of vision, often a Hardy poem seems to be going in one direction only to end up in another, or with just enough of a turn to deny the first intention without quite stating a new one: experience is caught in process. "The Darkling Thrush" (CP, 150) presents so unrelievedly gloomy a voice that one would expect an absolutely gloomy vision. Stanza 1 contains the language of death: "spectre-grey," "dregs," "desolate," "broken lyres," "haunted"; and stanza 2 presents the dead body: "The land's sharp features seemed to be / The Century's corpse outleant." Then, despite an appearance that blends with the persona's mood—"frail, gaunt, and small, / In blast-beruffled plume"—the thrush's entry is a remarkable contrast to the speaker's "fervourless[ness]" as the bird "fling[s] his soul / Upon the growing gloom." This "full-hearted" song "[o]f joy illimited," this "ecstatic sound," opens the speaker to possibilities outside his own bleakness, to "[s]ome blessed Hope, whereof he knew / And I was unaware." Stanzas 3 and 4, responses to the bird's song, are simpler and more literal, less weighted with the layers of metaphoric construction of stanzas 1 and 2. The heavy authority of doom is disrupted with a voice of modesty and need and, perhaps, hope. There is a question in the air, as there is in much of the poetry.

"Nature's Questioning" (CP, 66) muses, "We wonder, ever wonder, why we find us here!" and proceeds to guess at grim answers—grim and abstract: are we the result of a "Vast Imbecility" that has left nature "to hazardry" or an "Automaton" who is not even conscious of us or "Godhead dying downward" or a "high Plan" "[o]f Evil stormed by Good"? But the poem ends with the speaker's voice, the voice of an ignorant observer:

> Thus things around. No answerer I. . . .
> Meanwhile the winds, and rains,
> And Earth's old glooms and pains
> Are still the same, and Life and Death are
> neighbours nigh.

The poem presents a pessimistic voice of abstraction versus an observing voice of concreteness. In this final stanza we are presented with a new way of knowing: winds and rains are felt and seen, immediately sensed, and Life and Death are made not distant dreads but familiar experiences. The conclusion contains no fatalism, no pessimism, no hope, no despair, no answer, but a different way of seeing and feeling and naming. Again, there is an element of uncertainty—"No answerer I"; as Emma Clifford has noted about Hardy's changing world, "[E]ach event goes on to be an object of eternal questioning in space and time."[22]

Some poems are more explicit and dramatic in their turns from one view to another. Assumption is hardly allowed in "The Dream Is—Which?" (CP, 650). The speaker appears to be tossed through three stanzas containing contrasted views of three scenes. The images move back and forth from "laughing," "splashed," "tumbling," to "blankness," "haggard," "lonely"; from "radiant" and "rapid" to "bent and thin," "cinder-grey"; from "[w]eightless as thistleball" to "a mounded green." Stanza 1 of "Last Week in October" (CP, 709) contains a traditional vision of autumn, conventional enough to celebrate the inevitable cycle of nature: "The trees are undressing, . . . / Their radiant robes . . . / Here, there, another and another, still and still." But, in stanza 2, a spider's web catches one leaf:

> Like a suspended criminal hangs he, mumming
> In golden garb, while one yet green, high yon,
> Trembles, as fearing such a fate for himself anon.

The poem contains the kind of ambiguity and mockery mentioned earlier about the title *Far from the Madding Crowd*. "Like a suspended criminal, hangs he" is unexpected and grim while the words that follow, "Mumming / In golden garb," would be a lovely pastoral image except for the context, which makes it a mockery. The reader sees an ordered cycle of nature, a grotesque halting of that order with mockery and terror, and the ironic tone itself, which connotes a changing perspective. A sure pattern is broken; absoluteness is never the final form—only framings and disruptions.

The poetry can give one the sense of a door left only slightly ajar, a windowshade not quite reaching the sill. Readers may feel provoked into pressing eyes and ears against a keyhole, straining after sights and sounds to reach the whole feeling, to get the whole story, the truth. What Furbank notes about the existence of God in concrete things in modern poetry can be said of existence generally in much of Hardy's poetry: it is made up of "things glimpsed in the moment before the mind has had time to generalize and categorize them"[23]—before the mind has had time to frame them. Experience is in a state of perpetual disruption, an intentional formation of seeming incompleteness. "At the Wicket-Gate" (CP, 430) is about the story not told. Only the ending is pictured, and even that is blurred:

> And we slowly moved on to the wicket,
> And downlooking stood,
> Till anon people passed, and amid them
> We parted for good.

The people around them know nothing and the reader knows little more; but the speaker's response continues:

> But never will Fates colder-featured
> Hold sway there again.
> . . . .
> what a play was played under their eyes there
> As thence we withdrew.

Grim irony, slow movement, repetition of word and/or sound discover a barely discernible, yet exact and inevitable psychological state of depression. We almost see what the speaker can hardly endure to show us. Richard Swigg points out that what Hardy called his "grave, positive, stark delineations"[24] are achieved "by adjusting vision so precisely round the little that is understood . . . one feels . . . a completeness for which no key is sought or offered."[25] This is the experience of a poetry of personal, individual, unique consciousness, not a public voice of authority and generalization.

Even when we do get the whole story, there is an element of the untold. The ballad form Hardy uses at times has its built-in aspects of bareness with little but the stark outline of story that is called for in the ballad genre. Readers get the whole story, chronologically told, in "The Trampwoman's Tragedy" (CP, 195–99), but they do not enter characters' minds, get no complex analysis of people or things. When her lover speaks in a voice "I had never heard, / I had never heard," why does she continue "still to tease"? The poem does not invite the question. Furthermore, the accumulated specificity of places—"From Wynyard's Gap," where the poem begins, to "the Western Moor," where it ends—absorbs the passion, violence, and grief; we know them more than we (seem to) know the tragedy. The poem opens to us a minute but clearly etched view—names with brief suggestions of setting—of the worlds these lovers have lived in together. Readers encounter the trampwoman's tragedy in her compulsive memory of places attached to an extreme psychological experience, places that Donald Davie calls Hardy's "ghosts."[26]

> [A]s he travels, whole countrysides travel with him. Of poem after poem by Hardy, as of story after story, we can say that what occasions them is topography, a reality of place rather than time . . . , a mapping of physical space. What the reader of Hardy first needs . . . is not a history of nineteenth-century England, but a map.[27]

But of course the map is not all; the trampwoman—like so many other Hardy characters—has made the places her own:

III

> For months we had padded side by side,
>   Ay, side by side
> Through the Great Forest, Blackmoor wide,
>   And where the Parret ran.
> We'd faced the gusts on Mendip ridge,
> Had crossed the Yeo unhelped by bridge,
> Been stung by every Marshwood midge,
>   I and my fancy-man.

IV

> Lone inns we loved, my man and I,
> ·   My man and I;
> 'King's Stag', 'Windwhistle' high and dry,
> ·   'The Horse' on Hintock Green,
> The cosy house at Wynyard's Gap,
> 'The Hut' renowned on Bredy Knap,
> And many another wayside tap
> ·   Where folk might sit unseen.

And the poem's ending, not merely with place, "Western Moor," but with the personal, " 'tis past! And here alone I stray / Haunting the Western Moor," is consistent with the poem as a whole, a personal process of inconclusive—and exhausted—experience.

This study has at various points called upon the work of artists, art critics, art historians, and theorists of visual perception to help explain how Hardy sees and what he wants his readers to see. Recent experiments in photography by David Hockney support Arnheim's observation that "active selectivity is a basic trait of vision."[28] Hockney is critical of photography because it is "obsessed with subject matter"; he would place the emphasis elsewhere, on the "way things catch your eye. . . . Vision consists of a continuous accumulation of details perceived across time and synthesized into a larger, continuously metamorphosing whole."[29] He goes on to describe the way we actually see:

> [We see] not all at once but in discrete, separate glimpses which we then build up into our continuous experience of the world. . . . I look at your shoulder, and then your ear, your eyes (maybe, for a moment, if I know you well and have come to trust you—but even then only for a moment), your cheek, your shirt button, your shoes, your hair, your eyes again, your nose and mouth. There are a hundred separate looks across time from which I synthesize my living impression of you. . . . If, instead, I caught all of you in one frozen look, the experience would be dead . . . like . . . an ordinary photograph.[30]

This "continuous experience of the world" is a movement through framings and disruptions. One of Hockney's experiments involved taking a whole series of pictures of varied parts of a panoramic scene to try to reproduce the activity of seeing.

> Ordinarily, the photographer of such an expanse has to choose one point of focus, with the result that things closer or farther or to the sides are progressively more out of focus. This, according to Hockney, is another way in which photography falsifies the experience of looking. . . . "The actual size of the zone the eye can hold in focus at any given moment is relatively small in relationship to the wider visual field, but the eye is always moving through the field, and the focal point of view, though moving, is always clear."[31]

This selectivity and movement are perfect explanations of the way readers must come to know reality in Thomas Hardy's works. In describing Hardy's point of view—his "whole way of seeing"—Mark Kinkead-Weekes comes remarkably close to Hockney's descriptions of ways of seeing:

> [I]f a Hardy novel is a "series of seemings" or a "great web," it is because no single way of seeing will do. Vision, to be inclusive enough, must be from this angle, *and* that, *and* this; and the multiple perspectives do not fuse so much as sustain one another by a sense of interweaving. Hardy is . . . tentative, . . . aware of how one way of looking is different from as well as linked to another, . . . skeptical. He is also aware of . . . multiplicity, and of the sheer difficulty of seeing enough and of holding what one sees together. The "series of seemings" has to be articulated by a narrative which both allows for accident and holds design; and which, in moving narrator and reader from one location and mode of observation to another, never allows point-of-view to settle. . . . Hardy moves in and out of his fiction, now sympathetically involved, now wryly distanced, shifting stance from sentence to sentence or even within a sentence.[32]

One must see by many seeings.

From the above discussion on the multiple and varied and even contradictory points of view in Hardy, one can discover a tension between—on the one hand—the voice of authority, absoluteness, abstraction, generalization and—on the other hand—many voices of subjectivity, concreteness, indeterminacy, change. As discussed in Chapter 2, Virginia Woolf and Walter Pater also experimented with the enactment of empiricism in literature, but they do not exhibit this conflict. Pater's *Marius the Epicurian: His Sensations and Ideas* declares in its title that its center is the subjective experience and awareness of an individual human being. The narrator tells, as steadily as possible—with carefully nuanced and sensitive observation—the process of a human being's spiritual growth. And all of Woolf's novels, no matter who is speaking or thinking, are attempts to present thoughts and sensations without any single identifiable source. The extraordinary agility of that narrative voice to shift in and out of any mind, to alight on any object or sound or sense at all, is made up of a single texture whose source has been removed from the text itself: the imagination of Virginia Woolf. This is not true with Hardy; he creates vast numbers of imaginations to convey the tension, ambiguity, relativism so fundamental to his own vision.

Narrative voice in Hardy contains the full range of possibility felt throughout his works. The narrator can be omniscient about characters, holding years—even generations and centuries—of knowledge is his head. This distant voice has generalized, all-knowing philosophical views, often steeped in cynicism and pessimism. At times, however, it can be limited to the same source of knowledge available to everyone else in the text: the mere surface of things and subjective perception, the image and the eye. As Hardy obviously wishes to disrupt the concept of absoluteness and has this alternative to it, one might ask, why include the voice of authority at all? Literary critics do not seem to enjoy it. Hynes says that Thomas Hardy's "abstractions sometimes get in the way of his things"[33] and that at times he "violated the integrity of his materials to make his philosophical point."[34] Guerard notes his "abstract and even pedantic pessimism . . . , the dogged schematizings of gloom, . . . [the] impulse to systematize bad luck."[35] However, his way of working with framing and disruption is to disrupt but not to eliminate framings.

The broad spectrum of human error or insight includes the voice of authority, the huge generalization, the perspective that saw *Jude the Obscure* as "full of 'dirt, drivel, and damnation' and coined the sneer 'Jude the Obscene' " or wrote articles "entitled

'Hardy the Degenerate.' "[36] The voice of authority is a subjective projection of one way to read the world. And he does give the voice power, a power shown by both critics' and readers' responses, responses he felt the need to correct:

> In my fancies, or poems of the imaginations, I have of course called this Power [the Cause of Things] by all sorts of names—never supposing they would be taken for more than fancies. I have even in prefaces warned readers to take them as such—as mere impressions of the moment, exclamations in fact. But it has always been my misfortune to presuppose a too intelligent reading public, and no doubt people will go on thinking that I really believe the Prime Mover to be a malignant old gentleman, a sort of King of Dahomey—an idea which, so far from my holding it, is to me irresistably comic. (*Life*, 409)

The voice of abstraction and generalization is one kind of framing, of packaging reality—like shopping malls and spas. Hardy gives full voice to authority and abstraction only to pull them back into personal, particular, multiple subjective perceptions. The opposition is not between optimism and pessimism or any other -ism but between monistic abstraction and indeterminate particularity.

Furthermore, a controling narrative voice is Hardy's accommodation to traditional expectations of realistic fiction that there be some guiding voice, a universal truth, a clear resolution, a single position. The tension between the knowing and the ignorant narrator is Hardy's way to accommodate and to resist this traditional expectation and is analogous to the tension between storyteller and poet discussed in Chapter 2. The truth and authority of a tidy story or all-knowing narrator are present but also disrupted by multiple perspective and pictorial-poetic movement. He reflects his culture and the increasing assumptions of relativism by "enter[ing] the ironic gap, which now lies not between author or narrator and characters but between limited understanding which is real, and an ideal of absolute truth which is suspect."[37]

Hardy rejects two major forms of nineteenth-century realistic narration: (1) the eye-witness's limited perception of a single character inside or outside the action; (2) an omniscient narrator, outside the action, with special privileges of knowing, whose "multiple perceptions . . . coalesce into a single reality, a single truth."[38] While he permits a seemingly omniscient voice to exist, he disrupts its final authority by breaking through its frames of omniscience and abstraction with a multiplicity of voices. He also disrupts it by exposing it as something created, not by nature given. The very forcefulness of authority's overly simple and unexamined assumption, its arbitrariness, pomposity, and error reveal it to be not absolute and received but personal and subjectively constructed, like every other voice. While it would be precipitous to label Hardy—with all his novels' traditional characteristics—a writer of anti-narratives, his sense of disruption previsions post–modern novels that frustrate these conventions and codes, that "bring the codes themselves to the foreground of critical attention, requiring us to see them *as* codes rather than as aspects of human nature or the world."[39] We are shown what has been lost, the frames of monistic and universal truths about life and about narratives. However, we are also offered involvement in a new construction, an art of process. By frustrating readers' expectations of a consistent and orderly point of view, Hardy interrupts our habitual responses, tips us from our customary stances, pushes us into the process of making meaning.

Final Forms: White Glove or Red Fire?

Discussions of a Hardy novel as embodying a particular genre will almost inevitably lead to disagreement. The multiple and conflicting conclusions about the role of Eustacia in *The Return of the Native,* mentioned in Chapter 3, reflect disagreement about the novel itself. Is it tragic, pathetic, ironic, romantic, all of the above, none of the above? Questions also appear within the title of *Far from the Madding Crowd.* Alone, it suggests an idyllic green world, but within the novel grotesqueries disrupt any likelihood of an ideal pastoral land. Finally, the title must encompass ideal world, grotesque disruptions, and the ironic process of a changing perspective. *The Woodlanders* as pastoral is also problematic. The reader is struck with both the all-encompassing green world and this world's destruction, a destruction either self-inflicted or caused by outside forces: invasions from a modern, scientific, cosmopolitan world. Divisions between country and city, ideal and real are no longer clear and neither are the genre formations. This ambiguity is forcefully presented in what may at first appear to be Hardy's most formal attempt at a traditional form, *The Mayor of Casterbridge.*

Certainly Hardy intended the story of Michael Henchard to follow the pattern of tragedy, as, for example, John Paterson has amply documented.[40] Echoes of *Oedipus Rex* and *King Lear* are present, but to hear these echoes as if they had the clear and unmediated sound of tragedy is to lift Henchard out of a novel in which he is irrevocably placed. Like *The Woodlanders,* and unlike classical tragedy, *The Mayor of Casterbridge* takes place in history, and at a particular moment of historical change. In tragedy the hero's death should evoke meanings and values from a traditional and absolute moral order, and the new leader should reassert these past values for the future. But, like Giles Winterborne's death, Henchard's death provides no usable meaning from the past; the new leader, Donald Farfrae, begins a new order. By presenting a pattern of tragedy that is bold yet functionless in the context of this novel's world, by presenting a frame with a built-in disruption, Hardy uses a strategy of defamiliarization that leads the reader to see tragedy anew—as a thing now lost.

Though Michael and the narrator at times see "the Gods" as working against human efforts, Henchard does come very late in the novel to an understanding that life is "a mere painted stage" (MC, 340). The reader is made aware of this—or is at least shown it—much earlier, from the novel's opening view, so firmly fixed on the external appearance of the Henchard family, and from the novel's second "opening," as Susan and Elizabeth-Jane approach Casterbridge and the reader gets a camera's surface vision of Casterbridge. Both of these large scenes are followed by close-up views of Henchard, first within the furmity-woman's tent and second within the King's Arm's window. The close-up views become spotlighted stages with audiences, the first presenting Michael Henchard, the auctioneer, the second presenting Michael

Henchard, the mayor; however, both dramas end with a minor character stealing the scene from the potential tragic hero.

When the stranger answers "Yes" to Henchard's request, "Five Guineas. . . . Yes or No?," "[a]ll eyes were turned." The sailor is now the central actor, and shortly after Susan leaves with him, Henchard stands at the tent's entrance; outside, the rosy sky places him as one "looking at some grand feat of stagery from a darkened auditorium" (MC, 45). Henchard has been turned from subject to object; he has been tossed off the stage. So, too, in the King's Arm's window scene, while Henchard is telling a story of his feats as a businessman, a voice interrupts with a comment about the current bad bread, a business failure. After a few words of defense, Henchard remains silent and sits down. The chapter ends and the next chapter opens with the spotlight once more on a stranger, Donald Farfrae, and Henchard's receiving his note. Farfrae and his note are the subjects now; again, the former subject has become the object, tossed out of center stage.[41] Michael cannot or will not yet see the ephemeral texture of the world in which he plays though readers have been seeing "mere painted scenes" from the start. Here, as throughout Hardy, readers learn to know by learning how to see.

However, to say that Henchard is tossed off the potential stage of tragedy is not to say that Henchard is tossed out of the novel. Seymour Migdal observes that *The Mayor of Casterbridge,* among other Hardy works, presents a world "in which history and archetype exist in a permanent state of tension";[42] and Samuel Hynes speaks of the unresolved contradictions at the core of all Hardy material and, further, notes that the resulting irony does not function merely as an aspect of "tone or texture . . . but as a principle of structure. . . ."[43] Unresolved tensions are at the heart of Hardy, not only the tensions of oppositions but also of multiple perspectives, and it is the reader who must travel along these lines of tension. "Experience unteaches," but it is not meaningless. Henchard may be removed from tragic possibilities, obsolete, but he is not meaningless. Though the novel recognizes the unavoidable new world, unavoidable change, it does not hail this new world but only presents it.

Donald, the new world's man, is a fragmented personality

whose personal feelings and business sense are separate. He sings sentimental songs of the Scotland he never revisits and fits into the vicious life of Casterbridge, new business methods, and science. He may fall in love but is easily cured when his dead wife turns out to be an emotional liability. When the novel's ending places him side by side with Whittle's remarkable loyalty to Henchard, the reader bounds away from the emotional emptiness of Farfrae even though the movement is toward the inflexible and at times wrong-headed feelings of Henchard. Furthermore, while the hero is swept off the stage and out of sight, his final words occupy the center of a page and come close to being the center of a novel; Henchard's will contains the high and terrible standards he had set for his own life. His self-condemnation stands as an outline of his extraordinary and self-created values and maintains its everlasting presence on the page. He places in question values of both past and future, standing not for a final and total moral order but as a particular human being, living at a particular moment, governed by his particular values and acts. The classical tragic hero has become a generalized abstraction, a hardened symbol, a frame now disrupted and lost to the particular and the concrete.

Disruptions of traditional genre patterns are one more sign of the truth etched out repeatedly in Hardy's works: neither literary patterns nor the universe can be reduced to a single, significant form. Older forms, frames, still exist in mind and memory but inevitably they collide with new structures. This collision creates a new "truth" and new "reality"—the reality of change itself, of process. There is no final answer; the "final" form is movement. With no final answer, there can be no conclusive ending and, in fact, it is not only in genres but also in endings that some of Hardy's unresolved tensions are made apparent. Earlier this study pointed to conclusions upset by the reader's involved process of reading. In *The Mayor of Casterbridge* Elizabeth-Jane's controlling summary and the new leadership of Donald are merely icons of explanation; they cannot contain the reader's experience of other characters' intensely emotional lives or, placed at the end of the novel, the picture of Henchard's will. Chapter 3's discussion of Bathsheba Everdene connects the final visualized shape with earlier visualizations; readers break through the final figure to continue a fluid movement among frames. Often the poems end on a note of conflict or question or unresolved perspectives; at times they seem to contain neither beginnings nor ending, only a moment of untouched experience. Perhaps nowhere does Hardy more explicitly play at questioning the adequacy of conventional notions of endings than in *The Return of the Native.*

At the end of the penultimate chapter of *The Return of the Native,* Hardy includes a note:

> The writer may state here that the original conception of the story did not design a marriage between Thomasin and Venn. He was to have retained his isolated and weird character to the last, and to have disappeared mysteriously from the heath, nobody knowing whither—Thomasin remaining a widow. But certain circumstances of serial publication led to a change of intent.
>
> Readers can therefore choose between the endings, and those with an austere artistic code can assume the more consistent conclusion to be the true one. (RN, 413)

While Hardy says he is giving us two endings from which to choose, he is in fact doing something else altogether. For one thing, he does not give us two endings. He summarizes one, the one that—as far as our experience of the novel is concerned—would more logically follow the narrative thus far. And he most dramatically and fully unfolds the other before our eyes. We do not have a choice to make because Hardy has already chosen for us. Even if one elects the first, it cannot be chosen without the second—the romance and wedding—also in one's consciousness. And it is this ending that Hardy wants in our consciousness: a presentation of the content and form of conventional nineteenth-century closed endings and his exposure of that closure as inadequate.

When George Levine observes, "There is a violence implied in the conventions of narrative that wrests resolution from the muddle of experience,"[44] one gets some sense of the return of Diggory Venn, white, a sense shared by readers and characters:

"O, how you frightened me!" she said to someone who had entered. "I thought you were the ghost of yourself."

Clym was curious enough to advance a little further and look in at the window. To his astonishment there stood within the room Diggory Venn, no longer a reddleman, but exhibiting the strangely altered hues of an ordinary Christian countenance, white shirt-front, light flowered waistcoat, blue-spotted neckerchief, and bottle-green coat. . . . Red, and all approach to red, was carefully excluded from every article of clothes upon him. . . .

Yeobright went around to the door and entered.

"I was so alarmed!" said Thomasin, smiling from one to the other. "I couldn't believe that he had got white of his own accord! It seemed supernatural." (RN, 400)

Not only does Hardy choose to wave a supernatural wand over Diggory to make him a suitable husband for Thomasin and provide a suitable wedding ending for the novel; he also raises Diggory to the level of high romance.

This new and unfamiliar white figure searches in the moonlight for Thomasin's glove, the romantic hero's souvenir. We are for a moment reminded of the former, compulsive Diggory, the voyeur, waiting to catch sight of his prey:

> Diggory's form was now distinct on the green; he was moving about in a bowed attitude, evidently scanning the grass for the precious missing article, walking in zigzags right and left till he should have passed over every foot of the ground. (RN, 404)

And that unswerving, monomaniacal devotion to Thomasin is seen in his final movement, "in a mathematically direct line" (RN, 405), toward his home. In between is the lover in the moonlight who finds the glove: "At last Venn appeared to find it; whereupon he stood up and raised it to his lips. Then plac[ed] it in his breast-pocket—the nearest receptacle to a man's heart" (RN, 405). This vision of a white Diggory in the moonlight, conventionally kissing a lady's glove, is out of keeping with everything we have known of him throughout the novel. An object removed from its normal context may make us see it for what it really is. But this white image of Diggory is split as with a guillotine from what he was. There is no connection whatsoever. From first to last he is unfamiliar and unrecognizable.[45]

Furthermore, that this utterly domesticated, ordinary young man should so startle character and reader is a sign of the inadequacy of mere conventionality to contain the problems of the novel. The reader withdraws, distances himself or herself, rebounds to prior structures in which picture and emotion were more at one. Eyes seek out the red automaton, gambling by candlelight and glowworms; one looks yearningly for the picture of Eustacia-the-Turkish-Knight and Clym at their initial meeting in the moonlight, a scene of extraordinary sexual tension. One turns back from a white glove found on the grass to a red fire gleaming across Egdon Heath. As wrong-headed and blind as Eustacia, Clym, and even Wildeve have been and as peculiar as Reddleman Venn has been, they have governed one's responses to the novel. They have been at the emotional and visual center, far too dominant for a whitewashed Diggory to be any answer at all. Sending readers to prior frames, involving readers in the rejection of a reconstructed Venn, Hardy claims for Eustacia, Clym, and Wildeve a validity they may not have won before. Furthermore, the neatly packaged new Diggory—rather than inviting unconscious acceptance of a traditional, closed ending—defamiliarizes the convention, exposes the frame, initiates readers to a conscious awareness and a scrutiny of form itself.

In *The Return of the Native* Hardy goes beyond what he does in *The Mayor of Casterbridge* and *Far from the Madding Crowd*. Here again the reader is sent back to prior forms, pressed into movement, but in *The Return of the Native* he moves closer to the open-ended modern novel.[46] His ironic use of Venn is so fundamental an aspect of structure that it exposes not only this ending for this novel and these characters as inadequate but the whole idea of endings as inadequate. One is startled into seeing the machinery of fiction and the possibility that it is merely machinery. He even uses characterization, Clym's general habit of abstractedness, to develop a critical perspective within the text. Clym can hardly give the topic of Diggory's and Thomasin's marriage his briefest attention.[47] After Thomasin announces, "He's much more respectable now than he was then!" Clym replies, "Who? O yes—

Diggory Venn" (RN, 412). Following Humphrey's observation that Venn and Thomasin have become friends again, Clym responds, "Have they?" (RN, 412). When Thomasin prefaces the announcement of her wedding plans with, "What do you think I have to tell you, Clym?" and Clym responds, "I can guess," surely a tone of mockery and humor comes through. Hearing Clym accept Diggory as someone who has "turned over a new leaf" (RN, 412), one cannot take the language seriously. It is not a question of Diggory's character but of metaphor itself; the words must be taken literally. He *is* a new leaf, a page without print, white and spotless, with neither blemish nor origin nor history not credibility. Nothing emerges. The final form of Diggory Venn is Hardy's perhaps playful but decisive rejection of a final form.

Thus far this chapter on disruption has examined the disruptive quality in some of the larger elements of literature—point of view, genre formation, and endings. While all of these larger patterns include aspects of style and other elements of tone and texture, the next section, "Large and Startling Figures," will concentrate specifically on one aspect of Hardy's style, the grotesque. Also, while the disruptive elements of point of view, genre formation, and endings point to cultural changes—old and new "frames" existing simultaneously—the grotesque points with more violence to a change already taken place with, possibly, no new frames.

Large and Startling Figures

> And the great realistic fictions are exuberant with details, even when they are melancholy thematically. The alienation implied by description is partially compensated for by the sheer pleasure of being able to *see,* as though for the first time. . . . This very vitality of detail is part of the realist's gestures at life, for they will not succumb to the conventions of patterning.[48]

What George Levine notes about Victorian realism generally has frequently been noted about Hardy specifically: a high degree of tactility joined to tension and contradiction. In discussing Hardy, Albert Guerard observes this life of *"things* touched and tasted and seen."[49] He also senses an energy derived from the details of "absurd plotting" that brings character to life; it even "establish[es] a convention of feeling and make[s] the miraculous credible."[50] Samuel Hynes sees Hardy's ironic juxtaposition of actions and images as the linking of irreconcilable experiences and as central to the animating movement of his works: Hardy "saw experiences as a configuration of opposites, every event contradicted or qualified by a succeeding event, an infinite sequence of destructive tensions."[51] However, it is not destruction but antagonism that Hynes points to as Hardy's central emotion.[52] Events and images are contradicted but not eliminated; frames may be broken but they remain present. This dynamic, disruptive, chaotic quality in things seen and tension felt is found with great force in Hardy's use of the grotesque style.

The grotesque in literature is "an aesthetic category determined by the subjective perception of the viewer . . . , a mode of illusion."[53] The grotesque style assumes incongruity and juxtaposes the ludicrous and the fearful, real and fantastic, tragic and comic. It does not provide the conventional combinations because its purpose is to startle, enlarge, mythicize—to shake one into seeing by the use of ambiguity, complexity, distortion.[54] There is double vision, a clash between at least two assumptions of reality, which creates a tension without a resolution. It often appears during periods of cultural upheaval; point of view becomes more confused and subjective because the public element is gone.[55] Hardy was writing at a time of broad ideological upheaval, a time in which he could neither find belief nor succumb to cynicism. He felt no attachment to old traditions but found nothing to take their place. He is not unlike Tess: "The universe itself only came into being for Tess on the particular day in the particular year in which she was born" (TD, 195). Because there is no objective, orderly, meaningful universe to inherit, one longs to create an order; however, owing to the chaotic nature of life, almost all attempts are thwarted. One desires unity but discovers only fragmentation: the modern dilemma.

Hardy's works convey the dislocation, the disorientation of the modern dilemma, the absurd condition. Jean Brooks concludes that "Hardy's multiple vision of experience brings him close to the modern Absurd form of tragi–comedy or comi–tragedy."[56] Hardy himself wrote, "If you look beneath the surface of any farce you see a tragedy; and, on the contrary, if you blind yourself to the deeper issues of a tragedy you see a farce" (*Life*, 215). Possessing a non-rational and anti-systemic understanding of the universe, Thomas Hardy presented his view of a chaotic world. But there is a difficulty in such subjective and isolated perception. With traditional forms gone, or going, writers have a special challenge to convey a vision of reality that is private, subjective, and imaginative. An audience can easily ignore or misunderstand such vision. Flannery O'Connor—a Catholic mystic writing in twentieth-century, industrialized, secular America—saw the difficulty in communicating her views and explained her need for a grotesque style: "[T]o the hard of hearing one shouts, for the almost blind you draw large and startling figures."[57] The picture is disoriented and disorienting but necessary; a special kind of language is needed to generate a special kind of knowledge.[58] Hardy, too, drew "large and startling figures" to present an externalization—a visualization—of the absurd condition.

In examining the grotesque, a reader must learn to look not at the left or right, before or after, beginning or end, but precisely at the center where lines cross, at the point of contradiction itself. In "At Waking" the speaker sees his former love moved from a positive but generalized former image—"Love," "endowment / Of charm," "gilt," "Enrichments," "believed-in-thing"—to a negative and more particular image: "Dead-white as a corpse outlaid," "bare / Hard lines unfold," "killed," "common" "average," "blank" (CP, 224). We catch the speaker at the moment of disorientation, when former images still linger but they linger as a feeling of startling loss. As not infrequently happens in Hardy's works, love has briefly served to bring an order to one's life; however, inevitably, such subjectively-created structures end in alienation. Where before had been a center of meaning is now only a harsh outline containing nothing. Anguish is felt less for the lost object than at the fact that loss can take place at all:

> Off: it is not true;
> For it cannot be
> That the prize I drew
> Is a blank to me
>   (CP, 224).

"In her despair Tess sprang forward and put her hand upon the hole, with the only result that she became splashed from face to skirt with the crimson drops" (TD, 61). A moment of contradiction is pictured when Tess tries to stop Prince's death and, simultaneously, gets pulled into the spill of blood. She, like the speaker in "At Waking," is astounded and made to feel ridiculous by the fact of change and chance: "Why, I danced and laughed only yesterday!" (TD, 61). Unlike that speaker, however, she takes responsibility for her own ignorance about the nature of life, adding, "To think that I was such a fool!" (TD, 61). The same lines might be said by Bathsheba as she confronts the corpses of Fanny and baby. The fundamental and constantly potential contradiction between ignorance and knowledge, efforts and results, will and chance, desire and limitation is what waking scene, blood scene, and coffin scene evoke metaphorically. Grotesque images are not so much a result of the will to convert image into icon, as discussed in Chapter 2, as the reactive moment at which created meaning or the will to create is undercut. The grotesque occurs in large, revealing scenes, as in "At Waking" or the above scenes from *Tess* or *Far from the Madding Crowd;* but it is also sprinkled throughout in smaller structures, making this unresolved tension, contradiction, antagonism an integral and constant part of the visual texture of Hardy's world. Though antagonistic, the conjunction of forces is neither meaningless nor necessarily negative; it is part of a process that includes disorientation, during which change may become possible, the hidden may become known.

At times the grotesque moment is shown by objectifying human beings into images of nature or things. Tess, objectified and devitalized as she works on the threshing-machine, exists in a vision of hell. Her body must work at the same speed as the machine, the man who runs the machine looks like "a creature from Tophet" who "served fire and smoke" (TD, 373), "the workers look cadaverous," and the scene ends in a "confusion as of Pandemonium" (TD, 381, 2). Through this section the truth behind the surface, Tess's psychological state and awareness, is shown, and it is this grotesque vision of her life as Hell that she must confront before moving on to her next position. In *The Return of the Native,* the rustics, with all their ignorance and inaccurate perceptions, are first seen as "so involved with furze . . . that [they] appeared like a bush on legs" (RN, 43), which is a grotesque combination of the natural and the human, but as they sit about the fire the comic grotesque moves to the hideous: they are described as "Dureresque," having "eye-sockets, deep as those of a death's head," "nostrils like wells" (RN, 45). Wildeve and Diggory, in their crazed dice game with which they attempt—and fail—to mold chance to their wills, appear in bizarre forms: Wildeve screams and stamps and looks like a madman while Diggory is not human at all, but "a red sandstone statue" and a "red automaton" (RN, 252).

Clym, in his will to sacrifice his individual self to higher human goals, unconsciously becomes a heath insect; and Farfrae, in a multiplicity of wills, becomes an insect-machine-piano. Farfrae is like T. S. Eliot's hollow men, not in being nothing but in being everything. He is identified with progressive machines and machine-like modern accounting, but also with nostalgic song. For a moment he becomes both:

> The machine was painted in bright hues of green, yellow, and red, and it resembled as a whole a compound of hornet, grasshopper, and shrimp, magnified enormously. Or it might have been likened to an upright musical instrument with the front gone. (FFMC, 93)

The horse drill, presented in grotesque terms as looking like giant insects and like an x-rayed, skeletal musical instrument, contains Farfrae's singing voice coming from the center of it. Elizabeth-Jane responds to the machine—and its undercutting of Biblical meaning—by commenting, " 'Then the romance of the sower is gone for good.' " Donald answers, " 'Ay, ay. . . . It must be so,' . . . his gaze fixing itself on a blank point far away" (MC, 195).

In this scene we get the juxtaposition of many Donalds and no Donald at all: "his gaze fixing itself on a blank point far away." His many parts cancel each other out to a disconcerting blankness.

On the other hand, *Jude the Obscure*'s Father Time is startling not by his many selves but by his one self: absolute, undivided, single-minded, and dead. In his inability to believe in the present moment—"I should like the flowers very much, if I didn't keep thinking they'd be all withered in a few days" (JO, 316)—he becomes a thing, an abstraction, empty of concrete experience and possibility. Sue's cheeks reflect the color of pink roses, and her desire to grasp the enchantment of flowers—"I should like to push my face quite into them" (JO, 316)—is totally absent from this old child. Whereas Donald's chameleon quality leads one to question the existence of any central source of meaning in him, Father Time's insularity leads one to the same question. He is incapable of receiving or projecting meaning, processes that are necessary for survival. Each character lacks a creating center, a lack that disrupts the possibility of process.

Hardy made varied use of the grotesque in his poetry. We have already noted the cosmic terror in "At Waking." In *Satires of Circumstance in Fifteen Glimpses* we get glimpses of two views of the same situation, the second usually being the satiric reversal of what seemed to be the state of circumstances in the first. Satire can move in tone from gentle amusement to brutal attack, but the tone in these pieces is more that of a comic leer, like the carved mask on Lucetta's High Place Hall. They are not didactic, as satire usually is, but reveal the painful but contradictory circumstances in which people live without knowing it. The young wife, the aunt who saved her money and trusted her niece, the ignorant bridegroom, the squabbling mothers—all live (or lived) in illusions that we cannot quite laugh at because the truth would be so painful, so our smiles are twisted into leers. The structure of these poems, primarily made up of two stanzas with the view in one stanza clashing against the view in the other, and the number of them set side by side, help to impress grotesqueness upon the reader. In "The Convergence of the Twain" (CP, 306), where the satire carries a more didactic tone than that found in *Satires of Circumstance,* the grotesque tension is felt in the convergence of images used to convey the illusory nature of pride—opulent mirrors are covered with slimy worms; jewels are now lightless and blind—and in the ironically indifferent tone of the speaker. He can call the destructive iceberg "gaily great" and use the word "consummation," which usually connotes positive union, to describe the fulfillment of tragedy. The poem's steady beat and repeated sounds plus the idea of a great plan and pattern collide with actual human experience, chaos.

The most pervasive way in which the grotesque is used in Hardy's poetry is in the imagery. His poems are filled with images of ghosts, corpses, phantoms, spectres. One rarely finds the lengthy scenes of spectacular enlargement found in the novels but, as in those scenes, the imagery in the poems intensifies the experience and pushes toward a fuller revelation of the material and/or psychological situation. The tone can be lightly ironic as in "1967" (CP, 220) or filled with inexplicable, gothic dread as in "The Re-Enactment" (CP, 361) and "A January Night" (CP, 466) or weighted with anguish as in "A Commonplace Day" (CP, 115) or "Neutral Tones" (CP, 12). "Neutral Tones" is a description of situation and setting highly colored by the emotions of the persona. The title is an ironic commentary upon the description we are not getting. The sun looked "as though chidden by God," the sod is "starving." The person to whom he is speaking—literally or imaginatively—has a smile that is "the deadest thing alive enough to have strength to die; / And a grin of bitterness swept thereby / Like an ominous bird awing." There is dread and death throughout the poem; added to the dead smile and the word "ominous," the word "grin" (inappropriate for a literal picture of the situation) suggests a skeletal head. The love is now a corpse, but the corpse remains: the disorienting and alienating experience of loss. The speaker is left with a vision of fragmentation: a face, the sun, a tree, the pond—separate images with no unity. In "Wessex Heights" (CP, 319) the speaker is also haunted by ghosts; the past may be agonizingly dead, but in the persona's emotions and memory, it insists on being dreadfully alive as well. "The dread is what we do not and cannot know, the forces of the emptiness behind the actual."[59] The dread is the dread of an absurd universe.

The Dynasts, a work saturated with a devastatingly ironic vision of human efforts and with grotesqueries, frequently presents the "bird's-eye view" where people are seen "writhing, crawling, heaving, and vibrating" (Fore Scene, 6). At one point the Russian soldiers are crossing over a frozen lake, which begins to crack; Napoleon has his troops forward this disaster by firing upon the ice: "A ghastly crash and splashing follows the discharge, the shining surface breaking into pieces like a mirror, which fly in all directions. Two thousand fugitives are engulfed, and their groans of despair reach the ears of the watchers like ironical huzzas" (I, 6, iii, 121). Horses and people are frozen to death, Napoleon is shown as frantic as a wild animal, and the multitudes of dead bodies could drive one mad. The human troops with all their efforts are seen as "no more than a file of ants crawling along a strip of garden-matting" (II, 5, v, 278), and the entire English army looks like three caterpillars. Napoleon's ruined army in Russia is also pictured as a caterpillar that "gets more attenuated, and there are left upon the ground behind it minute parts of itself, which are speedily flaked over, and remain as white pimples by the wayside" (III, 1, ix, 354).

The grotesqueness increases as the work progresses, paralleling greater and greater human effort with more and more human devastation and a sense of the ridiculousness of the effort. Napoleon, seeing himself as finally attaining his victory when he reaches Moscow, says, "Yes: it was time. . . . Now what says Alexander!" (III, 1, vii, 347) and is answered by a creeping fire, "one huge furnace" (III, 1, vii, 347) that had been Moscow. Russian soldiers show the nobility of warriors by refusing to shoot sleeping enemies, but ideas such as "nobility" are undercut when the enemy has already frozen to death in sitting position. The reverence that the troops can still feel for Napoleon is violated when he abandons them, and we hear the "Mad Soldier's Song." There is also the juxtaposition between the gentle tone of a line and the destruction it connotes: "Till floats down one small morsel, which appals" (III, 1, ix, 353) introduces the snow that will destroy Napoleon's forces. The ballroom scene in Brussels is ghastly, with death surrounding it, and within the scene one moves from brilliant lights, music, dancing through rumors and premonitions of death to the final silence, stillness, and the barren light of dawn. Thwarted efforts and violence, rather than being shocking, become exhausting but ordinary, and in that matter of fact assumption of disaster is a sinister silence. The remainder of Chapter 4 will examine the many elements of *The Dynasts*, grotesque and otherwise, that mold this epic-drama into an entire work of disruption.

The End of Magic: An Anatomy of Fictions in The Dynasts

> When I set out for Lyonnesse,
>   A hundred miles away,
>   The rime was on the spray,
> And starlight lit my lonesomeness
> When I set out for Lyonnesse
>   A hundred miles away.
>
> What could bechance at Lyonnesse,
>   While I should sojourn there
>   No prophet durst declare,
> Nor did the wisest wizard guess
> What would bechance at Lyonnesse
>   While I should sojourn there.
>
> When I came back from Lyonnesse
>   With magic in my eyes,
>   All marked with mute surmise
> My radiance rare and fathomless,
> When I came back from Lyonnesse
>   With magic in my eyes.
>   (CP, 312)

"When I set out for Lyonnesse" is quintessential of much Hardy poetry. As has been said earlier, his poetry often combines a fullness of emotion with a limitation of knowledge; it is a poetry of complex and ambiguous experience—personal, individual, unique. The poem contains two experiences, the speaker's and, from the speaker's perception, those who observe him: "prophet," "wizard," and "All." The response to his adventure, both before and after, is beyond language: before, "No prophet durst declare,

/ Nor did the wisest wizard guess," and after, "All marked with mute surmise." The poem has visual details, yet they are always just out of reach, just out of sight. Lyonnesse is an exact place, spatially mapped out for us, "a hundred miles away," yet the reader never sees the place or even one mile of the journey. "Rime" and "starlight" are visually concrete, yet we can see them only as they effect the ephemeral, "spray," or the abstraction, "lonesomeness." The speaker's final state is expressed visually, a "radiance rare and fathomless," but not concretely; the "picture" is abstract and incomprehensible. The poem's central frame and picture, "the magic in my eyes," is vague and uncertain; magic can be approached only through "mute surmise," and "eyes" that frame magic contain, of course, a subjective and intuitive perception of reality. The ballad-like repetition of line helps lure the reader into mystery, where experience hangs in the air: concrete and ephemeral, geographic and spaceless, built on images not quite graspable but palpably felt.

If Thomas Hardy frustrates the reader at times—both in the poetry and in scenes from the novels—by seeming to be concrete but, finally, being less than absolutely knowable, he also rewards by giving the reader a sense of possibility, of meditation that lasts beyond the last line. It is this sense of the magical, of not clearly delineating how it all works—poetry, prose, or human experience—of insisting that readers "see in half and quarter views the whole picture,"[60] that creates fluidity and continuousness: process. And it is this sense of the magical that is withheld from *The Dynasts,* thereby disrupting a sense of possibility in creative structure and in human experience.

The Dynasts in no way lacks visualizations; it has been described as a transparency, an x-ray, an anatomy, a diorama, a shooting script, a stage setting with the ropes showing.[61] We see Immanent Will transparencies in the "key-scene to the whole" (General Chorus, Fore Scene, 6) through a specialized sight, granted only to the Spirit of the Years, that seems to be x-ray vision:

> The point of view . . . sinks downward through space, and draws to . . . where the peoples, distressed by events they did not

cause, are seen writhing, crawling, heaving, and vibrating in their various cities and nationalities. . . .

A new and penetrating light descends on the spectacle, enduing men and things with a seeming transparency, and exhibiting as one organism the anatomy of life and movement in all humanity and vitalized matter included in the display. (Stage directions, Fore Scene, 6)

On the surface, reality moves and glitters. The preface introduces "the Spectacle here presented,"[62] and the poem describes people as moving surfaces, "mov[ing] like figure[s] on a lanternslide" in a "phantasmagoric show" (I, 4, v, 76). Readers are informed of events through multiple visualizing techniques: stage directions that describe scenes, earthly dramatic scenes, dumb shows, Overworld dialogue, and the Immanent Will transparencies. Each kind of scene materializes in a dreamlike circus of continuous display. At the end of one of the poem's dumb shows, which, like all of the innumerable visual structures in the poem, is a minutely detailed description—this time of soldiers at varied activities, on land and sea, both close-up and in panoramic view—"The show presently dims and becomes broken, till only its flashes and gleams are visible" (I, 1, iv, 27). It sputters away in fragments, like fireworks, and is just as insubstantial. The question to be asked is, what is the purpose of this multi-media event?

Susan Dean, in her explanation of visual activity in *The Dynasts* as a diorama, sees the problem in this display:

> Hardy himself in the poem voices what we might call the informed criticism of his diorama. The words he uses for it—"spectacle," "exhibit," "display," "demonstration," "scene," "pictures of the play," and "show" (every kind of show: puppet show, lantern-show, . . .)—are all flat, static ones. They suggest magic shows, optical illusions designed to divert and to fool. . . . But as with all ingenious toys that offer the illusion of living movement, the time must come when its effects become repetitive, its illusion guessed, and it is proved to be a lifeless machine after all.[63]

But she solves her problem: "[W]hat begins in an arrangement of surfaces becomes a free-standing object of art and a freeing act of vision."[64] The solution is not final, however, and questions keep arising: What is dream, what reality? "And who knows anyway, in this performance of gauzes and screens, anatomies and transparencies and strange lights . . . [w]hat is real and awake and what is dream? . . . [Is it all] a conjuror's trick?"[65] And again she answers with description: "shadowy images" and repetitions are contained within "a sealed perpetual-motion box."[66] However, descriptions are not necessarily answers. Looking at the same materials, Emma Clifford concludes:

> All that the lonely and ghostly observer can expect is that the shifting moving scenes, whose common quality of vagueness is itself an arbitrary factor, will come together, part, fade, and finally dissolve, as the great confederacy of the nations dissolves, "like the diorama of a dream."[67]

One is left with nothing. Or, for Alexander Fischler, one is left with despair. In writing this epic drama, Hardy wished to depart from and replace former epics. This poem, a "modern expression of a modern outlook,"[68] is a work *sui generis,* yet despite its originality, it does not open to new possibility. Freed from traditional forms, Hardy

> can play freely, at last, with all the devices without the limitations imposed by genre. Here, indeed, the alternation between genres, the consequently changing manner of presentation, and the manipulation of protagonists with more-or-less obvious ropes were to become the very characteristic of a world presented on a huge stage, a stage on which direction as well as action seems magnificent because of its futility.[69]

What Hardy does once freed from the restrictions of genre is to create futility through an anatomy of fictions, both human illusions and art form. The pessimism of *The Dynasts* overwhelms any opening to new thought processes. The work's frame, the Overworld, is severely stunted in two ways. First, it is not new but is a seriously ineffectual version of an older form. Not only are the Spirits greatly diminished in comparison to the gods in former epics; they are powerless, merely seeing all, desiring little, and controlling nothing. The former frame is present but dead; the present disruption is present but devitalized; their meeting point is paralysis. Second, they are far less effective than characters in novels and personae in poems who can startle us into awareness and involvement with individuals and actions lifted to a level of complexity and myth. Here, the Spirits are lowered to embodiments of separate—and simplified—aspects of human beings. We get the views of resigned acceptance, of cynicism and irony, of pity. But they are views without a will, merely self-enclosed observations, and without dialogue, except in the most simplistic understanding of that term. There is a pretense of discussion among them without a trace of the dialectical. The actuality is of several parallel streams of observation without interaction or a sign of possible disruption among them. The Spirits are far more alike than different in their unswervingly monistic perspectives. Taken in combination, the Spirits might have been a conglomerate of many views of a particular situation or within a particular character. There could have been oppositions, tensions, disruptions that can lead to new meanings. However, the manner of presenting the Spirits—as an anatomy of humanity—works against complexity, contradiction, ambiguity. Each position is fixed, isolated, static, robotic, programmed for one generalized and abstract absolute: pity or irony or rumor or reason. Indeterminacy and change, possibilities of process, present in the novels and poetry, are not present in *The Dynasts*.

As for visual structures, though plentiful and various, they are devitalized by their repetitiveness, by a surplus of detail, and ultimately by a deadening perspective. Rather than being pulled into the process of making meaning, the reader is pummeled with repetitious sight, movement, and narrative into a position of disinterested passivity. The Napoleonic story exists first as a story already told in history, and Hardy's poem repeats that story repeatedly: in dramatic scenes, dumb shows, and the Spirits' commentaries. Again and again the hideousness of life is depicted:

> The lines . . . are beheld melting down like wax from an erect position to confused heaps. Their forms lie rigid, or twitch and turn, as they are trampled over by the hoofs of the enemy's horse. (II, 6, iv, 300)

> Hot corpses, their mouths blackened by cartridge-biting, and surrounded by cast-away knapsacks, firelocks, hats, stocks, flint-boxes,

and priming-horns, together with red and blue rags of clothing, gaiters, epaulettes, limbs, and viscera, accumulate on the slopes, increasing from twos and threes to half-dozens and from half-dozens to heaps, which steam with their own warmth as the spring rain falls gently upon them. (II, 6, iv, 301)

All scenes of human desire are unrelentingly undercut with irony and devastation. Over and over, humanity's lack of will is shown:

At once, as earlier, a preternatural clearness possesses the atmosphere of the battle-field, in which the scene becomes anatomized and the living masses of humanity transparent. The controlling Immanent Will appears therein, as a brain-like network of currents and ejections, twitching, interpenetrating, entangling, and thrusting hither and thither the human forms. (I, 6, iii, 118)

Meaning is established with the first question and answer of the poem: "What of the Immanent Will and Its designs?" (Fore Scene, 1). The Will controls all of life; no will is permitted to character or reader. The close-up views of the Immanent Will are actually views of humanity, *en masse,* as cosmic puppetry, not as personal, unique, subjective individuals. One of the most severe aspects of Hardy's anatomy of fiction is the fragmenting of human beings, the separation of will from human acts. We have already seen this tendency in the fragmentation of human experience depicted by the Overworld figures, and now we see it in the Immanent Will. Of course, people's belief that they can control, will events is always treated as an illusion in Hardy's world, but the violent mockery of this illusion is nowhere as powerful and diminishing as it is in *The Dynasts.* In other works the reader witnesses and becomes involved with the complex workings of individual characters as they assert or subject their wills—the becomings of a lifetime. But here there is no turning image into icon, metaphors do not open out to new possibilities, as there is only one meaning, one final form. It is not necessary to "see in half and quarter views the whole picture" because the whole picture is provided. The reader is pushed back, distanced from the work, to the position of perceiver, only, not creator. Subjective perception has been objectified into non-existence.

Disrupted Images 129

In the Fore Scene, the reader gets an early description of Europe, the setting for this epic-drama: "The nether sky opens and Europe is disclosed as a prone and emaciated figure, the Alps shaping like a backbone, and the branching mountain-chains like ribs" (Fore Scene, 6). One can view this skeleton not only as a metaphor for war-torn Europe but also as a metaphor for the end of fiction(s). It is a self-referential figure of literature in the modern world. The glittering spectacle, the activity of this poem which at first seemed magical, eventually begins to show its own workings. Chapter 2 pointed out the vital quality of Hardy's text, for example the way in which his excessively structured plots—his "blueprints"—were upset in a fruitful tension with poetic movement. The result is an indeterminacy that opens the way for reader involvement, new possibilities, new metaphors. In *The Dynasts* the blueprint is all there is. Readers, passive and uninvolved, have nothing to do but observe how the display works, watch the lantern slides, and the "magic" stands exposed—"with the ropes showing"—as automated trickery, as mechanized picture-making. The denial of will, central to *The Dynasts,* is the denial of imagination, of myth-making, of fictions, of process—in life and in art; it is the denial of metaphor and of metamorphosis—the end of magic.

In calling this work an epic-drama, Hardy immediately states the impossible: it is neither epic nor drama. Though printed on the page in the form of a drama, it was never meant to be performed, so one is left with the printed matter on the page, which, in this text, is a series of emphatically isolated parts. Throughout his writings, Hardy occasionally enlarged and separated words from the rest of the text, words like " 'MARRY ME' " in *Far from the Madding Crowd.* In so doing, he turns the words into signs that do not have signifieds; they are themselves the thing signified. In like manner, every page of *The Dynasts* can be seen as a shape of self-referentiality. One grows weary from repetition's assault upon nerves and curiosity, and ceases to see words; rather, the reader sees squares and rectangles of print with titles, like titles that might appear atop the individual frames in a slide show: names of people—PITT, KING, THIRD CITIZEN, BOY, LADY, LORD, NAPOLÉON, MURAT, SOLDIER, OFFICER, JOSEPH; of Spirits—SPIRIT OF RUMOUR, SPIRIT

OF THE YEARS, SPIRIT IRONIC; of places—PARIS, THE TUILERIES, VIMIERO, ELBA, THE QUAY, PORTO FERRAJO, LONDON, SPRING GARDENS; and DUMB SHOW, DUMB SHOW, DUMB SHOW, etc. These are the graphics of isolation and fragmentation. In his discussion of the realistic imagination, and the relationship between culture and art, Levine writes:

> The impelling energy in the quest for the world beyond words is that the world be there, and that it be meaningful and good; the persistent fear is that it is merely monstrous and mechanical, beyond the control of human meaning. Realism risks that reality and its powers of disruption.[70]

Hardy seems to have freed himself from the boundaries realism placed upon him in order to take the fullest risk, to present writing itself as monstrous and mechanical.

Hardy is the magician who knows that even the magic of art is really a science and is determined, at least this once, to reveal and expose fully the magical frames of fiction. This is not the Hardy who advised the reader in "The Profitable Reading of Fiction" (1888) to "catch the vision which the writer has in his eye, and is endeavoring to project upon the paper, even while it half eludes him."[71] Nor is he here the Hardy who, in "The Science of Fiction" (1891), wrote, "Nothing but the illusion of truth can permanently please, and when the old illusions begin to be penetrated, a more natural magic has to be supplied."[72] He has dispensed with vision, illusion, and magic. Reflecting about *The Dynasts* in 1904, Hardy observed,

> The old theologies may or may not have worked for good in their time. But they will not bear stretching further in epic or dramatic art. The Greeks used up theirs: the Jews used up theirs: the Christians have used up theirs. So that one must make an independent plunge, embodying the real, if only temporary, thought of the age. (*Life*, 319)

And *The Dynasts* is a real, if only temporary, end of process in Thomas Hardy. Chapter 1 ended with a quotation from the *Life*, written in 1901:

> I do not think that there will be any permanent revival of the old transcendental ideals; but I think there may gradually be developed an Idealism of Fancy; that is, an idealism in which fancy is no longer tricked out and made to masquerade as belief, but is frankly and honestly accepted as an imaginative solace in the lack of any substantial solace to be found in life. (*Life*, 310)

For a moment, *The Dynasts*'s long moment, imagination proves to be no solace. If *The Dynasts* provides one unquestionable value to this study on Thomas Hardy, it is the truth that emerges at the point of contradiction between *The Dynasts* and most other Hardy works: sixty years of a writer's literary production cannot be neatly framed or packaged in a single assumption, in this case the assumption of a theory of process.

Nor does *The Dynasts* represent a new, changed Hardy, neatly packaged in disruption forevermore. Many poems written after the epic-drama contain the visualized ineffability of unique experience, a will toward meaning, and life as process as in "When I Set Out for Lyonnesse" (1870), for example, its companion piece, "The Phantom Horsewoman" (1913). The earlier poem celebrates Hardy's meeting with his first wife, Emma; the second celebrates his dreaming memory of her, after her death. Again, there are several levels of experience, this time for the dreamer; the speaker; and a larger community, "they." The poem explores, among other things, one's imaginative involvement with others' private and unique experience. Again the experience is given a concrete yet ephemeral place, "As if on the air / It were drawn rose-bright—"; "On that shagged and shaly / Atlantic spot" (CP, 354). Again it is an experience beyond logic and explanation: "A phantom of his own figuring." And again, by the end of the poem all are lured into a communal image of ecstasy: an organic mingling of nature and myth. Dreamer, speaker, "they," and readers see with subjective imagination, as the ghost-girl–rider "as when first eyed / Draws rein and sings to the swing of the tide"—the magic in our eyes.

With this discussion of disrupted images, three of the fundamental structures of Thomas Hardy's visual art have been examined. The role played by disruption is demonstrated by its highly complex and far-reaching presence in both prose and poetry, narrative process, point of view, metaphoric movement, structure, style. Disruption dissolves, displaces, and exposes (former) images and values; but it neither destroys former meaning nor reconciles old and new meanings nor halts the continuing process of making meaning. It occupies an essential place in Hardy's iconology; as fully as the patterns of image into icon and framing are needed to create meaning, so disruption is needed, on the one hand to prevent the illusion of idealism, absolutes, stasis but on the other hand to permit new possibilities. It is with the arrival at and acceptance of contradiction that one can grapple with this fundamental element of Hardy's vision. The images discussed at the start of this chapter—shopping malls and advertisements and cartoons—were used in part to display metaphorically the precise ways in which Hardy's visual aesthetic works to reveal the relationship between literary tradition and literary disruption. However, these images from our culture have broad implication for seeing Hardy's iconology in its fullest outreachings: its revelation of the movement of the modern mind, plus signs of the culture in which that mind exists, expressed symbolically.

Chapter 5

Relationships within the Image

Throughout this study readers have been encountering the individual image: a gargoyle, a woman's figure, a red man, a scarlet ace of hearts, Christminster cakes, a pond, a woods, a heath. But even these solitary visual structures have stood in relationship to other matter within the image: water plunging from the gargoyle, a woman's figure atop her wagon, a woman's figure above a barrow, a red man on a heath, an ace of hearts on a ceiling, "a pond edged with grayish leaves," a woods or heath interacting with the human community that performs within it. Arnheim notes that "to see means to see in relation,"[1] even in seemingly simple perceptions. Chapters 3 and 4 analyzed primarily broad and complex interactions among images of framing and disruption. The present chapter will draw in and take close-up looks at the morphology of individual images to show the force of Hardy's visualizing power not only in the large pictorial scenes but also in the precise arrangements of myriad smaller and subtler visual structures. Whenever appropriate, this focused view will open up to consider aspects of relationship among a series of parallel imagistic constructions. Opening the view still wider, the disparate topics in this chapter—expressionism, social commentary, and topography—further demonstrate the pictorial aesthetics permeating every aspect of Hardy's art.

The Intensified Expression of Things

> Oak raised his head, and wondering what he could do, listlessly surveyed the scene. By the outer margin of the pit was an oval pond, and over it hung the attenuated skeleton of a chrome-yellow moon, which had only a few days to last—the morning star dogging her on the left hand. The pool glittered like a dead man's eye, and as the world awoke a breeze blew, shaking and elongating the reflection of the moon without breaking it, and turning the image of the star to a phosphoric streak upon the water. All this Oak saw and remembered. (FFMC, 73)

Preceding the above description, the narrator had explained Gabriel's humaneness, which took pity on the poor sheep, and his economic ruin, even quoting his practical response to feeling: " 'Thank God I am not married' " (FFMC, 73). However, no words of explanation about feelings can match this attempt to picture Gabriel's deepest emotional response to the current disaster. Unlike some other instances of the grotesque in Hardy, the words "skeleton" and "dead man" are not the major carriers of mood. Rather, mood is expressed in the objects themselves and the spatial arrangement and movement of these objects. The barrenness of the scene, in which very few objects are spread out across darkness, reaches down with the mirror-like pond and finds Gabriel's fundamental feelings. The absence of content in a fading moon, the repetition and exaggeration of that fragility in its reflection on the moving water, a single star—all contribute to the emptiness. Darkness alone could have been a comforting enclosure, but this darkness is used to reveal the depressing sparseness that remains. And the star's "phosphoric streak upon the water" pictures the unplanned, the unexpected yet indelible shock of trauma felt within Oak. Reflection has the claustrophobic effect of a character face to face with an inescapable reference to feeling. As in a camera's timed exposure, movement and the passing of time are captured in an everlasting frozen moment. "All this Oak saw and remembered."

Reaching after concrete expressions of inner qualities is a repeated pattern in Hardy. We see it again when Boldwood learns of Bathsheba's marriage to Troy:

> [Gabriel] saw the square figure sitting erect upon the horse, the head turned to neither side, and the elbows steady by the hips, the brim of the hat level and undisturbed in its onward glide, until the keen edges of Boldwood's shape sank by degrees over the hill. (FFMC, 268)

His immobility and steadiness do express an agony "deeper than a cry" (FFMC, 268), and they succeed because Hardy has arranged a picture that is more expressive than sound. Joan Grundy sees in Boldwood's squareness "the tensions of suffering within him, ... almost Spenserian in its capacity to incarnate an emotion."[2] The strong perpendicular and horizontal lines, "keen edges," exclude everything outside themselves.[3] The importance of exclusion is paramount; just as this shape of Boldwood glides and sinks and disappears over the hill, just as he is visually boxed off from his surroundings, so in fact he is emotionally cut off from any human contact that could possibly provide some outlet for grief. Visually and socially, he is in isolation, where delusions can flourish, and they do.

Elfride Swancourt will stand forever in a scene: "the dead and brown stubble, the weeds among it, the distant belt of beeches shutting out the view of the house, the leaves of which were now red and sick to death" (PBE, 358–59). As Knight departs, he turns back to see "the stubble-field, and a slight girlish figure in the midst of it—up against the sky: Elfride, docile as ever, had hardly moved a step, for he had said, Remain" (PBE, 360). The text notes that this picture was "engraved for years on the retina of Knight's eye" (PBE, 358), and well might it be with his sharpened ambiguity—attraction, contempt, terror—toward this "girlish figure." However, the picture speaks more directly to the reader, who is allowed a less conflicted compassion for Elfride. Ronald Blythe explains one source of this scene's power:

> The most intriguing thing about A Pair of Blue Eyes ... is not its picture of a delightful girl receiving no more consideration from

Nature than a blade of grass on the headland, but of a heroine being harried along to oblivion by her creator. She is even confined to a limited field like a coursed hare, and her escape made impossible. For, although she appears occasionally in London and three of her lovers . . . travel extensively, the pursuit takes place within the boundaries of a village and, in spite of its moor and ocean, Endenstow, like all villages, can close in without mercy upon those who belong to it. Visiting the same rocks, lanes, meadows and scenes with different men fills Elfride's mind with guilt and comparisons, and the reader's with a strong sense of her treachery. . . . Cruelly and remorselessy, [Knight] prises some of the past out of her, driving her foot by foot toward an abyss from which there can be no salvation. Oblivion.[4]

The roughness of a stubble-field, a slight figure made even slighter and lonelier "up against the sky" contribute the line and texture to an image harsh, mournful, oppressive—an appropriate metaphor for a life trapped in geography.

Such scenes as the above attract attention to Hardy's desire to "intensify the expression of things . . . so that the heart and inner meaning is made vividly visible" (*Life*, 177). He frequently works in an expressive style, reaching after a way to delineate human senses, emotions, even thoughts in terms of line, color, shape, spatial arrangement—an artist's style. Ruskin believed very human condition could be "illustrated, with mathematical exactness, by conditions of line and color,"[5] and Matisse carries this belief and desire even further:

> Painting, Matisse seems to say, is the rhythmic arrangement of line and color on a flat plane, but it is not *only* that; how far can the image of nature be pared down without destroying its basic properties? . . . "What I am after, above all, is expression. . . . The whole arrangement of my picture is expressive. The placement of figures or objects, the empty spaces around them, the proportions, everything plays a part."[6]

In the above examples of Gabriel, Boldwood, and Elfride, expression is what Hardy has achieved repeatedly. For him, paintings could contain human senses: "In Botticelli the soul is outside the body, permeating its spectator with its emotions. In Rubens the flesh is without, and the soul (possibly) within. The very odour of the flesh is distinguishable in the latter" (*Life*, 217). If it can be done in paintings, why not in writing? Why not write to make "every object, and every action, as composed, not of this or that material, this or that movement, but of the qualities pleasure and pain in varying proportions?" (*Life*, 217). And if one can make pleasure and pain seen, one can make every emotion seen.

The ordinary, dull, hopelessly painful repetition of every day is drawn in "A Commonplace Day" (CP, 115) with the neat and mechanical arrangement of a dying fire and a dying day:

> I part the fire-gnawed logs,
> Rake forth the embers, spoil the busy flames, and
>   lay the ends
>   Upon the shining dogs;
> Further and further from the nooks the twilight's
>   stride extends,
>   And beamless black impends.

There is an order of lines; the ends are placed in a line and darkness arrives in a moving line, quietly and orderly. This tone is shaped again in "At a Lunar Eclipse" (CP, 116), as the earth's shadow moves "[i]n even monochrome and curving line / Of imperturbable serenity." Yet, both poems move from seeming smoothness to bemused and troubled thoughts: the first speaker is pressed with regret and loss; the second, with frustration and even rage; and the early lines contain this tension. First, the minute precision of detail, the grid-lock arrangement, and the intrusive movement of a spreading mass of "beamless black" convey anxiety. Second, the redundancy of "even monochrome" and "imperturbable serenity" undermines the calm with an excess that makes way for irony. These peculiarly ambiguous images are appropriate for states of stress; one recalls the brim of Boldwood's hat, "level and undisturbed in its onward glide."

"Neutral Tones" (CP, 12) is a masterpiece of spatial arrangement used to depict experience, in Matisse's words, "pared down without destroying its basic properties." The first three stanzas paint the coldness of a dead love with a sun "white as though chidden by God"; leaves that "had fallen from an ash and were grey"; eyes "that rove / Over tedious riddles"; a grin that is ominous. In the last stanza memory pares down the images into confrontation with essential pain: "Your face, and the God-curst sun, and a tree, / And a pond edged with grayish leaves." It is as if the words themselves have become the things themselves and have shrunk into small but pointed objects.

The idea of turning words into things must have been a temptation for a writer who wanted "the heart and inner meaning . . . made vividly visible." One can grasp this desire in Hardy's description of the effect of cold weather upon human faces:

> Cold weather brings out upon the faces of people the written marks of their habits, vices, passions, and memories, as warmth brings out on paper a writing in sympathetic ink. The drunkard looks still more a drunkard when the splotches have their margins made distinct by frost, the hectic blush becomes a stain now, the cadaverous complexion reveals the bone under, the quality of handsomeness is reduced to its lowest terms. (*Life*, 177)

Both writers and painters have yearned to capture the thing itself on the canvas, on the paper—in the palm of one's hand.

> [Picasso] was after something [in his late work] that he had never quite achieved—to go beyond painting, perhaps, into that vortex of raw emotion where there was no difference between art and life. "I don't want to do the nude as a nude. I want only to *say* breast, *say* foot, *say* hand or belly. To find the way to say it— that's enough."[7]

Of course, Picasso's "enough" is too much; such efforts must fail. The thing to look for is what results when a writer (or painter) takes the risk of trying to turn art into life. The extra distancing necessary to remove the writer's hand from the written word may result in objectification, alienation. Readers may be made to feel objectified and alienated from the text. The cinematic method in literature runs this danger and, it seems to me, *The Dynasts* suffers somewhat from it.[8]

That Hardy's works are noticed for their quality of distancing —the non-authoritative narrator, the disinterested and/or ignorant observer—has been mentioned throughout this study. Chapter 1 stressed Tanner's response to Hardy's impressions: "[S]omething seen but not tampered with, something scrupulously watched in its otherness, something perceived but not made over. . . . [It is] something seen, it is something there, it is an effect on the retina, it is a configuration of matter."[9] William Pritchard's "Hardy's Anonymous Sincerity,"[10] in refuting critical assumptions that Hardy's poems are filled with personal feeling and sincerity, uses examples from two classes of poems: those with a distant tone, hardly human, like "The Convergence of the Twain," and those that are seemingly personal, certainly psychologically complex, such as "Poems of 1912–13." In all cases the speaking voice is anonymous in its indifference to the reader's emotional response. Neither "The Broken Appointment" nor "After the Journey" nor "The Voice" makes a clear request for help or gives a clear direction toward any one reaction. Subject matter may draw forth emotions, but the speaker's stance does not. This distancing between speaker and content is, in fact, part of the content of things and experiences "watched in [their] otherness, something perceived but not made over." In "Hardy and the Figure in the Scene" John Peck examines things not made over but made, Hardy's arrangements of scenes:

> [Scenery] becomes the reflective surface of the poem's moral life. It . . . is never simply . . . landscape alone. . . . [It] looms up into the convexities of foreground, until it stands as the runic, fated face of mature feeling . . . installed and revelatory, arranged and compelling. An obsessive memory or regret brings its own shape with it, insistent, crude and unmined, which requires a certain conscious display, disposition, arrangement.[11]

The intermingling of experience and composition arrives at a final vision, an intermingling of the image and the artist's eye, an eye that calls attention to its own absolute and unmediated structuring of matter. Peck concludes by pointing out what I believe to be a major key to Hardy's success at making his composed images installed, arranged, arbitrary—yet revelatory, compelling, and involving as well:

> In the face of pain, close observation can be threatening; so that observation, even with melodrama or occasional oddness of fit, testifies to fidelity. . . . [S]cenes . . . must be realized . . . even though the rendering tend toward the pace of muted strangeness.[12]

Of the poems Peck mentions, the most obviously uncanny lines are from "Near Lanivet, 1872" (CP, 436). The woman, tired, goes to rest against "a stunted handpost" "[a]t the crossways":

> She leant back, being so weary, against its stem,
>   And laid her arms on its own,
> Each open palm stretched out to each end of them,
>   Her sad face sideways thrown.

The subjectivity of the description is admitted by the speaker, who perceives that the woman looks "as one crucified / In my gaze at her." However, visual details rivet the woman's arms to the cross and the reader's eyes to the resulting arrangement: woman and post are one. The repetition in verbal form—"against its stem," "on its own," "each . . . to each"—and the unspoken assumption that the handpost has arms—"And laid her arms on its own"—and perhaps even palms, bring the picture of woman and post to startling life, eerie but felt.

This "muted strangeness," a certain tilt to the scene, complements the distancing in Thomas Hardy's best work, giving to language, as far as possible, its own life. The unique vantage point is present not only because of the pain or anxiety or fear or surprise through which some things are felt and seen. Often such strangeness is contained in contradictions within the image itself: the pond's still reflection of Gabriel's trauma, Boldwood's rigid body and gliding hat, stubble-field and fragility, smoothly moving celestial lines and jagged human thoughts, unified fragmentation in neutral tones. In an imagery that disorients both picture and reader, Hardy seems to have found one way to delineate experience. The uncommon quality of his vision defamiliarizes images to permit their reemergence from distancing into new and energetic shapes—the intensified expression of things.

The Power of Print

Symptomatic of defamiliarizing aspects in Hardy's imagery is the repeated appearance of print in his texts, not the entire printed work but print treated explicitly as an object, not as signifier but as the thing signified:

" 'MARRY ME' "

(FFMC, 131, 132)

THY DAMNATION, SLUMBERETH, NOT

2 Pet. II 3

(TD, 114)

THOU, SHALT, NOT, COMMIT—

(TD, 115)

Η ΚΑΙΝΗ ΔΙΑΘΗΚΗ

(JU, 63, 68)

THITHER ☞
J. F.

(JU, 94)

𝔄𝔩𝔩𝔢𝔩𝔲𝔍𝔄

(JU, 108)

'MICHAEL HENCHARD'S WILL

'That Elizabeth-Jane Farfrae be not told of my death, or made to grieve on account of me.

'&that I be not bury'd in consecrated ground.
'&that no sexton be asked to toll the bell.
'&that nobody is wished to see my dead body.
'&that no murners walk behind me at my funeral.
'&that no flours be planted on my grave.
'&that no man remember me.
'To this I put my name.
'MICHAEL HENCHARD'

(MC, 353)

Two of these examples, the valentine invitation and Henchard's will, have already been treated in Chapter 2 and will not be examined in great detail here but will be brought into discussion to reach some general conclusions. Let us look first at the two samples from *Tess of the d'Urbervilles*.

Tess meets these commandments as part of the setting, like modern-day obtrusive billboards. The first message appears:

> Against the peaceful landscape, the pale, decaying tints of the copses, the blue air of the horizon, and the lichened stile-boards, these staring vermilion words shone forth. They seemed to shout themselves out and make the atmosphere ring. . . . [T]he words entered Tess with accusatory horror. . . . "I think they are horrible. . . . Crushing! killing!" (TD, 114–15)

And then the painting preacher prints the second message:

> "Ah—there's a nice bit of blank wall up by that barn standing to waste." . . . The old gray wall began to advertise a similar fiery lettering to the first, with a strange and unwonted mien, as if distressed at duties it had never before been called upon to perform. . . . "Pooh—I don't believe God said such things!" [Tess] murmured contemptuously when her blush had died away. (TD, 115, 116)

Tess meets the Commandments in every corner of her life; they are powerful and absolute abstractions in her society but have a monstrously visceral presence in her being. To John Peck's description of the "muted strangeness" in Hardy's imagery must be added Emma Clifford's similar observation; she calls attention to

> Hardy's knowledge of the extent to which the shock of existence in a hostile and confusing environment can tamper with traditional characteristics of human awareness and cause his characters to live . . . in "an outer chamber of the mind [brain]." . . . There is no escaping the fact that Thomas Hardy had an uncommon flair for private worlds. Writing as he is of mankind in a strange and new universal scheme, he has few reticences about taking enormous liberties with human personality and many characters in his novels perceive realty in their own highly individual fashion.[13]

The last line of Part 1, "The Maiden," reads, "An immeasurable social chasm was to divide our heroine's pesonality thereafter from that previous self of hers who stepped from her mother's door to try her fortune at Trantridge poultry-farm" (TD, 108). Some months later, but fewer than five minutes in the reader's time, Part 2, "Maiden No More," opens with these "immeasurable" billboards. The signs are not literally gigantic, but they are startlingly framed in the text itself and placed in a monumental relationship to "Tess," the ordinary-sized word on a page. After the birth of her baby, when Tess walks alone at night, she imagines that nature chides her: "[A]irs and gusts . . . were formulae of bitter reproach. A wet day was the expression of irremediable grief at her weakness." She projects her psychological state upon nature, which seems to her "peopled by phantoms and voices antipathetic to her, . . . a cloud of moral hobgoblins by which she was terrified without reason" (TD, 120). Later on, in the midst of her joy with Angel, those billboards, those hobgoblins are still with her:

> Her affection for him . . . enveloped her as a photosphere, irradiated her into forgetfulness of her past sorrows, keeping back the gloomy spectres . . . —doubt, fear, moodiness, care, shame. She knew that they were waiting like wolves just outside the circumscribing light, but she had long spells of power to keep them in hungry subjection there.
> A spiritual forgetfulness co-existed with an intellectual remembrance. She walked in brightness, but she knew that in the background those shapes of darkness were always spread. They might be receding, or they might be approaching, one or the other, a little every day. (TD, 236–37)[14]

Tess's two responses to the signs—"I think they are horrible . . . Crushing! Killing!" and "Pooh—I don't believe God said such things!"—express a divided self of which she is unaware. These signs are social laws internalized by Tess and are magnified by the self-projection of a part of her. Their danger is less in their image of a person fragmented and alienated than in Tess's only partial and infrequent awareness of this state of being. The print has power over Tess not only because it is so deep a part of her but because the external and absolute social restraints it proclaims are only a part of her, existing in ignorant contradiction with her subjective and personal rebellion against them.[15]

Sue's and Jude's lives are surrounded by quackery, superstitions, dreams, fantasies, memories. Both characters easily create icons as expressions of themselves, Sue with her Greek statues and Jude with his message on the milestone. It is ironic that he responds to his own engraved words as if they were a positive sign of something outside of his self. While the letters, carved in stone, do represent to Jude his individual and ideal plans, they also seem to have an external power over him. He is a romantic, a perennial mythmaker, who grew to idolize his Old Testament study in Greek, and Greek letters, too, were placed on the page as items to worship. Between the two appearances of the Greek words, he betrays them for Arabella: "[T]he capital leters on the title-page regarded him with fixed reproach in the grey starlight, like the unclosed eyes of a dead man:

Η ΚΑΙΝΗ ΔΙΑΘΗΚΗ

(JO, 68)

The grotesque exaggeration here reflects both guilt and compulsive involvement; indeed, his milestone letters strike him so fully partially because they occur after his marriage to and separation from Arabella. They represent a return to the original adoration: Greek letters—scholarship, religion, and Christminster.

The next letterings from *Jude* are not only printed; they are elaborately designed characters in the style of church texts. And they are large, being cut into a piece of zinc three or four feet long. Though Sue is doing the lettering, Jude is surreptitiously watching her. They have never met, though his aunt has gossiped about this cousin, and he leaps—like Angel and Clym and Eustacia and so many other potential lovers—to the wrong conclusion: "A sweet, saintly, Christian business, hers!" (JO, 108). Just as he had eagerly sought for meaning in his self-carved milestone, here, too, he seeks meaning in print. These letters have about them as much multiple perception and irony as *Far from the Madding Crowd*'s "Marry Me." Sue and Jude view them from vastly different eyes, his with pleasure, hers with repugnance. Within two minutes of the reader's time, Sue purchases miniature reproductions of Venus and Apollo and proves herself to be not only a pagan but also, in her domestic environment, an adroit liar. The ironies accrue from there; while Jude is able to adopt Sue's paganism, by the end of the novel she rebounds with astonishing masochism to the Judao-Christian laws she had earlier abandoned—the letter of the law.

This enshrinement of print in Hardy stands as a paradigm of the enormous influence of institutionalized power upon the lives of Hardy's characters. Even Henchard, denying that his death be recognized by any social, religious, or psychological forms—in part from his sense of failure within social forms—excludes himself within the code of a Last Will and Testament. His formal act of self-obliteration places him within the social structure he foregoes. Boldwood's "Marry Me" results from the extremely lighthearted convention of Valentine's Day. His age, economic security, and place in the community make him an extremely attractive bachelor, revealing a conscious or unconscious determination on his part to reject the institution of marriage. The potentiality for personal ties to be destructive in his life is apparent: "Since receipt of the missive [the valentine] in the morning, Boldwood had felt the symmetry of his existence to be slowly getting distorted in the direction of an ideal passion" (FFMC, 132). Distortion increases to the novel's end and demonstrates strange and unanticipated responses to conventional structures. Discussion on *Tess* has already touched on the breaking of a religious and social code and the punishment that follows from others and from the codebreaker's internalization of law and punishment. By the novel's end, Tess does manage to have the ultimate confrontation with those towering letters, but she also pays society's ultimate price. All the above characters stand in some negative relationship to conventional social laws: the power of the print. The conventions in Hardy exist not as a general ideal but as a human fiction that is both necessary for society and destructive of its most interesting members. It is not a wonder, therefore, that opposition and anguish are felt nowhere more powerfully than in the text whose subtitle reads, "The letter killeth."

All the print from *Jude the Obscure* is related to academic and religious institutions. The power of knowledge and religion in Jude's and Sue's lives is one of the thematic centers of the novel. They believe one can cast off religion and take in knowledge in one's own, individual way. The largeness of the print in relation to the words "Sue" and "Jude," and the double engraving of the words—on stone or a book's cover or metal, as well as on the page—shows vividly the relationship between these social structures and individual needs and desires. One last lettering remains; though print is not enlarged upon a page, the enlargement may have been omitted because it could not be made large enough, the text of culture outsizing the literary text.

During their stay in Aldrickham, Sue and Jude are slowly but surely being ostracized, socially and economically; as their unconventional living arrangements become known, they become less and less tolerable to the townspeople. Ironically, as even they come to realize, Jude is given work to restore and reletter a large, plaster Ten Commandments, part of a whole wall, and Sue joins him to work on painting the letters: "She began painting in the letters of the first Table while he set about mending a portion of the second" (JO, 319). We get a picture of these two violators of church law, painting and mending the Word itself: their bodies in the foreground on raised platforms; the tables of Jewish law, the immediate backdrop, "tower[ing] sternly over the utensils of Christian grace, as the chief ornament of the chancel end" (JO, 329). Sue and Jude think they have rid themselves of idols, that they are to some degree free, but that is put in question visually as they stand so small before the huge letters. The picture questions their freedom; the novel's ending denies it.

In this series of images one can get some further idea of how Hardy arranges relationships within images so that the relationship itself is a shape of meaning. Further, an accumulation of similar structures, like the relationship between character and print, can produce a process that also gives revelation. While process has thus far been understood largely as a progression of framings and disruptions, movement as we see here can emerge through an accretion of similar images. Another example can be found in the relationship between characters and their varied placements along a vertical line. Elfride begins far above Stephen, on Pansy; is lowered to the stubble-field; and finally is placed lower still in a coffin. Eustacia appears atop the barrow and ends beneath ground level, drowned in a river. Bathsheba appears atop a wagon, a horse, a haystack, and ends on ground level within a containing frame. Lucetta moves up and down between High-

Place Hall and the marketplace, finally placed in the upper window of her home with Donald where the lower street moves up to her eye level to kill her with the form of a raised effigy, another shape of Lucetta. All of these movements are ironic comments on the possibility for fixed meanings, for everlasting good fortune, in human life. They are signs of the inescapable presence of chance and contingency, always a condition of life in Hardy's world.

In his discussion on visual thinking Arnheim writes,

> To see means to see in relation; and the relationship actually encountered in percepts are not simple. . . . Relation, . . . far from leaving related items untouched, works as a condition of the total context of which the items are parts and produces changes that are in keeping with the structure of that context. . . . At any level [of complexity] perception involves operations of a structural complexity similar to cognitive behavior more in general.[16]

To see is to know. Hardy communicates to our eyes and our understanding extraordinary and complex human experiences through relationships within the image.

Topography

"[A]s if a magic lantern threw the nerves in patterns on a screen,"[17] so Thomas Hardy projects psychological states upon the land. "One cannot write directly about the soul. Looked at, it vanishes," Virginia Woolf advised herself,[18] and Hardy, too, in his need and desire for concreteness, maps out the soul with a morphology of places. Donald Davie, strongly sensing Hardy's rootedness in topography, presents a writer for whom one needs not a "history of nineteenth-century England, but a map."[19] "The Trampwoman's Tragedy" occurs over a period of time, but its emotive texture lies embedded in the places the speaker has known. It is not only that Hardy's people become saturated with places, but that places become saturated with Hardy's people. The "Poems of 1912–13" are a great achievement of this engraining of self into place.

> You were she who abode
> by those red-veined rocks far West,
> You were the swan-necked one who rode
> Along the beetling Beeny Crest.
>
> (CP, 338)
>
> You did not walk with me
> Of late to the hill-top tree.
>
> (CP, 340)
>
> I found her out there
> On a slope few see.
>
> (CP, 342)

Up the cliff, down, till I'm lonely, lost,
    And the unseen waters' ejaculations awe me.
. . . .
Yes: I have re-entered your olden haunts at last;
    Through the years, through the dead scenes I have
        tracked you;
. . . .
I see what you are doing; you are leading me on
    To the spots we knew when we haunted here together,
The waterfall, above which the mist-bow shone
    At the then fair hour in the then fair weather,
And the cave just under, with a voice still so hollow.

(CP, 349)

> And looks at the sands
> And the seaward haze
> . . . .
>
> By that briny green
> . . . .
>
> On that shagged and shaly
> Atlantic spot.
>
> (CP, 353-54)

O THE opal and the sapphire of that wandering western sea
And the woman riding high above with bright hair flapping
    free—
. . . .

> The pale mews plained below us, and the waves seemed far
>   away
> In a nether sky, engrossed in saying their ceaseless
>   babbling say,
> . . . .
> A little cloud then cloaked us, and there flew an irised
>   rain,
> And the Atlantic dyed its levels with a dull misfeatured
>   stain,
> And then the sun burst out again, and purples prinked the
>   main,
> —Still in all its chasmal beauty bulks old Beeny to the
>   sky.
>   (CP, 350–51)

But when ontological significance rests in subjectivity—in emotions, will, and illusion—always there is doubt:

> Does there even a place like Saint-Juliot exist?
>   Or a Vallency Valley
>   With stream and leafed alley,
> Or Beeny, or Bos with its flounce flinging mist?
>   (CP, 348)

And often there is separation; place becomes a hardened, a "varnished" symbol:

> I look upon the map that hangs by me
> Its shires and towns and rivers lines in varnished
>   artistry—
>   And I mark a jutting height
>   Coloured purple, with a margin of blue sea.
> . . . .
>   The charted coast stares bright,
> And its episode comes back in pantomine.
>   (CP, 321–22)

In "Wessex Heights" (CP, 319) the speaker, without either problem or relief of separation, has so successfully, if unwillingly, permeated the land that he must withdraw not from the old places but from his old self that they now are:

Down there I seem to be false to myself, my simple self that was,
And is not now, and I see him watching, wondering what crass cause
Can have merged him into such a stranger continuator as this."

His fragmented existence "know[s] some liberty" only in a state of self-extinction: on "some heights in Wessex, . . . / I seem where I was before my birth, and after death may be." Except for "one rare fair woman," all of his ghosts are visually vague: "a figure against the moon," a "form," "a ghost . . . in a shroud of white," or a "profile against the pane." Those "phantoms having weird detective ways" are so successful at locating him, and so vague, because they are an emptied identity filled by imagination, a self-haunting.

At times the changing background of a scene, as when snow falls, becomes a fresh canvas on which the world can be painted anew. So in "A Light Snow-Fall after Frost" (CP, 733), formerly invisible cobwebs now hang like "thick white worsted." And a man passes by:

> His ruddy beard brings fire to the pallid scene;
> His coat is faded green;
> Hence seems it that his mien
> Wears something of the dye
> Of the berried holm-tree that he passes nigh.

One might say the world becomes unpainted in a scene from *The Dynasts* in which foreground obliterates any place or person. A devastating snow storm, during the Russian campaign, makes the French troops—whose activities normally create whole landscapes—disappear. We see "one white morsel, which appals."

> What has floated down from the sky upon the Army is a flake of snow. Then come another and another, till natural features, hitherto varied with the tints of autumn, are confounded, and all is phantasmal grey and white.
> The caterpillar shape still creeps laboriously nearer, but instead of increasing in size by the rules of perspective, it gets more attenuated, and there are left upon the ground behind it minute parts of itself, which are speedily flaked over, and remain as white pimples by the wayside. . . . The snow storm increases, descending in tufts which can hardly be shaken off. The sky seems to join

itself to the land. The marching figures drop rapidly, and almost immediately become white grave-mounds.

Endowed with enlarged powers of audition as of vision, we are struck by the mournful taciturnity that prevails. Nature is mute. (III, 1, ix, 353–54)

Egdon Heath, that "vast tract of unenclosed wild" (RN, 33), has more than one geography and not only because of subjective perception. On 5 November it is transformed into a new shaping of its old self:

While the men and lads were building the pile, a change took place in the mass of shade which denoted the distant landscape. Red suns and tufts of fire one by one began to arise, flecking the whole country round. . . . Some were distant, and stood in a dense atmosphere, so that bundles of pale strawlike beams radiated around them in the shape of a fan. Some were large and near, glowing scarlet-red from the shade, like wounds in a black hide. Some were Meanades, with winy faces and blown hair. . . . Perhaps as many as thirty bonfires could be counted within the whole bounds of the district; and as the hour may be told on a clock-face, when the figures themselves are invisible, so did the men recognize the locality of each fire by its angle and direction, though nothing of the scenery could be viewed. . . . It seemed as if the bonfire-makers were standing in some radiant upper storey of the world, detached from and independent of the dark stretches below. The heath down there was now a vast abyss, and no longer a continuation of what they stood on. . . . Then the whole black phenomenon beneath represented Limbo as viewed from the brink by the sublime Florentine in his vision. (RN, 43–44)

People may still be able to read the "old" heath like a clock, but this new shape to reality also provokes new readings: fans, Maenades, Dante's Limbo, ancient gods and priests, rebellion: "Black chaos comes, and the fettered gods of the earth say, Let there be light" (RN, 45). Like Hardy's observation that the effect of cold weather on people's faces is to bring out otherwise hidden character traits, so the effect of a black backdrop upon fire is to bring out an otherwise muted intensity. However, the moving, flickering fires against black night are analogous to another form or intensity; they map out the narrator's imagination bringing light to black chaos. This may be the need of a character who, instead of "wandering in an unmapped no-man's land 'between two worlds,' "[20] finds a way to fill up the void by mapping out a multitude of worlds. And we are off to the process of metamorphosis.

This arrival at metamorphosis moves us on to Chapter 6; however, its presence here should point out once again what has been said earlier in this study. No single part—part of this chapter or any one of the four major visual structures—is meant to be seen as separate; rather, they should be understood interactively. As to relationships within the image, Hardy is always to some degree after expressionism; these efforts to express emotion in artistic form are regularly worked out in spatial arrangements; and in one or a series of images both style and meaning are signs of the culture in which they are written: "essential tendencies of the human [modern] mind" expressed symbolically.[21]

By now those oft-quoted Hardy words, introduced in Chapter 1, have a more exact meaning than when first encountered here: "impressions of the moment," "unadjusted impressions have their values," "idiosyncratic mode or regard," "non-rational subjects," "half and quarter views," "vision which the writer has in his eye and is endeavoring to project upon the paper while it half eludes him." Hardy wished to capture the most fundamental and/or fleeting aspects of human life in a picture-making language. Rather than translate unique experience into explanatory definitions, categories, detailed descriptions, or broad generalizations, he repeatedly located experience in the precise image, showing the particular feeling or the exact moment and allowing meaning to radiate from the image, not logically but emotively. This chapter has looked at diverse categories of subject matter as filtered through Hardy's particular—"idiosyncratic"—eye. He has attempted to capture human emotion and thematic concerns through (1) the expressive mode of line, shape, color, and the arrangement of matter within the image; (2) the projection of subjective experience upon the landscape; (3) metalanguage; (4) and repetition of particular imagistic formulations. The whole world of human concerns seems to have passed through his imagination to become knowledge in the form of visual structures. Attending with precision to an enormous breadth of human experience, absorbing his observations in images, Hardy attempted to place the experience visually upon the page. Of course, he could not quite do it, which is why the quest is always elusive; nevertheless, the result of his will and his imagination is far from failure. One does not travel to Wessex to verify Hardy; one turns to Hardy to verify a "partly dream-country"[22] called Wessex.

PART THREE

THE WHOLE PICTURE

Chapter 6

Metamorphosis

Metamorphosis has never been out of sight. The many framings and disruptions described throughout this study—heath, woods, landscape. autumn leaf, valentine, painted sign, cycle of seasons, rituals in white dresses or in red fires, white man or red man, road speck, point of view, narrative voice, endings, genre, Lucetta at a window, Bathsheba on a horse, Henchard within a window, Eustacia in costume, Tess in blood—all participate in variations, changes, exchanges; all are part of a larger series; all are in process. Chapters 2, 3, 4, and 5 have been directed primarily to slowing down process, to catching Hardy's "impressions" while they move to make more graspable their intermingling as a moving whole. This concluding chapter brings forth the whole picture, not only individual brush strokes but the whole design. The panoramic view will follow a prominent Hardyan image, the road, as it moves through Hardy's entire text, and will study perspective and image as they metamorphose through several poems. Finally, it will trace, in *Jude the Obscure* and *Tess of the d'Urbervilles,* the metamorphosis of visual structures as they move through the counterpoints of both Hardy's epistemology and his aesthetics: fact, authority, the absolute versus imagination, change, process; abstraction and generalization versus concreteness, particularity, the personal; skepticism versus idealism; story versus poem. It is these tensions, antagonisms, incongruities, contradictions that form—with visual structures and subjective vision—the theoretical assumptions of this iconological study of Thomas Hardy's visualizing imagination.

Roads

The roads of England actually did surround Hardy, the country boy and man, and that his works are filled with them is a product of autobiography and of realism. However, the degree to which roads are a powerful presence in his writings does attract attention. Hardy knew roads, yes, but why did he decide to use them in his art? They may be essential for what Tanner calls "the most searching of all Hardy's preoccupations—walking, travelling, movement of all kinds. Somewhere at heart of his vision is a profound sense of what we may call the mystery of motion."[1] Donald Davie, strongly sensing Hardy's rootedness in topography, presents a writer for whom one needs not "a history of nineteenth-century England, but a map.... And it will be noticed too that location matters so much, and it changes into phantasmagoria, only for a man who is on the move; on the move, for instance, between *cultures,* mobile in more than a physical sense."[2] Roads and places may be the most useful and most felt images in Hardy's works. Joan Grundy's examples of Hardy's "figure in a landscape" inevitably repeat images of the road:

> [Hardy is] as lonely in his "pilgrimage" as Mrs. Yeobright, Tess or Jude. The "onward earthtrack" of "The Temporary the All" leads him for a time to "paths through flowers" (CP, p. 349), but his common complaint is that "Life's bare pathway looms like a desert track to me" (p. 269); "Ever the road!" (p. 742)[3]

While examining the preponderance of circuses, fairs, and other forms of garish and bizarre fantasy in *Jude the Obscure,* Emma Clifford comments upon Hardy's attention to nomadic life: "[M]any characters in the novel regard nomadic life as a suitable form of existence. . . . When respectable society seems likely to reject Jude, Sue, or Arabella, they make their own plans to follow the life of the wanderer." The tightrope walker and the juggler use movement to maintain balance. Even someone as stable as Gabriel Oak must be willing to travel once his sheep are destroyed, and Tess knows she must move on, repeatedly, if she is to survive. Clifford concludes, "In a changing universe nothing has overcome the eternal stability of those who wander."[4]

J. Hillis Miller responds to Hardy's roads:

> To see time as a pattern in space is to see it as determined to follow just the sequence it does follow. Space fatalized. . . . To represent time as a movement through space is already implicitly to be a fatalist. . . . Often the motif which organizes a Hardy novel or poem . . . is the image of travel across the land. . . . To express the temporality of human life in this way is to suggest covertly that the future already virtually exists just as the past cannot fade from existence.[5]

Dorothy Van Ghent, who also senses fatality in Hardy, presents the earth, including roads, as an antagonist to human beings, their antagonism being most dramatically conveyed by the amount of land that must be covered with exhaustion and pain and uncertainty of what lies at the end of the journey. She does, however, perceive its functioning in varied ways: as a metaphor in *The Return of the Native*—a "reflection of the loneliness of human motive, of the inertia of unconscious life, of the mystery of the enfolding darkness"; as a real thing in *Tess of the d'Urbervilles*—"*a real thing* that one has to move on in order to get anywhere or do anything, and it constantly acts upon people . . . to encounter, to harass them, to detour them, seduce them, defeat them."[6] She finds the road responsible for Prince's death. (Yet John Holloway, commenting on this same scene, places the responsibility not on the road but on Tess, who "has a weakness . . . an alienation, a dreaminess," a tendency within herself that causes the accident.)[7] Tony Tanner, joining in the fatalist view, sees Tess's walks get longer and harder, in daylight and in darkness, and explains her appearance as "a moving spot intruding on the white vacuity"

(TD, 435) of the road as "a visible paradigm of the terms of human life—a spot of featured animation moving painfully across a vast featureless repose" and ending in the horizontal position of death.[8]

Certainly one hears fate on the road in the opening lines of *Tess of the d'Urbervilles* in the conversation between John Durbeyfield and the parson, in which the parson, so to speak, knights drunken John. John gets drunk again because of the good news heard on a road and Tess must take responsibility for her father's drunkenness by driving the wagon of beehives on a road. This trip leads to Prince's death on a road, which makes Tess travel on the road again, to Trantridge. She ultimately returns from Trantridge on a road and "ruined." She then departs again on a road to be "ruined" again, this time psychologically, directly by Angel but indirectly by Alec, whom she meets because of an accident on a road. The novel bludgeons one with a fatalistic view. Life on the road, which is to say "life," provides trouble. We meet Henchard on a road, hear him sell his wife, hear him make his vow of abstinence, and know the wife-selling will return to haunt his life. The novel is structured to make us know. That Susan appears soon thereafter (in the reader's time; twenty-one years later in the novel's time), on the road to Casterbridge or that Henchard leaves, a broken man, on the road from Casterbridge, does not terribly surprise the reader. What we cannot know about Tess or Henchard or many other Hardy characters, at first, is what—if anything—they will do to create meaning for the earth and for themselves as they travel the road. But what we do learn after reading a bit of Thomas Hardy is that they will do something. The road is static, present, engraved into the land; just as surely, it enables movement, permits people to be absent, somewhere else, never in any one spot but rather, like the road itself, in process. One learns another version of the tension between the image and the eye—obstructions, chance, change versus will, choice, action; we learn to see this tension everywhere, including on the road. To see the road as one thing, "space fatalized," for example, denies its multiple functions and overlooks its protean form and the fact that its spatialization makes it similar to much else in Hardy: a visual structure, a metaphoric construction with possibilities for new meanings.

Of course, to neutralize the constant presence of the road or to avoid the fact that roads—in Hardy and in vast numbers of other writers—are especially connected to the concept of fate, on the one hand, or a quest, on the other, would also be shortsighted. Nevertheless, to summarize, generalize, schematize Hardy's roads as a symbol of fate or the human quest for meaning would limit their full value as a vital symbol that is itself in process. The varied kinds of detail given to roads and to land in general can be seen on one of Tess's roads:

> Thus absorbed she recrossed the northern part of Long-Ash Lane at right angles, and presently saw before her the road ascending whitely to the upland along whose margin the remainder of her journey lay. Its pale surface stretched severely onward, unbroken by a single figure, vehicle, or mark, save some occasional brown horse-droppings which dotted its cold aridity here and there. (TD, 354)

It is austere and familiar, obstacle and vehicle—containing the appropriate tensions not for preordination but for something new to emerge, including a new meaning for the word "quest" itself.

One spring, after her baby's death, Tess feels a "spirit" rise within her "as the sap in the twigs. It was unexpected youth, surging up anew after its temporary check, and bringing with it hope, the invincible instinct toward self-delight" (TD, 139). Her descent into the Valley of the Great Dairies, on a "pilgrimage," reminds one of another spring:

> When that Aprill with his shoures soote,
> The droghte of March hath perced to the roote,
> . . . .
> Thanne longen folk to goon on pilgrimages.[9]

In Hardy, despite all the pain to which he subjects characters, still remains the bouyancy of Chaucer's pilgrims, the inexplicable renewal and joy in life, the quest. There is also, and more frequently, the will to survive with little joy. Why does Tess work on that threshing machine at Flintcomb-Ash? Why do Beckett's Estragon and Vladimir choose to stay on a country road, "waiting for Godot"? Why should *Oedipus the King*, a play that drives with unrelenting speed and anguish toward unavoidable and terrible revelation, put such repeated stress on the conjunction between an anonymous wanderer and a spot where three roads meet? All three writers—Ancient Greek, Medieval, or Modern—give to human beings the fundamental prerequisite for making the quest: responsibility, choice, will, self-creation.

Though it is essential to be on the road, in life, the presence of the road promises choice no more than it announces fate. The indeterminancy fundamental to Hardy hovers over any single understanding of his roads. *Jude the Obscure* is encircled with roads. Sue and Jude, by foot or train, continually travel. Early in the novel we are treated to a great variety of words for "road": "path," "track," "highway," "ridge-way," "road," and the Brown House near the road that is one of the visual focal points of the novel. There they are, road and place, those ever-constant engravings all over Hardy's text. The deadly touch of this novel may be in the irony of all these seeming opportunities for movement, choices, the will toward one's desires. For, with all their travels, all their places—Marygreen, Christminster, Melchester, Shaston, Aldbrickham—Sue's and Jude's feet barely touch the road at all. Elizabeth Hardwick notes "the unreality of themselves as a plan of life":

> In the absence of *surroundings*—they are like itinerants with no articles to offer as they wander in a circle from town to town—in the way their need has no more claim upon society than the perching of birds in the evening, they come to fall more and more under the domination of the mere attempt to describe themselves. They live under the protection of *conversation,* as many love affairs without a fixed meaning, without emotional space to occupy, come to rest in words. Their drama is one of trembling, inner feeling and of the work to name the feeling.[10]

Nevertheless, to reverse the ironic perspective, roads as metaphors of the process of self-creation are nowhere more suitably placed than in this novel and surrounding these characters. Sue and Jude, more than any other Hardy characters and despite whatever limitations they may have, disrupt belief in former structures of meaning and realize that self is a matter of self-creation.

Readers may arrive at particular meanings for the roads they meet in particular texts, but underlying all those interpretations is its emblematic existence in Hardy's whole text. As cosmic as Tess's "road ascending whitely . . . [i]ts pale surface stretched severely onward" or as concrete and familiar as the "occasional brown horse-droppings" found on it, the image of the road is the potentiality for metamorphosis in Hardy's modern world.

"But to Impose Is Not / To Discover"[11]

"Under the Waterfall" (CP, 335–37) is like many other Hardy poems in its movement from the present, into memory, and then back to the present. Its sound is full—with a strong lilting beat, rhyming couplets, and ubiquitous assonance and alliteration. The rhythm plus the concreteness and eternal quality of the dream world pull us into the speaker's memory:

> the purl of a little valley fall
> About three spans wide and two spans tall
> Over a table of solid rock
> And into a scoop of the self-same block;
> The purl of a runlet that never ceases
> In stir of kingdoms, in wars, in peaces;
> With a hollow boiling voice it speaks
> And has spoken since hills were turfless peaks.

Furthermore, one is pulled further and further into the dream, along with the narrator, as she works through several levels of subjective creation: first the effort of memory, "The sweet sharp sense of a fugitive day / Fetched back from its thickening shroud of gray"; second, the acknowledged self-creation of the original day itself when the lovers "[w]alked under a sky / Of blue with a leaf-wove awning of green, / In the burn of August, to paint the scene"; and finally, the return to the present, but with a difference. Originally, we are told, "Whenever I plunge my arm, like this, / In a basin of water, I never miss" remembering that past day. But in the return, that original description grows, spontaneously and unexpectedly, into not only the similarity between basin and pool, but also an added transformation: "And the leafy pattern of china-ware / The hanging plants that were bathing there." For a moment we get a sense of the myth-making of "The Phantom Horsewoman": speaker and vision—domesticity (humanity), imagination, and nature—inextricably interwoven. The poem might have ended here but, like many a Hardy character's quest, it cannot be content in experience alone, in "being," in discovery alone; it must find a final meaning, interpretation, absolute.

A wish for eternity has been suggested throughout the poem. Memory is explicitly fetched out of death, and the pool has "spoken since hills were turfless peaks." The worshipped item—called a "drinking-glass," a "vessel," a "glass"—becomes in the final stanza "a chalice," which takes on the mysteriously eternal quality of the falls. None of this would necessarily cut off the exquisite moment in which hanging plants grow out of chinaware. But the trite rhetoric of the last couplet does: "No lip has touched it since his and mine / In turns therefrom sipped lovers' wine." The everlastingness, earlier felt in the transformed beauty of "smoothness opalized," now takes on the aspects of interpretation and possessiveness, revealing a speaker unconvinced of her own momentary, imaginative experience. We have witnessed a quest to make the past present on a "road" of discovery curve into the imposition of rationalized explanation and definition.

A very different movement is felt in "The Voice" (CP, 346), in which the speaker's efforts to grasp the ineffable are never realized, but the failure, rather than being rationalized, is realized. The speaker starts, in a very musically modulated stanza, "Woman much missed, how you call to me, call to me"; stanza 2, however, asks, "Can it be you that I hear? Let me view you, then." Doubt takes over and wants proof, possession of the dream. Instead, he can discover only insubstantial language: "listlessness," "dissolved," "wistlessness." Finally, however, it is in a picture—active and concrete—of the speaker's yearning and failure that one feels the most intense and immediate experience:

> Thus I; faltering forward,
> Leaves around me falling,

> Wind oozing thin through the thorn from norward,
>   And the woman calling.

The stanza's power exists not in a successful retrieval of the past and not only because the external world takes on its greatest concreteness here, but because the speaker enters the present and reaches a consciousness of his own place in relation to that external world. Of course, the dream need not be lost for one to achieve a correct consciousness of one's place in the external world. Hanging plants do not grow out of chinaware, yet one could have believed in them. "The Phantom Horsewoman," already discussed several times in this study, pulls an "uninvolved" observer into the dreamer's vision in which both are carried onto rocks and waves where the "ghost-girl-rider" "sings to the swing of the tide" (CP, 354). J. I. M. Stewart calls it "a splendid taunt hurled at oblivion by the imagination." [12] The poem moves toward the discovery of the impossible made possible through language.

Metamorphosis exists in multiple forms: the changing shapes of Bathsheba Everdene, the self-framings of Eustacia Vye or Lucetta Templemen, the stream of images provoked by the Fifth of November firelight on Egdon Heath. Metamorphosis also exists in multiple levels in a single text or changes nature as it moves through a text. In the poems discussed above, the texture of experience is changed through a metamorphosis of images, and in "The Trampwoman's Tragedy" a series of places turns, by the poem's end, from external geography to a process of internalized and compulsive memory. The following and final section of this chapter will look at yet another level of the movement of metaphors in *Tess* and *Jude*, not print or roads this time but, in *Jude,* a series that spans the entire text like a swaying bridge moving above and counter to what seems to be the novel's dominant direction; and in *Tess,* a series of images constructed toward the end of the text that, like a dam, halts the novel's prior movement. As in much Hardy poetry, these new levels turn the perspective of each text, not enough to banish other perspectives but enough to disrupt them with an indeterminacy and a call for the reader's involvement in making meaning.

Over-arching Halo; Bodies in a Row; Reverberations

Very early in *Jude the Obscure* we get pictures of Sue and Jude that will stay with the reader throughout the novel. There is extrasensitive Jude in the fields, unwilling to scare and starve the birds, just as, later, he is unwilling to kill the pig. Being twirled about by Farmer Troutham or staring at the blood-stained snow, he discovers repeatedly that life is "illogical," that it does not quite add up to one's values or desires. Yet between these two "illogical" occurrences, Jude commits himself to a dream, the overarching halo that is Christminster. And there is vulnerable Jude who is not only in pain for all living creatures but also ignorant about formal education and about human beings. He believes that one rule, one clue, can unlock a whole language and is easily duped by the shrewdness and trickery of Arabella and of Vilbert. Nevertheless, despite his realization of the fact that pigs must die and that people can be brutal, despite the plodding labor needed to learn languages, he remains idealistic and a mythmaker: glorifies Christminster, studies Latin and Greek, falls in love, and tries to create a life according to his own "logic."

Our early pictures of Sue are of a spirit free, idealistic, intellectual, insecure, ambivalent, and rebellious. She spontaneously buys her pagan images, the naked Venus and Apollo; lies her way into her living place; reads Gibbon and Swinburne; and throughout the night gazes at her pagan symbols in the surrounding of Christian artifacts. Sue's ambivalence is practically notorious—about appointments, about marriage, but most importantly about her radical disbelief in Christianity and all social conventions alongside her terror of her own disbelief. Despite her violent criticism of Christminster and Christian rituals, she is too superstitious to meet Jude at a religious crossmark symbolizing martydom. The many images of Sue and Jude (see above, Chapter 3) with both passion and a window frame between them picture the constant contradictions within her. Sue's mercurial nature changes so rapidly from position to position that she is never in any position, is always between, seeming to fear landing in any one spot.

These two characters, similar in their sensitive natures, alienated from the world around them, join one another to form a separate world, without a teleology, in a frame of their own design. In following the outreachings of these early visualizations associated with Sue and Jude, I will explore the whole of *Jude the Obscure* to bring forth two interrelated "series of seemings": (1) the earlier images as they culminate in later images; (2) a panoramic view of visual structuring that spans the entire novel—over-arching halo, bodies in a row, and reverberations.

Sue and Jude try to act out in the domestic realm their idealistic values, but the community makes no place for them; they become excluded and self-enclosed.[13] At first talking—especially Sue's talking—creates an atmosphere, a "place"; however, it does not suffice. Hardwick (above) captures the feeling of this couple when she speaks of the "insecurity," "the unreality of themselves as a plan of life," and their falling "under the domination of the mere attempt to describe themselves." These are Hardy's two most educated characters, highly verbal and intellectually self-aware, at home with "modern views," excellent and tireless at analysis; yet their agility with ideas and with language gets them nowhere. Unlike Tess, Sue can tell Jude about her past and, unlike Angel, Jude can accept it. Nevertheless, the endless talk, juxtaposed against the endless failure, is the most powerful conveyer of tragedy and hopelessness in the novel. Their definitions and explanations, such as that they are ahead of their time, fifty years too soon, are not acts and do not curve into actions. Theirs is not "the act of finding / What will suffice"[14] but the act of the effort to find and the failure of that effort.

When Father Time attacks Sue for being pregnant again, adding to all their trouble, she fails to find the right words to comfort him. Instead, she speaks of things being out of control because she desperately feels in turmoil herself. Earlier in the day Jude had spoken to the Remembrance Day crowd about his own chaos and failure and choices:

> It is a difficult question . . . for any young man . . . whether to follow uncritically the track he finds himself in . . . or to consider what his aptness or bent may be, and reshape his course accordingly. I tried to do the latter, and I failed. But I don't admit that my failure proved my view to be a wrong one, or that my success would have made it a right one. . . . However it was my poverty and not my will that consented to be beaten. It takes two or three generations to do what I tried to do in one . . . I am in a chaos of principles—groping in the dark—acting by instinct and not after example. . . . I perceive there is something wrong somewhere in our social formulas: what it is can only be discovered by men or women with greater insight than mine. (JO, 345–46)

He is a bit morbid, bitter, self-pitying, but also independent and aware of choices, of self-creation, of possibility, of the future. While he had been speaking, Sue had seen Phillotson. Later on, Jude asks, "What made you tremble so?" Sue answers, "I saw Richard. . . . Although I know it is all right with our plans, I felt a curious dread of him; an awe, or terror, of conventions I don't believe in. It comes over me at times like a sort of creeping paralysis" (JO, 34). This contradiction within Sue is her emotional need for a system. As Perry Meisel notes, Jude's advanced ideas and ideals have been formed out of experience and they can survive experience;[15] Sue's ideas and ideals have been formed more from abstraction and fall apart when they clash with experience. Though she may not want the old law, Sue does lean toward systematic thinkers; she wants an answer with which to order the radical confusion within her. Indeed, Jude's reconstruction of dead buildings, etching words and designs into stone, studying Latin and Greek, and Sue's learned and intellectual analysis all point to a search for some means to explain and/or express a self. Definitions and explanations declare a need for an answer, a sign, to sum up or refute—to test—their experience. And they get it.

> At the back of the door were fixed two hooks for hanging garments, and from these the forms of the two youngest children were suspended, by a piece of box-cord round each of their necks, while from a nail a few yards off the body of little Jude was hanging in a similar manner. (JO, 355)

This scene is perhaps the most terrible scene in all Hardy and may strike many readers as Hardy taking his "full look at the worst"[16] a bit further than necessary. Nevertheless, the disruptive quality of Father Time generally and this final visual structure of his being that erupts from the novel serve to test Sue and Jude together and individually and to test the novel itself.

Those vertical bodies become a row of bars that entrap Sue forever. This event, however, does not create the Sue who returns to Phillotson; it releases her. Frozen within her has always been a fear of self-creating acts, demonstrated from the start in a highly visualized picture of her unease after buying the treasured Venus and Apollo: "They seemed so very large now that they were in her possession, and so very naked. . . . [S]he trembled at her enterprise. . . . [W]hite pipe clay came off on her gloves and jacket" (JO, 114). Unable to tolerate a life whose values must be found in living experientially, fearing the markings of pipe clay, losing the ability of savor the moment and the courage to imagine the next one, like Father Time at the flower show, she withdraws from the progressive tense to a past tense—a world already made.[17]

Sue has her ambivalence resolved in a self-created (though unacknowledged by her as such) abstraction: the absolute law of self-sacrifice, guilt, masochism, dogma; the letter of the law: "[H]e led her through the doorway, and lifting her bodily, kissed her. A quick look of aversion passed over her face, but clenching her teeth she uttered no cry" (JO, 417). As Elizabeth Hardwick notes, "In this ending Sue is faithful to her passion for an examined life; for indeed religion is at least an idea for her, not a mere drifting. . . . [But] [t]he defeat of Sue is total."[18] Finally we reach the end of the delightful young woman who sat up one night watching pagan gods surrounded by Christian artifacts. One cannot know the turn of a person or a metaphor until the final scene. Earlier, the pagan gods stood as a picture of ironic commentary upon Christianity and were reflective of Sue's free spirit; she does lose her lodging because of them. However, even then she sits up reading about the end of paganism—" 'Thou hast conquered, O pale Galilean' " (JO, 115)—and she does desire " 'I-i-i-mages!' " (JO, 113) of some kind. And now let us look at Jude's images.

Early in *Jude,* the boy Jude sets out one evening to see his dream place, Christminster. "He was rewarded; but what he saw was not the lamps in rows, as he had half expected . . . only a halo or glow-fog over-arching the place against the black heavens behind it" (JO, 42). Writing on modern fiction, Virginia Woolf states, "Life is not a series of gig lamps symmetrically arranged; but a luminous halo, a semi-transparent envelope surrounding us from the beginning of consciousness to the end.[19] Thomas Hardy did not read those lines, nor is it essential that he thought of "lamps in rows" as opposed to an over-arching halo when he created a row of dead children. His extraordinary visualizing sensibility saw the difference between objects in rows and a glowing curve. At the start of the novel Hardy hands Jude Fawley a visual structure, the glowing halo, to see what this character—sensitive, vulnerable, lonely, isolated but also eager and curious and idealistic and inventive—will do with it. And what is also important, he makes the reader want to see, too.

What Jude does is cherish it, for itself. In part he glorifies Christminster beyond even his own simultaneous objective criticism of it. When he sees a cab driver kick his horse in the stomach he remarks, "If that can be done . . . at college gates in the most religious and educational city in the world, what shall we say as to how far we've got?" (JO, 346). The forces of his criticism can be felt in the policeman's recalling him to order. Nevertheless, immediately thereafter, his old yearning is also shown. Looking at the Theatre, he longs to get in or, at least, to hear the Latin through open windows. "The indifferent universe does not dehumanize his spiritualizing vision. Rather, in a world without value, Jude's way of seeing becomes the only source of value," concludes Richard Benvenuto, who sees in Jude, despite his occasional will to suicide, a positive "will to live."[20] Jude's devotion appears less absurd, more meaningful, when one reflects upon the justice of his desire for education and when one recalls that Christminster is the magical place for Jude—the place haunted with phantasmagoria—with ghosts not only of the university but also of his love for Sue Bridehead.

The halo image, in fact, unites Christminster and Sue the first time Jude "sees" her: between brass candlesticks on his aunt's mantlepiece sits "the photograph of a pretty girlish face, in a broad hat with radiating folds under the brim like the rays of a halo. . . . The picture haunted him" (JO, 97). Sue, unlike the university, is willing to cultivate his mind, lead it from narrowness into visionary possibilities already seeded by an over-arching halo. Christminster, as a literal place, is at times placed on an ordinary level of importance, such as when Sue and Jude bake and sell Christminster "in pastry" (JO, 331). Though the Christminster cakes reflect Jude's obsession, they are also a diminishment to which he does not subject Sue Bridehead.

Regardless of Sue's horrifying, final regression, one must keep in view Jude's view of her, a perspective colored by agonizing love and loss but, to a large degree, accurate. He repeatedly sees her in images of light, illumination, possibility—further connections to his glowing image of Christminster. After the death of the children, he notices her change: "She was no longer the same as in the independent days, when her intellect played like lambent lightning over conventions and formalities which he at that time respected, though he did not now" (JO, 364). When she condemns herself, he calls her, "a woman-poet, a woman-seer, a woman whose soul shone like a diamond—whom all the wise of the world would have been proud of, if they could have known you" (JO, 370). When he mocks her, it is not to diminish but to provoke her into sight: "Can this be the girl . . . who brought the Pagan deities into this most Christian city?—who mimicked Miss Fontover when she crushed them with her heel?—quoted Gibbon, and Shelley, and Mill? Where are dear Apollo, and dear Venus now!" (JO, 371). Sue is one of the major choices of Jude's life, and as such it is vital that she be a valid choice. His ideals have not reached their full potential in reality, but he asserts the necessity for the human activity of mythmaking—despite the harsh contrasts in concrete reality—as the only remaining source for creating values. As he becomes sicker and sicker, he thinks of her and of them: "[S]he was once a woman whose intellect was to mine like a star to a benzoline lamp. . . . As for Sue and me . . . we were at our own best, long ago—when our minds were clear, and our love of truth fearless" (JO, 419). Jude's glowing metaphors of Sue, lightning and diamond and star, and the reader's devastation at Sue's self-denunciation, and thereby her or his acceptance to some degree of Jude's perception, keep Jude's vision from ending in a vision of total despair.

Furthermore, for Sue to have been so forceful an agent in Jude's development yet for him to renounce totally her return to Phillotson and her present dogmatism allows a character who has, at times, seemed weak, now to appear in unquestionable strength. Nothing could convince him more than Sue's present position that life is hopelessly "illogical"; yet he calls her return a "fanatic prostitution" (JO, 380) and rewords Sue's "right thing"—his remarrying Arabella—as "degrading, immoral, unnatural" (JO, 408). To Sue's "[w]e must conform. . . . It is no use fighting against God!" he answers, "It is only against men and senseless circumstance" (JO, 362). Jude does not give in to any form but his own and maintains to the end his belief in vision or, at the very least, in his final moments, the necessity of vision for him to live.

Despite Jude's rejection of Sue's position, however, the terrible power of the line-up of dead children and the picture of Sue's clenched return to Phillotson cannot be exaggerated. For William E. Buckler, Father Time "shatters the textuality of both *Jude* and the canon by the very violence of his metaphoric eruption."[21] For Gillian Beer, "Plot—that combination of the inexorable and the gratuitous—in *Jude* annuls writing. In all other of Hardy's works there is, as in Darwin, a strongly surviving belief in the 'recuperative powers' which pervade both language and the physical world."[22] These are both powerful statements and difficult to refute. My own analysis of Hardy in terms of visual structures, metaphoric movement, could reach as deadly a conclusion if one views the poetic process as a movement from a mythical misty halo to a factual row of corpses. This latter visualization is an antithesis to Jude's early vision of Christminster as a glowing halo —hazy, indefinite, visionary, mythical. This is a clearly delineated fact—blank, barren, unquestionable, absolutely authoritative.

Chapter 5 spoke of images accreting not only through framings and disruptions but also through repetition and contrast. These two metaphors, row of bodies and glowing halo, stand as the contrasting points between which one creates reality in Hardy's epistemology and aesthetics: external fact and subjective perception; the absolute and the personal; the general and the particular; skepticism and idealism. Father Time's explanation, "Because we were too menny" (JO, 356), is a paradigm of the inadequacy of all the general explanations in this novel of explanations, but it is joined to an act and a picture of self-annihilation that turn inadequate explanation into rigid dogma. The novel's subtitle, "The letter killeth," could mean the letter of the law—the Ten Commandments, Sue's return to Phillotson—or it could mean all writing. Chapter 5 discussed the oppressive power of print in *Jude,* and this chapter has suggested the seeming uselessness of analysis. Can we be sure "the letter" is only the language of dogma that kills, not also the inadequacy of any imaginative processes to save? Yes, to a degree, we can; *Jude the Obscure* is not *The Dynasts,* and Father Time's act is not the end of this novel's metamorphosis.

> An occasional word, as from some one making a speech, floated from the open windows of the Theatre across to this quiet corner, at which there seemed to be a smile of some sort upon the marble features of Jude; while the old, superseded, Delphin editions of Virgil and Horace, and the dog-eared Greek Testament on the neighboring shelf, and the few other volumes of the sort that he had not parted with, roughened with stone-dust where he had been in the habit of catching them up for a few minutes between his labours, seemed to pale to a sickly cast at the sounds. The bells struck out joyously; and their reverberations travelled round the bedroom. (JO, 428)

To have this last view of Jude and the unendurable anguish that precedes his death unite with a visualized sound, "The bells struck out joyously; and their reverberations travelled round the bedroom," gives the reader just the tiniest opening needed to remember the joyousness of this novel. When they are about to be married, the first time, in Albrickham, Sue hesitates and talks of fears, making Jude afraid, too; so they return home arm in arm to "think it over. . . . They thought it over, or postponed thinking. Certainly they postponed action, and seemed to live in a dreamy paradise" (JO, 291). The high point of our view of their joy is at the Great Wessex Agricultural Show. In physical movement, speech, feeling, and thought they move along as if "two parts of a single whole" (JO, 311). Throughout the scene the reader sees a series of metaphors that repeat this image of their unity. We move along with Arabella, watching them take pride in their joint work: " 'Model of Cardinal College, Christminster; by J. Fawley and S. F. M. Bridehead' " and take pleasure in each other: "Jude's hand sought Sue's as they stood, the two standing close together so as to conceal, as they supposed, this tacit expression of their mutual responsiveness" (JO, 314). There is affection and teasing between them:

> "I should like to push my face quite into them—[the flowers] the dears!' she had said. 'But I suppose it is against the rules to touch them—isn't it, Jude."
> "Yes, you baby," he said; and then playfully gave her a little push, so that her nose went among the petals.
> "The policemen will be down on us, and I shall say it was my husband's fault!"[23]
> Then she looked up at him, and smiled in a way that told so much to Arabella.
> "Happy?" he murmured.

D. H. Lawrence captures the form of their connectedness and the way in which it translates the world:

> The roses, how the roses glowed for them! The flowers had more being than either he or she. But as their ecstasy over things sank a little, they felt, the pair of them, as if they themselves were wanting in real body, as if they were too unsubstantial, too thin and evanescent in substance, as if the other solid people might jostle right through them, two wandering shades as they were.
> This they felt themselves. Hence their uncertainty in contact with other people. . . . But they had their own form of happiness, nevertheless, this trembling on the verge of ecstasy, when, the senses strongly roused to the service of the consciousness, the things they contemplated took flaming being, became flaming symbols of their own emotions to them.[24]

The form of their happiness is a vision founded upon childlike sensibilities—neither character wished to grow up—innocent and fragile and separate from all structures, all conventions. It is a willed escape from a nightmare world, and of course it is destroyed by physical reality, fact. Nevertheless, despite love being a frequent theme in Hardy, no other couple reaches anything near the spiritual intimacy and ecstasy—Greek joyousness—of Sue and Jude. In the final scene, Jude's corpse is viewed by the kind and caring Mrs. Edlin: " 'How beautiful he is!' " she says and the more prosaic Arabella: " 'Yes. He's a 'andsome corpse' " (JO, 427). The narrator gives him the conventional, formal dignity of "marble features." Conversations continue; in the background, from out the window and from within the room, words are what we hear. But in the foreground—mixed with worn-out books and stone-dust and defeat—joyous and reverberating soundwaves traveling round the room are what we see. There is still some magic in our eyes.

There can be no attempt to present *Jude*—or any other Hardy novel discussed in this study—as cheerful. The entry of those unexpected and almost unbelievable bells does not work upon the text like the ending of *The Return of the Native,* to deconstruct itself and return the reader to earlier images. Nor does it work like the final framing of Bathsheba to send us back to all the frames, moving as an intermingling whole. Father Time is a murder-suicide; Sue is among the living dead; Jude is dead. It is a fragile metaphor, this joyous vision of a sound, to be etching its way into and opposed to the devastating events of this novel. Not despite its fragility, however, but because of it, this metaphor is the perfect reestablishment of the possibilities for imagination, self-creation, ideals as they have lived in this novel. D. H. Lawrence and Elizabeth Hardwick speak of Sue's and Jude's love as "trembling on the verge of ecstasy" or as a "trembling inner feeling." Chapter 2 discussed Hardy's need to teach readers how to see, to read, his writings; in *Jude the Obscure* he has had to teach us in a most particular way. No one could miss the deadly touch of Father Time: absolute, general, factual reality. In such a world, imaginative quests are bound to be tenuous, trembling, so we have been carefully attuned to even the subtlest images. It is in precisely such visual structures that we locate the unresolved tensions at the core of Hardy's writings. In this novel the tension between plot and poem is pushed as far as it can go without breaking, but Gillian Beer's "plot . . . annuls writing," while certainly a valid response, is not necessarily a final view.

John Bayley notes, "The small things are more important in Hardy than the big things, but in so being they become the big things," and he goes on to explain the quality of these small-big things as "situated at some meeting-point of space and time with consciousness, like a crossroads in solitary country."[25] This is what we must look for to read the small-big images in *Jude the Obscure*. The novel's images move, like modern poetry, without transition. Ian Gregor described *Jude* as having "constant oscillations of interest . . . a series of significant but isolated moments."[26] *Jude* moves not only like a "series of seemings"[27] but, more precisely, like a series of poems, each one carrying out the subjective experience of characters; the intermingling of these poems carries out the writer's subjective creation, and demands the reader's creation, of the entire text. Chapter 5 speaks of Hardy's saturation of places with people—Beeny Crest does not mean something; it is a subjective and private embodiment of feeling. A landlady opens her door on Jude's words, "Why the bells—what church can that be? The tones are familiar" and impatiently replies, along with another "peel of bells," "I don't know! . . . Did you knock to ask that?" (JO, 348). They are Jude's bells. Not only Christminster as place but also, repeatedly, the Brown House and the road to Alfredston resonate with experience; Latin book and stone dust; language engraved in stone and stone engraved in gingerbread—all are moments in Jude's subjective awareness of life. Allusions to outside texts, quotations from texts, pagan statues, weightlessness, roses, her own speaking voice are Sue's subjective awareness. Arabella, Phillotson, Vilbert, the people in the street and in the taverns of Christminster: everything has its poem. The density of such private images reflects fragility, yes, and also a phenomenal sense of presence. They put an emphasis on the subjective element, the element of pure consciousness, reverberating within this text, an emphasis that enacts the increasing subsuming of the image by the eye in the "movement of the [modern] mind" expressed symbolically.[28] Therefore, when "[t]he bells struck out joyously; and their reverberations travelled round the bedroom" (JO, 428), the sensitive reader is ready to see them even in this novel's bleak ending. We've been taught "to see in half and quarter views the whole picture,"[29] the inexorable movement of plot and the poetic movement of images: the impossible made possible through language, through imagination.

Hardy, experimenting with the centrality of private consciousness in fiction, goes as far as he can. But it is not his final position. Empiricism, Darwinism, a practical materiality in his social views insist that consciousness live in history, in culture.[30] Mythmaking is an essential activity for the human imagination and is necessary to create and preserve ideals, visions of possibility. Yet it can also be dangerous—entrapping and self-destructive. The recognition of material fact is essential to maintain one's sanity; unfortunately, there is always the danger of its destroying human creativity. This unresolved tension is enacted in the series of visual structures that span *Jude the Obscure*. This text is a novel of subjective consciousness, of possibility and imagination, of an over-arching halo. Father Time disrupts it with the limitations of existence, being, and becoming; with the confines of chance and change, the unknown and unknowable internal and external aspects of life; with dead bodies in a row. This image is disrupted in its turn by the creative suggestiveness of willed vision: "reverberations travelled round the bedroom," a visual structure evoking its own reality. This over-arching metamorphosis of metaphors pictures *Jude the Obscure* as a novel of fruitful contradiction, the contradiction at the center of Thomas Hardy: the uncertainties and limitations of "reality" and the imaginative will to negotiate with this unknown, through rhetoric, to make it known and to make it magic.

"Tess Is Queer." / "Call Me Tess"

To get a sense of the particular quality of *Tess of the d'Urbervilles*, one only need compare it to another Hardy novel with a seemingly similar surface, *Far from the Madding Crowd*. Both have as central characters independent, strong-willed women whose lives are greatly affected by the men who take interest in them, both are set in agricultural worlds, and both are highly episodic, containing large scenes that present in strongly visualized terms the state of the heroine and the process of the novel. One could move through scenes of Tess in white, Tess pulled into Prince's blood, the absent "scene" of rape/seduction, theological billboards, Paradise at Tolbathays, red glow and dark shadows of a confession scene, the Satanic machine at Flintcomb-Ash, an ace of hearts, and Stonehenge. However, what these similarities do is point up the vast differences. Like the Great Barn scene in *Far from the Madding Crowd,* Tolbathays speaks fleetingly of an ordered rural world, but the former novel does not have economic precariousness as a dominant theme (though that theme is present), nor does it have anything like the raw and decaying nature scene in Tolbathays' "paradise" or the violence of agricultural machinery upon human beings at Flintcomb-Ash. Though Troy's swordplay, Boldwood's monomania, Fanny's coffin, and even Gabriel's spying do objectify Bathsheba Everdene, their actions do not approach the repeated objectification of Tess by parents, Alec, Angel, men in general, field labor, and machinery. Tess's repeated journeys, alone, across open expanses of land depict conditions for living that are far grimmer, and the landscape takes on qualities less local, more cosmic. Both in content and in quality, scenes and setting have changed. The novel, like *Jude the Obscure* that follows it, comes closer to fundamental questions of existence, of a character's inward state of being; Tess moves along a continuum of scenes in which she must continually fight for the survival of her spirit.

Therefore, this discussion will view visual structures and the process of metamorphosis within a text by concentrating on two movements: first, the effort of external forces around Tess to split her body—her surface, external presence—from her spirit—the complex self-identity she feels and tries to live;[31] and, second, the response of Tess and of the novel to this attack. Similar to the analysis of *Jude,* earlier discussions will at times be broadly summarized, in this instance to encompass the unyielding objectification of Tess and her persistent resistance, and to prepare for a detailed look at the final sequence of bold visual structures that constitute Tess's and this novel's ultimate self-definition. Again, as in the examination of *Jude,* visualizations will be apparent even in summary as Hardy has worked them into every element of his fictional/poetic constructions.

Tess's father's "Tess is queer" (TD, 55) is emblematic of the way all the others see her as something other than what she is "supposed to be," according to their needs, conveniences, assumptions. Of course, Tess is queer, unfamiliar, to her parents:

> Between the mother, with her fast-perishing lumber of superstitions, folk-lore, dialect, and orally transmitted ballads, and the daughter, with her trained National teachings and Standard knowledge under an infinitely Revised Code, there was a gap of two hundred years as ordinarily understood. When they were together the Jacobean and the Victorian ages were juxtaposed. (TD, 51)

Nevertheless, John Durbeyfield shows greater perception than his wife in his openness to seeing something different in Tess. Joan's response, "But she's tractable at bottom" (TD, 55), is entirely inaccurate, for it is at the core of her being ("at bottom") that Tess is not "tractable." And Joan is wrong again, as Tess goes off with great misgivings to Trantridge Farms, in assuming that Tess will play her life, her "trump card," as her mother did. John asks, "What's her trump card? Her d'Urberville blood, you mean?" and Joan answers, "No, stupid; her face—as 'twas mine" (TD, 82). Again John comes closer by looking at the internal: blood; for Tess's "trump card" will turn out to be a blood-red, enormous ace of hearts. Toward the end of the novel it is with complete honesty that Joan can reply to Angel's "I know her better than you do," "That's very likely, sir; for I have never really known her" (TD, 424).

Tess's father's perception that Tess is unusual is also noted but even more fiercely resisted by Alec d'Urberville. After passively receiving his kiss, she wipes it away with her handkerchief. "His ardour was nettled at the sight for the act on her part had been unconsciously done. . . . 'You're mighty sensitive for a cottage girl!' " (TD, 85). It is his insight to her internal being that he immediately obscures, replacing the particular individual with the general packaging of "cottage girl." The label is a desire to make her an object he can control; her repeated rejection of his initially only half-interested wish to master her and her repeated projection from the labels he places upon her escalate Alec's desire into an implacable will and need to destroy Tess's being and to own her body. The machine scene carries Tess far toward this division between self and body. Machinery represents one of humanity's most advanced scientific developments. The scene depicts culture's structures—science, sexism, social class—and the individual human ego—Alec and his use of those structures—working toward a complete obliteration of Tess:

> She was the only woman whose place was upon the machine so as to be shaken bodily by its spinning. . . . The incessant quivering, in which every fiber of her frame participated, had thrown her into a stupefied reverie in which her arms worked on independently of her consciousness. . . . She beheld always the great upgrown strawstack, with the men in shirtsleeves upon it, against the gray north sky; in front of it the long red elevator like a Jacob's ladder, on which a perpetual stream of threshed straw ascended, a yellow river running up-hill, and spouting out on the top of the rick. (TD, 380–81)

This scene is mapped out in layers of visualized oppression: within, body and spirit are fragmented; without, chaos stands in a vertical stream looming above Tess and, insisting that he be the circumference of her life, Alec circles round. Alec is the greater danger, not to her physical self but to her spirit. Alec has his "trump card": a contradictory responsibility within Tess—responsibility to herself versus responsibility to her family, one aspect of her self.

What makes Tess unknowable both to her parents and to Alec is her particular response to "the ache of modernism" (TD, 165), the modern dilemma. (This is further elaborated in Chapter 4, above.) Tess is alienated from her past, from her surrounding; if she is to have a life, it must be built not on past structures—d'Urberville nobility or Durbeyfield peasantry—but on a present self-creation. "Upon her sensations the whole world depended to Tess. . . . The universe . . . came into being for Tess on the particular day in the particular year in which she was born" (TD,

195). Tess, Alec, and Angel are all deracinated people (as are the farm women, frequently drunk, with whom Tess works, and even the machine's Satanic-seeming engineer), living out this condition of life in a variety of ways. Tess's whole mode of being is toward the creation of values, responsibilities, choices—structures of meaning. This aspect of Tess, her incorruptible sense of her own integrity, Alec finds incomprehensible; and it is Tess's vision of Angel as a prophet of new views and new values grown out of experience, not superstition or dogma, that helps her to fall in love with him. Actually, he is a split person, who believes one thing and feels another, whose ideals, like Sue Bridehead's, break down when confronted with experience.[32] Angel is far more dangerous than Alec because he does not know himself. Tess's monumental lapse from her desire to live without "d'Urberville air castles" (TD, 136), without dreams and illusions, is her establishment of Angel Clare as God, a turning from concrete reality toward drifting fantasy.

Tess yearns for a shape to her universe, "and he was so godlike in her eyes" (TD, 222):

> There was hardly a touch of earth in her love for Clare. To her sublime trustfulness he was all that goodness could be—knew all that a guide, philosopher and friend should know. She thought every line in the contour of his person the perfection of masculine beauty, his soul the soul of a saint, his intellect that of a seer. The wisdom of her love for him, as love, sustained her dignity; she seemed to be wearing a crown. The compassion of his love for her, as she saw it, made her lift up her heart to him in devotion. He would sometimes catch her large, worshipful eyes, that had no bottom to them, looking at him from their depths, as if she saw something immortal before her. (TD, 234)

After the confession scene when, in his sleepwalking, Tess permits Angel to risk her life, and Angel finally places her in the coffin, both characters participate in the separation between Tess Durbeyfield's body and being. She does so in her passive subjugation of will to God; Angel does so when his loss of a myth (Tess) reduces all reality to meaningless matter. When he returns from his travels, he will find his dream turned reality: "[H]is original Tess had spiritually ceased to recognize the body before him as hers—allowing it to drift, like a corpse upon the current, in a direction dissociated from its living will" (TD, 429). From the start, Angel had wanted to rename and redefine Tess. He wanted to replace "Durbeyfield" with "d'Urberville," an early indication of contradiction within himself, and to replace this unique milkmaid with "a visionary essence of woman—a whole sex condensed into one typical form. He called her Artemis, Demeter." And she would reply, "Call me Tess" (TD, 170).

Though Tess's words to Angel—"Call me Tess"—are a gentle request, the novel ultimately makes of them a demand; they represent her fight for integrity against the external forces, personal and cultural, that wish to categorize and divide her. Early we witnessed her rebellion when she baptizes the baby and, while the theological billboards make her blush, they also draw her contempt. Tess's resistance to Durbeyfield values is also strong: she rejects the d'Urberville dreams and does not take her mother's advice regarding Angel. She sacrifices one set of principles for the family not because of an external law but because of another set of principles. She even corrects her single act of bad faith by pulling her false god out of the sky in a final and justified letter of outrage to Angel: "O why have you treated me so monstrously, Angel! I do not deserve it. . . . It is all injustice I have received at your hands!" (TD, 405). To Alec she responds with absolute resistance, and it is only to him that she reacts with a physical violence. Earlier in the novel she had wiped away his uninvited kiss with her handkerchief. At Flintcomb-Ash that former gesture escalates into a vividly pictured attack:

> One of her leather gloves . . . lay in her lap, and without the slightest warning she passionately swung the glove by the gauntlet directly in his face. It was heavy and thick as a warrior's, and it struck him flat on the mouth. . . . Alec fiercely started up from his reclining position. A scarlet oozing appeared where her blow had alighted, and in a moment the blood began dropping from his mouth upon the straw. (TD, 379)

When he visits her at home and tries to touch her through the window, "With stormy eyes she pulled the stay-bar quickly, and caught his arm between the casement and the stone mullion" (TD, 404). Now, as always, Alec will not believe his own (visual) experience with a particular human being who does not fit the mold; he senses that "Tess is queer" but rejects "call me Tess." John Bayley observes, "Hardy's engrossment, and ours, is in the particular: the general is a kind of insult to it, as the conditions of the world are to consciousness";[33] more than an insult, Alec's attitude and behavior are assaults upon Tess's consciousness. It is at his peril that he does not give others the right to exist, for "Tess was no insignificant creature to toy with and dismiss; but a woman living her precious life" (TD, 195). A final sequence of bold visualizations defends and presents that life.

As the landlady looks up at the ceiling her eyes

> were arrested by a spot in the middle of its white surface which she had never noticed before. It was about the size of a wafer when she first observed it, but it speedily grew as large as the palm of her hand, and then she could perceive that it was red. The oblong white ceiling, with this scarlet blot in the midst, had the appearance of a gigantic ace of hearts. (TD, 433)

Terry Eagleton observes that "Tess struggles against her reduction to a thing; but the only successful tactic is to reduce *herself* to impassive objectivity, making herself 'dead' when Alec kisses her." She further abandons herself by allowing her body to drift like a corpse "in the moment before it is formally destroyed by society."[34] This is a somewhat eclipsed reading of the novel. She also affirms herself by fighting back physically, violently, animatedly, and nowhere more dramatically than in the last section of the novel, "Fulfilment." There is a terrible gap between the life Tess has wished to live, the person she has felt she was, and the life she has lived, the person other people have seen her as being. That gap could be an abyss, a void, and Tess could be seen as moving in David DeLaura's "no-man's land 'between two worlds.' " Hardy, as DeLaura further notes, refused to make a compromise via neo-Christianity, Angel's position, but demanded a greater honesty in facing a barren world; it is hard to find a strong affirmative position in Hardy, easier to find a skeptic.[35] Nevertheless, his works are also textured with an existential perspective that demands responsibility and choice and process—an affirmation found in poetic process. Like the narrator in *The Return of the Native,* looking beyond fires into the black unknown, Thomas Hardy's imagination wills to fill the void with a series of worlds: an ace of hearts, a figure on a road, and Stonehenge.

John Bayley sees Tess as "at once the symbol of consciousness imprisoned in life and the justification for living. To imagine Tess, to write a poem, to see, to read and to dream, are immanent throughout *[Tess of the d'Urbervilles]* as the romance that makes life possible for Hardy."[36] These final images cut across story line as Hardy hands Tess a gift—a visual structure—of ample size and space and possibility for the full life of her consciousness, her self, and for the full life of his creating and visualizing imagination. Poetic form and poetic process emerge from chronological narrative as the ace of hearts disrupts the frame of a white ceiling and the seemingly unrelenting movement of this novel. Tess bursts startlingly, energetically, arbitrarily back into the text. The image of blood, of course, has its history in this novel. Prince's blood pulled Tess into her painful pilgrimage; blood on Alec's face and blood on the ceiling are her retaliation. Also, Tess's extraordinary loyalty, endurance, and resistance—even ferocity—in facing overwhelming obstacles are solid origins out of which a violent and self-defining image might germinate. Our last view of her is as a drifting corpse, a Sue Bridehead in Phillotson's arms, but Tess has decided to declare the terms under which she will live and die: as a self-creating human being in the full splendor of that activity. A violent and shocking—unexpected—blood-red, gigantic ace of hearts pictures the energy needed to resist the onslaught of forces that have tried to oppress her. Tess's explosion from background is repeated in a second visualization at the start of the next chapter when one sees a road:

> The tape-like surface of the road diminished in his rear as far as he could see, and as he gazed a moving spot intruded on the white vacuity of its perspective. . . . It was a human figure running. . . . The form descending the incline was a woman's. . . . It was not

until she was quite close that he could believe her to be Tess. (TD, 436)

Out of the vacuity comes the form of Tess, an image of onward and positive movement. As Tess and Angel proceed to walk along and talk of the past and the future, she states, "I am not going to think outside of now" (TD, 441). Tess will live precisely at the moment; neither Alec's "cottage girl" nor Angel's "Artemis, Demeter," she is her self.

Stonehenge calls attention to itself as something unexpected: "They had almost struck themselves against it" (TD, 444). It is a new world, beyond measurable time or space: "solid stone, without joint or moulding"; "a colossal rectangular pillar"; "indefinite height"; "vast architrave." Slowly they discover their way amongst the pillars until they can name it, Stongehenge; it is a visual structuring of the process of discovery. The heathen temple is a place so old, it gives the sense of having always existed. It cannot be categorized. It has no "inside" or "outside," no etchings upon it, only the wind and the sun. Whereas she had been frightened by the "shapes of darkness" (TD, 237) (see above, Chapter 5) she had seen at Tolbathays or the "raging tiger," "giant's head," or other "fantastic scenes" (TD, 58–60) on the night ride of Prince's death, she feels at home in the darkened shapelessness of Stonehenge. Killing Alec brings body and soul together; she confirms and accepts herself and her integrity in a self-generating creative act. In contrast to former scenes in which Tess dangerously drifted into states outside of time and space and body, away from concrete reality, this scene is positive. In Stonehenge Hardy has given to Tess the meeting point of time and space with consciousness. It is the appropriate surrounding for the person who can live consciously in process: " 'I am ready,' she said quietly" (TD, 447).

"Call me Tess," she had requested earlier, and Hardy here permits himself to respond with his ideal of the human being in a world without meaning who can live a life in process with the full consciousness that she is her own being. He has made subjective choices of images—an ace of hearts, a figure on a road, and Stonehenge—to affirm and immortalize the spirit of Tess

Durbeyfield; in so doing he has, for a moment, affirmed imaginative processes and committed himself to mythmaking. The positive quality of the novel must reside in imagination. Hardy has created "A Pure Woman, Faithfully Presented, by Thomas Hardy" (title page); "Placed, so, beyond the compass of change, / Perceived in a final atmosphere; / For a moment final."[37]

This final chapter on metamorphosis has explored widely varied enactments of process to make apparent the ever-present nature of movement within and among images and perspectives in Hardy's works. Images, such as the remembered drinking cup or the basin of water, can be an opening to imaginative outreachings toward further images, or they can provoke a withdrawal from possibility and creation into abstraction and generalizations. The cup's presence is absolutely felt, but neither its meaning nor its function is absolute. The poem itself may have a resolution in the final withdrawal from imagination, but the images, as instigators of thought, have no final position. So, too, is this true for frequent Hardyan images, be they the road, as discussed in this chapter, or places, or landscape scenes. Their "meanings" will reside finally in the changing perspectives brought to them by characters, narrators, readers: in process.

The metamorphosis of visual structures in particular novels has been examined in earlier chapters. For example, we have viewed Lucetta's process of self-framing, *Far from the Madding Crowd*'s process of framing Bathsheba Everdene, and Eustacia the Knight's process of framing Clym and herself. These kinds of analyses could be used to approach *Tess* and *Jude,* as evidenced by the series of large visualizations of framings and disruptions that frame the experience of Tess. However, *Tess* and *Jude* have instead been used to carry the examination of metamorphosis a step further: first, to the element of multilevel metamorphosis within an individual text and, second, to the continuum along which visual structures move and change between fundamental oppositions in Hardy's values and in his text: imagination and fact, image and abstraction, belief and skepticism, humanity's mythmaking tendencies and material reality, poem and story. In so doing, this chapter demonstrates the power of visual structures; they metamorphose these two novels from texts that end with a single, negative conclusion to texts in which fact and figure are still at play, in process. There is no final resting point, only framing, disruption, process.

Chapter 7

A Final Frame

Oppositions are central to forming meaning in the irrational world of Thomas Hardy. Along with visual thinking, contradiction—unresolvable tensions, incongruity, ambiguity, ambivalence—rests at the core of his writing. This study has demonstrated the dynamic sense of opposition that keeps readers from adopting monistic interpretations of a text and that provides vitality to the texture of images. In short, intensely realized visualizations placed in the context of intense antagonisms are precisely what produce Thomas Hardy's poetic process and reinvest his world of surface visualizations with a new significance, creative process itself. Impressions, unexplained and unsystematized, emerge spontaneously and chaotically; they change, disappear, reappear; the reader is pulled toward their surfaces to create a sense of the relationship among the images: to create reality.

We have seen, for example, in Chapter 4, how Hardy's introduction of a whitened Diggory Venn renders *The Return of the Native*'s conclusion unbelievable, disrupts the novel's systematic —patterned—ending, removes the novel form's circumference— its customary frame—enabling content to move around with no form but the energy of images themselves intermingling with the reader's imaginative processes. Hardy permits and demands that the reader choose between white gloves and red fire in order that she or he become involved in the process of making meaning. He chose to use so fluid a form in almost everything he wrote, or at least to include this poetic movement as a somewhat submerged but subversive presence even in his most highly structured novels, and to confront the farthest points on his spectrum of oppositions. These choices present not a commitment to pessimism or a surrender to despair, but an awareness of human possibilities demonstrated by his texts' open-ended, poetic processes and in the opening up of these texts to the imaginative processes of readers.

Tom Paulin, in *Thomas Hardy: The Poetry of Perception*, emphasizes the connection between Hardy and positivism and skeptical empiricism but also recognizes a visionary aspect to Hardy. He notes that while some poems separate fact and vision to make "the external world terrifyingly dead and threatening and imagination just a flimsy fantasy," other poems "have transcendental capabilities that float them above the ruck of wind, weather, and disappointment." These latter poems contain images "packed with facts which have been totally transformed by the imagination. . . . [T]hey exist in . . . a timeless reality. . . . beautifully and freshly present . . . uniquely human in their details and visionary in their total composition."[1] Paulin's quintessential poem of "visionary freedom" is "During Wind and Rain" (CP, 495–96); there could hardly be a better choice. After looking at this poem's images, I will suggest why it is not the images alone that enable it to float above life's inevitable limitations.

Each seven-line stanza contains five lines that develop a positive image, but ends with two lines of ruthlessness and anguish. The first stanza depicts communal singing, "With the candles mooning each face," but ends with the repeated refrain, "Ah, no; the years O!" and "How the sick leaves reel down in throngs!" The next stanza shows people clearing out overgrown nature to make "the garden gay" with "a shady seat," but ends with the refrain, "See, the white storm-birds wing across!" The third stanza presents the group breakfasting together, "Under the summer tree, / With a glimpse of the bay," but, also, "the rotten rose is ript from the wall." Finally, they are moving: "Clocks and carpets and chairs / On the lawn all day, / And brightest things that are theirs." are placed beside, "Down their carved names the rain drop ploughs."

The two kinds of images cannot possibly be reconciled or compromised. The positive images combine movement, suggestions of light and of containment, the intermingling of humanity and nature, and some degree of defamiliarization; they are exceptionally powerful in their fullness and warmth. The faces are made bright and safely secured in moon-light; the garden workers create a bright ("gay") place and a domestically enclosed seat; the breakfasters are enclosed beneath a tree yet are privileged to see beyond to the (sparkling?) bay; and, finally, most vivid of all, perhaps, domesticity and nature are joined in the startling placement of household furnishings, "brightest things"—like jewels —on a lawn. However, the negative images are also powerful. They are not mere generalizations but particular, active, brutal: sick leaves reel; storm birds wing across, the rotten rose is ript, and rain-drops plough into carvings.

The sense of awe within the poem and within the reader is attained not by the images alone but by the fierce effort needed to establish a clear outline of these bright images in juxtaposition with their clear negation. Hardy, true to his best work, presents only the visualizations, not explanations. The viewer must enter the contradiction as if stepping upon a borderline along which each series of images outlines itself against the other and against the reader. No one can question the obliterating facts of nature; however, a poetic energy is released in the repeated imaging of light, enclosure, and the human use of, rather than destruction by, nature. The felt presence of the material world, in its insistent resistance to time, is staggering. It has the unsettling effect of freeing us, for a moment, to hang suspended above the line of tension.

If on occasion Hardy seems to stand outside his world, as if he were writing from the margins of a map, it may be that an extra frame of stark outline is needed to bring forth vision against a chaotic backdrop of conflicting visions. And on infrequent occasions, Hardy overwhelms contradiction in such extraordinarily vital images arranged in so precise, albeit fragile, an equilibrium, that the reader gains access to a bright safety, above the contradictions, in a moment of poise and rest. This he has done in "During Wind and Rain." Such moments are rare, but they are magnificent achievements of a poet's imagination, enacting poetic vision in process. Nevertheless, reviewing Hardy's works as a whole demands an oscillation between opposing points. In poems such as "On the Departure Platform" or novels such as *Jude* or *Tess,* there are positive images; the presence of life, including the imagination's processes, is known and felt. Simultaneously, however, the anguish of loss is engrained throughout these works. At their highest moments, characters (and readers) do not overcome pain but do manage involvement, confrontation, acceptance of change. Thomas Hardy's world is "a yearning world [in which] cosmic agony is overwhelmed by cosmic energy";[2] its processes go on forever.

Notes

1. The Image and the Eye

1. Thomas Hardy, *Thomas Hardy's Personal Writings,* ed. Harold Orel (Lawrence: University of Kansas Press, 1966), 27.
2. Ibid., 33.
3. Ibid., 38–39.
4. Ibid., 39.
5. Ibid., 49.
6. Ibid., 117.
7. Hardy, *Personal Writings,* 115.
8. Ibid., 117.
9. Morton Zabel, "Hardy in Defense of His Art," in *Hardy, A Collection of Critical Essays,* ed. Albert Guerard (Englewood Cliffs, N.J.: Prentice Hall, 1963), 24–45.
10. Albert J. Guerard, *Thomas Hardy* (Cambridge: Harvard University Press, 1964), ix, 4.
11. David DeLaura, "The Ache of Modernism," *ELH* 34 (September 1967): 381.
12. Charles E. May, "Thomas Hardy and the Poetry of the Absurd," *Texas Studies in Literature and Language* 12 (Spring 1970): 165.
13. David Perkins, "Hardy and the Poetry of Isolation," in *Hardy, A Collection of Critical Essays,* ed. Albert Guerard (Englewood Cliffs, N.J.: Prentice Hall, 1963), 143.
14. Emma Clifford, "The Child: The Circus: and *Jude the Obscure,*" *Cambridge Journal* 7 (June 1954): 536.
15. For a variety of approaches on Hardy and art, visualizations, and seeing, note the following: Alistair Smart, "Pictorial Images in the Novels of Thomas Hardy," *Review of English Studies* 12 (1961): 262–80; Richard C. Carpenter,

"Thomas Hardy and the Old Masters," *Boston University Studies in English*, 5 (Spring 1961), 18–28; David Lodge, "Thomas Hardy as a Cinematic Novelist," in *Thomas Hardy after Fifty Years*, ed. Lance St. John Butler (London: Macmillan, 1977), 78–89; Richard C. Carpenter, "Hardy's Gargoyles," *Modern Fiction Studies* 6 (Autumn 1960): 223–32. Though the function of "seeing" may change from study to study, its centrality is not questioned. For example, see George Fayen, "*The Woodlanders:* Inwardness and Memory," *Studies in English Literature (1500–1900)* 1 (Autumn 1961): 81–100, who notes, "Elective affinities in the structure of Hardy's novels derive from the construction his characters are prepared to put on all they see and remember," 96; and Robert Kiely, "Vision and Viewpoint in *The Mayor of Casterbridge*," *Nineteenth Century Fiction* 23 (September 1968): 189–200, who notes, "The way people look at themselves and one another is the central concern of the novel. What each character sees defines, to a great extent, what he is," 190. Also illuminating are two full-length studies, one of Hardy's poetry—Tom Paulin, *Thomas Hardy: The Poetry of Perception* (Totowa, N.J.: Rowman and Littlefield, 1975)—and one of his fiction—J. B. Bullen, *The Expressive Eye: Fiction and Perception in the Work of Thomas Hardy* (Oxford: Clarendon, 1986).

16. Smart, 263.
17. Ibid., 263.
18. John Ruskin, *The Works of John Ruskin* (New York: Merrill and Baker, n.d.), 4: 318.
19. Tony Tanner, "Color and Movement in *Tess of the d'Urbervilles*," in *Hardy, The Tragic Novels*, ed. R. P. Draper (London: Macmillan, 1975), 200.
20. Ibid., 205.
21. Ibid., 206.
22. J. Hillis Miller, "Fiction and Repetition: *Tess of the d'Urbervilles*," in *Forms of Modern British Fiction*, ed. Alan Warren Friedman (Austin: University of Texas Press, 1975), 60.
23. Ibid., 64.
24. Ibid., 65.
25. Ibid., 66.
26. J. Hillis Miller, "Stevens' Rock and Criticism as Cure, II," *Georgia Review* 30 (Summer 1976): 344.
27. Ibid., 338.
28. James Gibson, ed., *The Complete Poems of Thomas Hardy* (New York: Macmillan, 1976), p. 460. All future references in the text will be to this edition.
29. William E. Buckler, "Thomas Hardy's Sense of Self: The Poet Behind the Autobiographer in *The Life of Thomas Hardy*," *Prose Studies* 3 (May 1980): 75–76.
30. Robert Kiely, "Vision and Viewpoint in *The Mayor of Casterbridge*," *Nineteenth Century Fiction* 23 (September 1968), 196.
31. Harold Rosenberg, *Saul Steinberg* (New York: Alfred A. Knopf in Association with the Whitney Museum of American Art, 1978), 19.
32. Hardy, *Personal Writings*, 25.

33. Ian Gregor, *The Great Web* (Totowa, N.J.: Rowman and Littlefield, 1974), 40.
34. David Lodge, Introduction to *The Woodlanders*, by Thomas Hardy (New York: St. Martin's, 1977), 18–19.
35. George Fayen, "*The Woodlanders:* Inwardness and Memory," *Studies in English Literature (1500–1900)* 1 (Autumn 1961), 95–96.
36. Stanley Kunitz, *The Poems of Stanley Kunitz, 1928–1978* (Boston: Little, Brown, 1979), 187.
37. Wallace Stevens, *The Palm at the End of the Mind* (New York: Random House, 1967), 133.
38. Ibid., 174.
39. Ibid., 98.
40. William E. Buckler, *The Victorian Imagination: Essays in Aesthetic Exploration* (New York: New York University Press, 1980), 355.
41. Ibid., 347.
42. Hardy, *Personal Writings*, 137.
43. Douglas Brown, *Thomas Hardy* (London: Longmans, Green, 1961), 30–32.
44. John Holloway, *The Victorian Sage* (London: Macmillan, 1953), 283.
45. Lodge, Introduction to *The Woodlanders*, 29.
46. Dorothy Van Ghent, *The English Novel: Form and Function* (New York: Harper, 1953), 208.
47. Lodge, Introduction to *The Woodlanders*, 25–28.
48. Lodge, Introduction to *The Woodlanders*, 28.
49. Charles E. May, "*Far from the Madding Crowd* and *The Woodlanders:* Hardy's Grotesque Pastorals," *English Literature in Transition* 17 (1974): 147–55.
50. Lodge, Introduction to *The Woodlanders*, 29.
51. John Holloway, "Hardy's Major Fiction," in *Hardy, A Collection of Critical Essays*, ed. Albert J. Guerard (Englewood Cliffs, N.J.: Prentice Hall, 1963), 62.
52. Van Ghent, 206.
53. J. Hillis Miller, *Thomas Hardy: Distance and Desire* (Cambridge: Harvard University Press, 1970), 22.
54. Hardy, *Personal Writings*, 135.
55. Tanner, 183.
56. Miller, *Distance and Desire*, 27.
57. Stevens, *The Palm at the End of the Mind*, 174.

2. Image as Icon

1. W. K. Wimsatt, *The Verbal Icon* (Lexington, Ky.: University of Kentucky Press, 1967), x.
2. W. J. T. Mitchell, "Editor's Note: The Language of Images," *Critical Inquiry* 6 (Spring 1980): 360–61.

3. Erwin Panofsky, *Studies in Iconology* (New York: Harper and Row, 1962), 14–15.
4. Ibid., 17.
5. Elizabeth K. Helsinger, *Ruskin and the Art of the Beholder* (Cambridge: Harvard University Press, 1982), 14–15.
6. Norman Page, "Hardy's Pictorial Art in *The Mayor of Casterbridge*," *Etudes Anglaises* 12 (1972): 487.
7. Ibid., 489–92.
8. David Lodge, "Thomas Hardy as a Cinematic Novelist," in *Thomas Hardy after Fifty Years,* ed. Lance St. John Butler (London: Macmillan, 1977), 82.
9. Ibid., 87.
10. It is interesting to note D. H. Lawrence's response to the surfaces in Hardy. He is seeing with Hardy's eyes when he criticizes Clym, who lived in abstractions. The emphasis on seeing as knowing in Hardy denies the validity of excessive abstraction. However, he is reading Hardy incorrectly in stressing the internal and powerful fecundity that works from below the surface of the heath. Lawrence sees a primal morality operating in the great Hardy backgrounds, a "vast, uncomprehended and incomprehensible morality of nature or of life itself, surpassing human consciousness." This speaks far more of Lawrence than of Hardy. Taking the incomprehensible universe as a given, Hardy gives attention to the morality human beings can either comprehend or create, just as he attends to a consciousnesss that is capable of being known and lived. D. H. Lawrence, *Phoenix* (New York: Viking, 1936), 416–19.
11. Rudolf Arnheim, *Visual Thinking* (Berkeley: University of California Press, 1969), 13.
12. Rudolf Arnheim, *Art and Visual Perception* (Berkeley: University of California Press, 1974), 5.
13. E. H. Gombrich, *Art and Illusion* (New York: Pantheon, 1960), 28.
14. Alan Spiegel, *Fiction and the Camera Eye* (Charlottesville: University Press of Virginia, 1976), 24–27.
15. Virginia Woolf, *Collected Essays* (London: Hogarth Press, 1963), 1:256–57. That Hardy's novels pull in contradictory directions has been noted by others. Eugene Goodheart, in "Thomas Hardy and the Lyrical Novel," *Nineteenth Century Fiction* 12 (December 1957), states, "Hardy's story-telling is midway between lyric poetry, the affirmation of the individual personality over and against those forces, social and natural, that would threaten its integrity, and the novel as more or less fixed by tradition, the subsuming of individual men and women as [elements of social institutions]" (220). John Bayley, in *An Essay on Hardy* (Cambridge: Cambridge University Press, 1978), perceives a "radical disunity" (40) in Hardy's writing "between attention and inattention, [a] shifting between the language itself and what it describes, . . . [between] what could be called Hardy's conscious and unconscious; and our feeling is for the alternation of the two" (31). The conscious Hardy constructs plots and literariness; the unconscious Hardy presents individual inner consciousness. And Gillian Beer, in *Darwin's Plots: Evolutionary Narrative in Darwin, George Eliot, and Nineteenth-Century Fiction* (London: Routledge and Kegan Paul, 1983), comments upon

Hardy's "strongly surviving belief in the 'recuperative powers' which pervade both language and the physical world" (258). Readers respond to "the contradiction of plot and writing . . . We are filled with intolerable apprehensions of what future events may bring, while yet the text in process awakens us to sensations full of perceptual pleasure" (238).

16. Thomas Hardy, *Thomas Hardy's Personal Writings,* ed. Harold Orel (Lawrence: University of Kansas Press, 1966), 117.

17. Robert Scholes, "Language, Narrative, and Anti-Narrative," *Critical Inquiry* 7 (Autumn 1980): 210.

18. Albert J. Guerard, *Thomas Hardy* (Cambridge: Harvard University Press, 1964), 11-12.

19. Woolf, *Collected Essays,* 1:258-59.

20. Hardy, *Personal Writings,* 117.

21. Ibid., 137.

22. Penelope Vigor, *The Novels of Thomas Hardy: Illusion and Reality* (London: Athlone Press, 1974), 14.

23. Ezra Pound, *Selected Poems* (New York: New Directions, 1957), 35.

24. George Levine, *The Realistic Imagination* (Chicago: The University of Chicago Press, 1981), 21.

25. A violent, chaotic, and objectified entry to adulthood is not unusual in Victorian fiction. Dickens's Pip finds his identity as "a small bundle of shivers" in a cemetery. A stranger violently turns him upside-down, making the church "go head over heels before me . . . I saw the steeple under my feet." Soon afterwards, he is again tilted into "a most tremendous dip and roll, so that the church jumped over its own weather-cock." Charles Dickens, *Great Expectations* (New York: Bobbs-Merrill, 1964), 3-4. Or note Jane Eyre's stay in the redroom: Rage turns to terror as she sees a "swift darting beam . . . from another world" and feels "my heart beat thick, my head grew hot, and a sound filled my ears, which I deemed the rushing of wings: something seemed near me; I was oppressed, suffocated." Only a fit and unconsciousness give her escape from the red-room violence. Charlotte Brontë, *Jane Eyre* (New York: Norton, 1971), 14.

26. Judith Ryan, "The Vanishing Subject: Empirical Psychology and the Modern Novel," *PMLA* 95 (October 1980): 858.

27. Virginia Woolf, *Mrs. Dalloway* (Middlesex, England: Penguin, 1969), 5.

28. Virginia Woolf, *To the Lighthouse* (New York: Harcourt, Brace, 1927), 160.

29. Ibid., 100.

30. James Naremore, *The World without a Self* (New Haven: Yale University Press, 1983), 225.

31. Virginia Woolf, *The Common Reader* (New York: Harcourt, Brace, 1925), 154.

32. Walter Pater, *The Renaissance* (New York: New American Library, 1959) 158.

33. William E. Buckler, *The Victorian Imagination* (New York: New York University Press, 1980), 262.

34. Woolf, *To the Lighthouse,* 95.

35. Ryan, 867.
36. Carol T. Christ, *The Finer Optic* (New Haven: Yale University Press, 1974), 13.
37. Ibid., 106.
38. Ryan, 867.
39. Christ, 109.
40. P. N. Furbank, *Reflections on the Word "Image"* (London: Secker and Warburg, 1970), 119.
41. Ibid., 103.
42. C. Day Lewis, *The Poetic Image* (London: Oxford University Press, 1947), 72.
43. Karsten Harries, "Metaphor and Transcendence," *Critical Inquiry* 5 (Autumn 1978): 73.
44. Paul Ricoeur, "Metaphorical Process as Cognition, Imagination, and Feeling," *Critical Inquiry* 5 (Autumn 1978): 154.
45. J. Hillis Miller, *Thomas Hardy: Distance and Desire* (Cambridge: Harvard University Press, 1970), 6.
46. Ibid., 22.
47. Ibid., 9.
48. Lawrence O. Jones, "Imitation and Expressionism in Thomas Hardy's Theory of Fiction," *Studies in the Novel* 7 (1975): 513.
49. Robert Kiely, "Vision and Viewpoint in *The Mayor of Casterbridge*," *Nineteenth Century Fiction* 23 (September 1968): 197–98.
50. Ibid., 198.
51. Ibid., 199–200.
52. Guerard, *Thomas Hardy* 43.
53. Tony Tanner, "Color and Movement in *Tess of the d'Urbervilles*," in *Hardy, The Tragic Novels*, ed. R. P. Draper (London: Macmillan, 1975), 200.
54. George Fayen, "*The Woodlanders:* Inwardness and Memory," *Studies in English Literature (1500–1900)* 1 (Autumn 1961): 96.
55. Jean R. Brooks, *Thomas Hardy: The Poetic Structure* (Ithaca: Cornell University Press, 1971), 228.
56. Wallace Stevens, *The Palm at the End of the Mind* (New York: Random House, 1967), 136.
57. Miller, *Distance and Desire*, 187.
58. Miller, *Distance and Desire*, 154.
59. Christ, 12.
60. Stevens, *The Palm at the End of the Mind*, 190.
61. Emma Clifford, "The Impressionistic View of History in *The Dynasts*," *Modern Language Quarterly* 22 (1961): 30.
62. Panofsky, 14–15.

3. Framed Images

1. David Lodge, Introduction to *The Woodlanders,* by Thomas Hardy (New York: St. Martin's, 1977), 38.
2. Robert Kiely, "Vision and Viewpoint in *The Mayor of Casterbridge,*" *Nineteenth Century Fiction* 23 (September 1968): 199.
3. Wallace Stevens, *The Palm at the End of the Mind* (New York: Random House, 1967), 46.
4. Thomas Hardy, *Thomas Hardy's Personal Writings,* ed. Harold Orel (Lawrence: University of Kansas Press, 1966), 9.
5. David Lodge, "Thomas Hardy as a Cinematic Novelist," in *Thomas Hardy After Fifty Years,* ed. Lance St. John Butler (London: Macmillan, 1971), 87.
6. Alistair Smart, "Pictorial Images in the Novels of Thomas Hardy," *Review of English Studies* 12 (1961): 271.
7. Ibid., 263.
8. Ibid., 271.
9. Ibid.
10. Joan Grundy, *Hardy and the Sister Arts* (London: Macmillan, 1979), 19.
11. Ibid., 18.
12. Lloyd Fernendo, "Thomas Hardy's Rhetoric of Painting," *Review of English Literature* 6 (October 1965): 63–71.
13. Ibid., 71.
14. Grundy, 23.
15. H. W. Janson, *History of Art* (New York: Harry N. Abrams, 1974), 494.
16. E. H. Gombrich, *Art and Illusion* (New York: Pantheon, 1960), 298.
17. Janson, 494.
18. Joan Grundy calls Hardy a "chameleon painter." "The whole realm of painting is at his command: he can adopt the style of any individual artist or school that he wishes" (26). His "command" is no coincidence; the *Life* describes his museum habits during the early years as a London architect. In 1866, "his interest in painting led him to devote for many months . . . twenty minutes after lunch to an inspection of the masters hung there, confining his attention to a single master on each visit, and forbidding his eyes to stray to any other. He went there from sheer liking, and not with any practical object; but he used to recommend the plan to young people, telling them that they would insensibly acquire a greater insight into schools and styles by this means than from any guide-books to the painters' works and manners" (*Life,* 51). Tom Paulin, in *Thomas Hardy, The Poetry of Perception* (Totowa, N.J.: Rowman and Littlefield, 1975), describes the above self-discipline as "behavioristic." "The aim is to school the mind to receive the imprint of a particular style through the disciplined observation of successive examples of that style, and though he disclaims any 'practical object,' he clearly developed an intensely practical method of study and learning. . . . Like thousands upon thousands of other people he stood in

front of those paintings and looked at them, but he trained himself to remember them with an unusual clarity and then—which is something else—he made them part of his imagination" (115).

19. Rudolf Arnheim, *Visual Thinking* (Berkeley: University of California Press, 1969), 20.

20. Keith Cohen, *Film and Fiction* (New Haven: Yale University Press, 1979), 62.

21. Arnheim, *Visual Thinking*, 20.

22. Arnheim, *Visual Thinking*, 54.

23. Alan Spiegel, in *Fiction and the Camera Eye* (Charlottesville: University Press of Virginia, 1976), notes the anatomical form of motion description that frequently appears in the cinematized narrative, and he discusses some modern novelists who make use of this camera eye to see according to the image on the retina. This kind of seeing "represents the findings of a 'trained' eye, an analytic and self-conscious eye, conscious of what it sees and the way it sees; the kind of eye that teaches us to see those retinal images that we rarely take note of apart from the assumptions, protections, concealments, and transformations of the ordinary human mind" (112). It is what Francois Truffaut sees when he says, "If you tell me a story . . . I see the different scales while you're talking: a two-shot here, a close-up there. I still see stories in terms of shots. . . . Filmmaking is a very special discipline." Francois Truffaut, "Francois Truffaut's 'The Last Metro,'" *New York Times,* 8 February 1981, sec. 2, p. 21, col. 3.

24. Hardy, *Personal Writings,* 137.

25. There is a clear analogy between the context of Clym's and Eustacia's meeting and a particular way in which we see and know external reality. "In many instances, vision, instead of contenting itself with the visible section completes the object. A box, partly covered by a flowerpot, is seen as a complete cube partly hidden. This means that perceptual organization does not limit itself to the material directly given but enlists invisible extensions as genuine parts of the visible. Similarly, objects are often perceived as three-dimensionally complete although only a frontal part of their surface is directly given. What happens here is not that the beholder completes by non-visual knowledge the fragment he actually sees. No, a cylindrical pot is *seen* as a complete, all-around thing; an incomplete cylinder looks quite different. . . . The cognitive feat involved in such a process consists in rejecting the wholeness of a shape that presents itself and in reinterpreting it instead as a part of a larger and structural whole." (Arnheim, 33–34). The way we see is the way we know; Clym and Eustacia reject the whole shape before them and reinterpret it instead as a part of a larger and better whole. Since this latter "whole" does not actually exist, it is an illusion.

26. Eustacia's role and the narrator's commentary upon her have been given ample critical attention. John Paterson, in *The Making of "The Return of the Native"* (Berkeley: University of California Press, 1963), presents Hardy's own changing conception of Eustacia from a less to a more attractive figure. Robert Evans's "The Other Eustacia," *Novel* 1 (1968): 251–59, concludes that Eustacia's

heroic role is undercut by the reader's increasing awareness of her as immature and foolishly romantic. Richard Benvenuto, in "Another Look at the Other Eustacia," *Novel* 4 (1970): 77–79, sees conflicts around Eustacia's character caused by Hardy's own ambiguous views of her individualistic values. David Eggenschwiler's "Eustacia Vye, Queen of Night and Courtly Pretender," *Nineteenth Century Ficiton* 25 (1971): 444–54, understands the ambiguity in the text and the character as a conscious and intentional design to produce a double perspective on the romantic heroine. He concludes, "One could legitimately claim that this novel is not generically pure, either as a tragedy or as a satire. But these familiar objections are too concerned with what the book is not, and not enough with what it is" (454), which is the point. However, it is less important for this study's purposes to evaluate varied interpretations of Eustacia's role than to observe that the novel presents ambiguity and invites complicated responses.

27. Derwent May, Introduction to *Return of the Native,* by Thomas Hardy (New York: St. Martin's, 1974), 16.
28. Hardy, *Personal Writings,* 32.
29. Ibid., 49.
30. Ian Gregor, *The Great Web* (Totowa, N.J.: Rowman and Littlefield, 1974), 64.
31. Ibid., 51.
32. Grundy, 32.
33. J. Hillis Miller, *Thomas Hardy: Distance and Desire* (Cambridge: Harvard University Press, 1979), 123–24.
34. Such an intense vision of a woman's grace, energy, and sexuality is not unusual in Hardy. *A Pair of Blue Eyes* presents Elfride Swancourt on her horse and Stephen, who loves her, at her feet as she shows herself off to him: " 'See how I can gallop.' . . . and Stephen beheld her light figure contracting to the dimensions of a bird as she sank into the distance—her hair flowing" (PBE, 89). The end of the novel places this energy in a coffin. In *A Laodicean* Paula Power, as the modern woman, informed on new ideas of physical culture, works out in her modern gymnasium, "bending, wheeling and undulating in the air like a goldfish in its globe" (*Laodicean* 196–97). Unfortunately, she is a goldfish in a globe; a secret watcher is spying on her and another secret watcher is spying on the first one. At this early point in the novel, the reader has already witnessed Paula Power's control of the baptism scene and now we witness her control of her body. Yet there are always those secret watchers, out of her control.
35. Arnheim, *Visual Thinking,* 27.
36. Gregor, *Great Web,* 120.

4. Disrupted Images

1. Erwin Panofsky, *Studies in Iconology* (New York: Harper and Row, 1962), 14, 15.
2. The Talk of the Town, *New Yorker,* 25 July 1983, p. 19.

3. Ibid., p. 20.
4. P. N. Furbank, *Reflections on the Word "Image"* (London: Secher and Warburg, 1970), 119.
5. Vincent B. Leitch, "The Lateral Dance: The Deconstructive Criticism of J. Hillis Miller," *PMLA* 6 (Summer 1980): 594, 5.
6. Ibid., 597.
7. Sandra M. Gilbert and Susan Gubar, *The Madwoman in the Attic* (New Haven: Yale University Press, 1979), xi, xii.
8. George Levine, *The Realistic Imagination* (Chicago: University of Chicago Press, 1981), 331. Studies on varied understandings of the term "disruption"— in Hardy, specifically, and/or in nineteenth-century literature generally—seem to be reaching their critical moment. See, for example, Cathy Comstock, *Disruption and Delight in the Nineteenth-Century Novel* (Ann Arbor: UMI Research Press, 1988); John Goode, *Thomas Hardy: The Offensive Truth* (Basil Blackwell, 1988); John Kucich, *Repression in Victorian Fiction* (Berkeley: University of California Press, 1987).
9. Levine, 24.
10. Ibid., 4.
11. Albert Guerard, *Thomas Hardy* (Cambridge: Harvard University Press, 1964), 21.
12. Thomas Hardy, *Thomas Hardy's Personal Writings*, ed. Harold Orel (Lawrence: University of Kansas Press, 1966), 52.
13. Marshall Brown, " 'Errours Endlesse Traine': On Turning Points and the Dialectical Imagination," *PMLA* 99 (January 1984): 21.
14. Levine, 12.
15. Panofsky, 14, 15.
16. Norman Page, "Hardy's Pictorial Art in *The Mayor of Casterbridge*," *Études Anglaises* 12 (1972): 487, 8.
17. David Lodge, "Thomas Hardy As a Cinematic Novelist," in *Thomas Hardy after Fifty Years*, ed. Lance St. John Butler (London: Macmillan, 1977), 80.
18. Hardy, *Personal Writings*, 33.
19. Ibid., 38, 39.
20. Ibid., 119.
21. Ibid., 38.
22. Emma Clifford, "The Impressionistic View of History in *The Dynasts*," *Modern Language Quarterly* 22 (1961): 30.
23. Furbank, 84.
24. Hardy, *Personal Writings*, 51.
25. Richard Swigg, "Hardy's 'even monochrome and curving line,' " *Agenda* 10 (1972): 86, 88.
26. Donald Davie, *Thomas Hardy and British Poetry* (New York: Oxford University Press, 1972), 51.
27. Ibid.
28. Rudolf Arnheim, *Visual Thinking* (Berkeley: University of California Press, 1969), 20.

29. Lawrence Weschler, "Art World," *New Yorker*, 9 July 1984, 63.
30. Ibid., 62.
31. Ibid., 66.
32. Mark Kinkead-Weekes, "Lawrence on Hardy," in *Thomas Hardy after Fifty Years*, ed. Lance St. John Butler (London: Macmillan, 1977), 102.
33. Samuel Hynes, *The Pattern of Hardy's Poetry* (Chapel Hill: University of North Carolina Press, 1961), 5.
34. Ibid., 39.
35. Guerard, *Thomas Hardy*, 174.
36. Robert Gittings, *Thomas Hardy's Later Years* (Boston: Little, Brown, 1978), 80.
37. Robert Scholes and Robert Kellogg, *The Nature of Narrative* (New York: Oxford University Press, 1966), 277.
38. Ibid., 273.
39. Robert Scholes, "Language, Narrative, and Anti–Narrative," *Critical Inquiry* 7 (Autumn 1980): 211.
40. John Paterson, "*The Mayor of Casterbridge* as Tragedy," *Victorian Studies* 3 (December 1959), 151–72.
41. Judith Bair sees Henchard's displacement, his removal from the center stage, repeated throughout the novel and concludes: "Rather than depicting the plight of the tragic hero, such a design seems to present the course of his extinction, closing the curtain on his final act. The novel suggests there is something in the very nature of inflexible will, doggedness, and energy that is bound to crumble when the criteria of success are dispassionate flexibility and rational, level-headed calculation. His inability to adapt to such standards renders the traditional hero inarticulately and awkwardly obsolete, just as failing to meet those standards will come to distinguish the modern anti-hero." "*The Mayor of Casterbridge:* 'Some Grand Feat of Stagery,' " *South Atlantic Bulletin* 42 (1977): 21.
42. Seymour Migdal, "History and Archetype in *The Mayor of Casterbridge*," *Studies in the Novel* 3 (1971): 283.
43. Hynes, 42.
44. Levine, 21.
45. Critics have not been silent about their incredulous—and even amused—responses to whitened Diggory. Albert Guerard noted, "The original ending of *The Return of the Native* would have been more satisfactory even for Diggory, who was certainly the kind of man to prefer Thomasin's lost glove to Thomasin herself" (119). Derwent May, in his Introduction to *The Return of the Native*, by Thomas Hardy (New York: St. Martin's, 1974), does not accept him as white at all and predicts that he will be a terribly difficult husband: "Washing off the reddle isn't going to change Venn, and all we see of him can only lead us to suppose him a man tormented by psychological problems. . . . For a champion of virtue he spends an inordinate amount of time prying on the couple whom he thinks are behaving wickedly among the gorse and heather—he is a most accomplished *voyeur*, and it is about the only accomplishment he has. So one may infer him to be a man obsessed by sexual fears and anxious sexual curiosity

—and it seems proper to feel some anxiety for Thomasin when he is finally in her arms" (23).

46. For a discussion of Hardy's experiments with endings, from the "closed experience" to the "open experience"—and his movement toward the open-ended modern novel—see Alan Friedman, *The Turn of the Novel* (New York: Oxford University Press, 1970). Friedman examines the containment strategies of weddings, funerals, and a "return" to the beginning. He sees Hardy move from *Desperate Remedies* (1871), with a conventional ending of wedding and return, through *Far from the Madding Crowd* (1874), with a somewhat mediated convention of wedding and return, to *Tess* (1891) and *Jude* (1895), with their fierce attacks on conventionality. He suggests that the efforts to contain *Tess* with outreachings to Christianity and *Jude* with double marriages, double funerals, and double returns are fiercely ironic commentaries on traditional resolutions for character and for form. On Sue Briedhead's efforts to order the lives of Jude and herself, Friedman notes, "It is as if Hardy had arranged matters so that his own skepticism may undercut and shatter Sue Bridehead's fanatical, unreasonable dedication to the principles of Fielding, Austen, Brontë, Dickens, and Eliot" (71).

47. Though Clym offers a few reservations about Venn as a husband for Thomasin—his mother's objection and Venn's inferior social class—his fundamental boredom with the fact of Diggory is consistent with the movement of his own life, the stand he has taken. Venn, by joining the community and making economic and social progress, has chosen the life that Clym had rejected. Indeed, while Diggory has removed the heath—the reddle—from his skin, Clym has returned to the heath where for a time he has been content to be "a brown spot and nothing more" (RN, 273). While Diggory has conformed to the social expectations of those on the heath, Clym and, for that matter, Eustacia revolt against those narrow views. Clym's mother cannot understand his movement, which, to her, is backward; she complains, "You are getting weary of doing well." He responds, "Mother, what is doing well?" (RN, 202). Raymond Williams, in *The Country and the City* (New York: Oxford University Press, 1973), in a discussion of the late nineteenth-century tensions between education and social advancement, between country and city, observes about Clym's question, "The question is familiar but still after all these years no question is more relevant or more radical" (202). Clym's life cannot stand as a resolution to the novel, but he does question social assumptions, the community's formal expectations, and as such is a most appropriate figure to question the value of a domesticated Diggory Venn.

48. Levine, 21.
49. Guerard, *Thomas Hardy*, 47.
50. Ibid., 52.
51. Hynes, 44.
52. Ibid., 45, 46.
53. Lewis A. Lawson, "The Grotesque in Recent Southern Fiction," in *Patterns of Commitment in Southern Literature*, ed. Marston La France (Toronto: University of Toronto Press, 1967), 166, 7.

54. Ibid., 171.
55. Ibid., 170.
56. Jean Brooks, *Thomas Hardy: The Poetic Structure* (Ithaca: Cornell University Press, 1971), 113.
57. Ruth M. Vande Kieft, "Judgment in the Fiction of Flannery O'Connor," *Sewanee Review* 76 (1968): 356.
58. Pierre Schneider, "All That Jazz," *The New York Review of Books* 32 (11 April 1985), 28. Painters show a parallel need for change in the texture and scale of their works in relation to the culture. Fernand Léger found it necessary to paint for an industrialized society: "In a museum, a private house, a picture could whisper; on the walls of a factory, in a street, it must shout. 'I hate discreet painting,' Léger said. To reach people in the modern world, one had to be broad, unequivocal, simple. . . . He turned increasingly from complex compositions to the representation of single objects or even of fragments of objects." Flannery O'Connor saw the need and the danger: "The direction of many of us will be toward concentration and the distortion that is necessary to get our visions across; it will be toward poetry, rather than toward the traditional novel. The problem of such a novelist will be to know how far he can distort without also destroying." Lewis A. Lawson and J. Friedman, *The Added Dimension* (New York: Fordham University Press, 1966), 279.
59. Hynes, 62.
60. Hardy, *Personal Writings*, 137.
61. For a variety of responses to *The Dynasts*'s extraordinary sense of the visual, see the following: Tom Paulin, *The Poetry of Perception* (Totowa, N.J.: Rowman and Littlefield, 1975); Susan Dean, *Hardy's Poetic Vision in "The Dynasts"* (Princeton: Princeton University Press, 1977); John Wain, Introduction to *The Dynasts,* by Thomas Hardy (New York: St. Martin's, 1979), ix–xiv; Alexander Fischler, "The Theatrical Techniques in Thomas Hardy's Short Stories," *Studies in Short Fiction* 3 (Summer 1966), 444, 5.
62. Hardy, *Personal Writings*, 39.
63. Dean, 43, 44.
64. Ibid., 44.
65. Ibid., 61.
66. Ibid. 63.
67. Clifford, "The Impressionistic View," 30.
68. Hardy, *Personal Writings*, 41.
69. Fischler, 444, 5.
70. Levine, 22.
71. Hardy, *Personal Writings*, 117.
72. Ibid., 135.

5. Relationships within the Image

1. Rudolf Arnheim, *Visual Thinking* (Berkeley: University of California Press, 1969), 54.

2. Joan Grundy, *Hardy and the Sister Arts* (London: Macmillan, 1979), 48.

3. H. W. Janson, *History of Art* (New York: Harry N. Abrams, 1974), in discussing Georges Seurat's style, states about his figures, "[T]hey appear mostly in either strict profile or frontal views, as if Seurat had adopted the rules of ancient Egyptian art. . . . Moreover, they are fitted very precisely into a system of vertical and horizontal coordinates that holds them in place and defines the canvas as a self-contained rectilinear field" (503). In just such an arrangement of lines we are allowed to see the self-enclosed psychological state of Boldwood.

4. Ronald Blythe, Introduction to *A Pair of Blue Eyes,* by Thomas Hardy (New York: St. Martin's, 1975), 27.

5. John Ruskin, *Works of John Ruskin* (New York: Merrill and Baker, n.d.), 4:318.

6. Janson, 515. Gauguin's description of his works also describes Hardy's most abstract experiments with visual structures: "By arrangements of lines and colors, using as pretext some subject borrowed from human life or nature, I obtain symphonies, harmonies that represent nothing absolutely *real* in the vulgar sense of the word; they express no idea directly but they should make one think, as music does, without the aid of ideas or images, simply by the mysterious relationships existing between our brains and such arrangements of colors and lines." John Rewald, *The History of Impressionism* (New York: The Museum of Modern Art, 1961), 574.

7. Calvin Tompkins, "The Art World," *New Yorker* 16 April 1984, 130.

8. Keith Cohen, *Film and Fiction* (New Haven: Yale University Press, 1979), 110–15, discusses the aspect of cinema that reduces people to the state of objects, and cinematic experiments in novels that externalize consciousness. "Thus characters are portrayed more and more objectively, the victims of their own thoughts, actions, and words rendered immediately to the reader. Furthermore, according to the leveling process of self and object, typified most concretely by the cinema, there was a growing temptation to treat characters with the same dispassionate air that was beginning to circulate with greater frequency among objects" (115).

9. Tony Tanner, "Color and Movement in *Tess of the d'Urbervilles,*" in *Hardy, The Tragic Novels,* ed. R. P. Draper (London: Macmillan Press, 1975), 183, 85.

10. William H. Pritchard, "Hardy's Anonymous Sincerity," *Agenda* 10 (1972): 110–16.

11. John Peck, "Hardy and the Figure in the Scene," *Agenda* 10 (1972): 124–25.

12. Ibid., 125.

13. Emma Clifford, "The Child: the Circus: and *Jude the Obscure,*" *Cambridge Journal* 7 (June 1954): 536.

14. Note Hardy's expressive style in his use of light and darkness in this scene. While the line between in this case moves forward and back, it recalls the steadily moving lines in "A Commonplace Day" and "At a Lunar Eclipse." In all cases, the moving line between light and dark, between brightness and shadow, pictures states of tension and anxiety. See further examples of light-darkness structures, below, in the discussion on Egdon Heath.

15. Terry Eagleton, "Thomas Hardy: Nature as Language," *Critical Quarterly* 13 (Summer 1971), discusses fragmentation as a general mode of imagery in Hardy, "one which depicts a peculiar tension, and occasionally an outright contradiction, between 'subjective' and 'objective' forms of existence or perception; but its implications spread outwards, into reflections on the relationship between mind and body, Nature and meaning, the self and others" (155). His application of this contradiction to *Tess of the d'Urbervilles* finds the novel's central crisis in a "wrenching apart of personal identity and the physical body" (159).

16. Arnheim, *Visual Thinking*, 54, 62–63.

17. T. S. Eliot, *The Complete Poems and Plays* (New York: Harcourt, Brace, 1952), 6.

18. Virginia Woolf, *A Writer's Diary* (London: Hogarth, 1969), 85.

19. Donald Davie, *Thomas Hardy and British Poetry* (New York: Oxford University Press, 1972), 52.

20. David DeLaura, "The Ache of Modernism," *ELH* 34 (September 1967): 381.

21. Irwin Panofsky, *Studies in Iconology* (New York: Harper and Row, 1962), 15.

22. It is worth noting Hardy's consistency about the imaginative nature of his writings. In 1874, in the preface to *Far from the Madding Crowd,* he called Wessex his "partly real, partly dream country." Harold Orel, *Thomas Hardy's Personal Writings* (Lawrence: University of Kansas Press, 1966), 9. In 1910, on the occasion of receiving the freedom of Dorchester, Hardy commented, "My Casterbridge . . . is not Dorchester—not even the Dorchester as it existed sixty years ago, but a dream-place that never was outside an irresponsible book" (*Life,* 351).

6. Metamorphosis

1. Tony Tanner, "Color and Movement in *Tess of the d'Urbervilles,*" in *Hardy: The Tragic Novels,* ed. R. P. Draper (London: Macmillan, 1975), 197.

2. Donald Davie, *Thomas Hardy and British Poetry* (New York: Oxford University Press, 1972), 52.

3. Joan Grundy, *Hardy and the Sister Arts* (London: Macmillan, 1979), 68.

4. Emma Clifford, in "The Child: the Circus: and *Jude the Obscure,*" *Cambridge Journal* 7 (June 1954): 546.

5. J. Hillis Miller, *Thomas Hardy: Distance and Desire* (Cambridge: Harvard University Press, 1970), 201.

6. Dorothy Van Ghent, *The English Novel* (New York: Harper, 1953), 202.

7. John Holloway, "Hardy's Major Fiction," in *Hardy, A Collection of Critical Essays,* ed. Albert J. Guerard (Englewood Cliffs, N.J.: Prentice Hall, 1963), 55.

8. Tanner, 202.

9. Geoffrey Chaucer, *The Works of Geoffrey Chaucer,* ed. F. N. Robinson, 2nd ed. (Boston: Houghton Mifflin, 1957), 17.

10. Elizabeth Hardwick, *Bartleby in Manhattan and Other Essays* (New York: Random House, 1983), 243.

11. Stevens, *The Palm at the End of the Mind*, 230.

12. J. I. M. Stewart, *Eight Modern Writers* (New York: Oxford University Press, 1963), 61.

13. Janet Burstein, in "The Journey Beyond Myth in *Jude the Obscure*," *Texas Studies in Literature and Language* 15 (1972), 499–515, notes the problems of Jude as isolation, alienation, and the absence of any activities to combat these existential problems. To return to past forms—Sue's final stance—is impossible with modern consciousness. What Burstein suggests as one way to endure the change is greater unification with other human beings, an attempt never made by Sue and Jude. One problem in this resolution, of course, is that most of the structures of community, such as marriage, are presented in the novel as threats equal to the dangers of isolation.

14. Stevens, *The Palm at the End of the Mind*, 174.

15. Perry Meisel, *Thomas Hardy: The Return of the Repressed* (New Haven: Yale University Press, 1972), 127.

16. Thomas Hardy, *Thomas Hardy's Personal Writings*, ed. Harold Orel (Lawrence: University of Kansas Press, 1966), 52.

17. Sue's collapse must not be put down too easily as a split in her self. Though ambivalence seems to be quite deeply rooted within her, on one topic she has been unswervingly consistent: she does not want a conventional married life, she does not want a sexual life, she does not want children. In this firmness, she shows self-knowledge. Giving in to Jude's need and her own jealousy is, finally, her own choice, but both William E. Buckler, in *The Victorian Imagination: Essays in Aesthetic Imagination* (New York: New York University Press, 1980) and D. H. Lawrence, in *Phoenix: The Posthumous Papers of D. H. Lawrence* (New York: Viking, 1963) see the validity of her original position. Buckler observes, "[Jude] requires of [Sue] what she simply cannot give, and the compromises she makes end catastrophically. . . . The integrity of her desire to be the soul-mate of sensitive men is not violated by their inability to adjust their desires to hers. Her life is ravaged, not by her self-myth, but by her weakness in succumbing to the very chaos against which that self-myth was her one dependable intuition" (368). Lawrence, too, sees Sue's authentic uniqueness: "Sue had a being, special and beautiful. Why must not Jude recognize it in all its speciality? Why must man be so utterly irreverent, that he approaches each being as if it were no-being? Why must it be assumed that Sue is an 'ordinary' woman—as if such a thing existed? Why must she feel ashamed if she is specialized? And why must Jude, owing to the conception he is brought up in, force her to act as if she were his 'ordinary' abstraction, a woman? She was not a woman. She was Sue Bridehead, something very particular. Why was there no place for her? Cassandra had the Temple of Apollo" (510).

18. Hardwick, 243.

19. Virginia Woolf, *The Common Reader* (New York: Harcourt, Brace, 1953), 154.

20. Richard Benvenuto, "Modes of Perception: The Will to Live in *Jude the Obscure,*" *Studies in the Novel* 2 (Spring 1970): 39–40.

21. Buckler, *The Victorian Imagination,* 368.

22. Gillian Beer, *Darwin's Plots* (London: Rutledge and Kegan Paul, 1983), 254.

23. Emma Clifford, in "The Child: the Circus: and *Jude the Obscure,*" *Cambridge Journal* 7 (June 1954), calls attention to the terrifying world of the novel: "It is a dark world and full of nightmares, where any child might be afraid. Jude and Sue . . . live in an anonymous world of Kafka-like nightmares as they wander from one community to another. . . . And there are policemen everywhere. . . . [W]hen he is very near to death and sees the ghosts of great scholars and famous men as he walks through Christminster with Arabella, all she can see is 'a damn policeman' " (545). Yet, in Sue's and Jude's present state of protective bliss, the policeman is present only as a joke.

24. D. H. Lawrence, 506.

25. John Bayley, *An Essay on Thomas Hardy* (Cambridge: Cambridge University Press, 1978), 19.

26. Gregor, *The Great Web,* 208–9.

27. Hardy, *Personal Writings,* 32–33.

28. Irwin Panofsky, *Studies in Iconology* (New York: Harper and Row, 1962), 15.

29. Hardy, *Personal Writings,* 117.

30. Mark Kinkead-Weekes, "Lawrence on Hardy," in *Thomas Hardy After Fifty Years,* ed. Lance St. John Butler (London: Macmillan, 1977), 101. In his discussion of D. H. Lawrence's study of Hardy, Kinkead-Weekes notes that though Hardy's "characters already existed in terms of being and consciousness rather than the conduct of sensibility of 'the old stable ego,' [they are] conditioned and action limited by place and time, by being-in-society and being-in-history."

31. Terry Eagleton, "Thomas Hardy: Nature as Language," *Critical Quarterly,* 13 (Summer 1971): 160.

32. Meisel, *Thomas Hardy,* 127.

33. Bayley, 204.

34. Eagleton, 161.

35. David DeLaura, " 'The Ache of Modernism' in Hardy's Later Novels," *Journal of English Literary History* 34 (September 1967): 381, 382, 395.

36. Bayley, 203.

37. Stevens, *The Palm at the End of the Mind,* 135–36.

7. A Final Frame

1. Tom Paulin, *Thomas Hardy, The Poetry of Perception* (Totowa, N.J.: Rowman and Littlefield, 1975), 210.

2. Emma Clifford, "The Impressionistic View of History in *The Dynasts,*" *Modern Language Quarterly* 22 (1961): 30.

Bibliography

Alexander, B. J. "Criticism of Thomas Hardy's Novels: A Selected Checklist." *Studies in the Novel* 4 (Winter 1972): 630–54.
Allen, Walter. *The English Novel*. New York: E. P. Dutton, 1958.
Anderson, Carol Reed. "Time, Space, and Perspective in Thomas Hardy." *Nineteenth Century Fiction* 9 (December 1954): 192–209.
Arnheim, Rudolf. *Art and Visual Perception*. Berkeley: University of California Press, 1974.
────── *Visual Thinking*. Berkeley: University of California Press, 1974.
Ashton, Dore. "On Harold Rosenberg." *Critical Inquiry* 6 (Summer 1980): 615–24.
Barthes, Roland. *Elements of Semiology*. New York: Hill and Wang, 1968.
────── *Image, Music, Text*. New York: Hill and Wang, 1977.
Barzun, Jacques. "Truth and Poetry in Thomas Hardy." *Southern Review* 6 (1940): 179–92.
Bayley, John. *An Essay on Thomas Hardy*. Cambridge: Cambridge University Press, 1978.
Beatty, C. J. P. Introduction to *Desperate Remedies*, by Thomas Hardy. New York: St. Martin's, 1977.
────── "The Part Played by Architecture in the Life and Work of Thomas Hardy with Particular Reference to the Novels." Diss., London University, 1963.
Beebe, Maurice, Bonnie Culotta, and Erin Marcus. "Criticism of Thomas Hardy: A Selected Checklist." *Modern Fiction Studies* 6 (Autumn 1960): 258–79.
Beer, Gillian. *Darwin's Plots: Evolutionary Narrative in Darwin, George Eliot, and Nineteenth Century Fiction*. London: Routledge and Kegan Paul, 1983.
Benvenuto, Richard. "Modes of Perception: The Will to Live in *Jude the Obscure*." *Studies in the Novel* 2 (Spring 1970): 31–41.
Berger, John. *Towards Reality: Essays on Seeing*. New York: Knopf, 1962.

Berger, John. *Ways of Seeing.* New York: Viking, 1973.
Blanchard, Leonard Albert. "The Limits of Fiction: Thomas Hardy's Dilemma As a Novelist in the Eighteen-Nineties." Diss., Emory University, 1975.
Bloom, Harold. *Wallace Stevens: The Poems of Our Climate.* Ithaca: Cornell University Press, 1976.
Blythe, Ronald. Introduction to *A Pair of Blue Eyes,* by Thoams Hardy. New York: St. Martin's, 1975.
Boumelha, Penny. *Thomas Hardy and Women: Sexual Ideology and Narrative Form.* Totowa, N.J.: Barnes and Noble, 1982.
Brick, Alan. "Paradise and Consciousness in Hardy's *Tess.*" *Nineteenth Century Fiction* 17 (September 1962): 115–34.
Brontë, Charlotte. *Jane Eyre.* New York: Norton, 1971.
Brooks, Jean R. *Thomas Hardy: The Poetic Structure.* Ithaca: Cornell University Press, 1971.
Brown, Douglas. *Thomas Hardy.* London: Longmans, Green, 1961.
Brown, Marshall. " 'Errours Endlesse Traine': On Turning Points and the Dialectical Imagination." *PMLA* 99 (January 1984): 9–25.
Buckler, William E. " 'The Thing Signified' in *The Dynasts:* A Speculation." *The Victorian Newsletter* 57 (Spring 1980): 9–14.
—————. "Thomas Hardy's Sense of Self: The Poet behind the Autobiographer in *The Life of Thomas Hardy.*" *Prose Studies* 3 (May 1980): 69–86.
—————. *The Victorian Imagination: Essays in Aesthetic Imagination.* New York: New University Press, 1980.
Buckley, Jerome H., ed. *The Worlds of Victorian Fiction.* Cambridge: Harvard University Press, 1975.
Bullen, J. B. *The Expressive Eye.* Oxford: Clarendon, 1986.
Burstein, Janet. "The Journey Beyond Myth in *Jude the Obscure.*" *Texas Studies in Literature and Language* 15 (1972): 499–515.
Carpenter, Richard C. "Hardy's 'Gurgoyles.' " *Modern Fiction Studies* 6 (Autumn 1960): 223–32.
—————. "The Mirror and the Sword: Imagery in *Far from the Madding Crowd.*" *Nineteenth Century Fiction* 18 (1964): 331–45.
—————. "Thomas Hardy and the Old Masters." *Boston University Studies in English* 5 (Spring 1961): 18–28.
Caudwell, Christopher. *Illusion and Reality.* New York: International Publishers, 1937.
Caws, Mary Anne. *Reading Frames in Modern Fiction.* Princeton: Princeton University Press, 1985.
Chaucer, Geoffrey. *The Works of Geoffrey Chaucer.* Edited by F. N. Robinson. 2nd ed. Boston: Houghton Mifflin, 1957.
Christ, Carol T. *The Finer Optic: The Aesthetics of Particularity in Victorian Poetry.* New Haven: Yale University Press, 1975.
Clayborough, Arthur. *The Grotesque in English Literature.* Oxford: Oxford University Press, 1965.
Clifford, Emma. "The Child: the Circus: and *Jude the Obscure.*" *Cambridge Journal* 7 (June 1954) 531–46.

——— "The Impressionistic View of History in *The Dynasts.*" *Modern Language Quarterly* 22 (1961): 21–31.

Cohen, Keith. *Film and Fiction: The Dynamics of Exchange.* New Haven: Yale University Press, 1979.

Cohn, Dorrit. *Transparent Minds: Narrative Modes for Presenting Consciousness in Fiction.* Princeton: Princeton University Press, 1978.

Comstock, Cathy. *Disruption and Delight in the Nineteenth-Century Novel.* UMI Research Press, 1988.

Covolo, John Joseph. "The Critique of Illusion in Thomas Hardy's Novels." Diss., Kent State University, 1977.

Cox, R. G. *Thomas Hardy: The Critical Heritage.* New York: Barnes and Noble, 1970.

Culler, Jonathan. *Structuralist Poetics.* Ithaca: Cornell University Press, 1975.

Davie, Donald, ed. *Agenda* 10 (1972).

——— *Thomas Hardy and British Poetry.* New York: Oxford University Press, 1972.

Deacon, Lois, and Terry Coleman. *Providence and Mr. Hardy.* London: Hutchinson, 1966.

Dean, Susan. *Hardy's Poetic Vision in "The Dynasts": The Diorama of a Dream.* Princeton: Princeton University Press, 1977.

Deen, Leonard W. "Heroism and Pathos in Hardy's *Return of the Native.*" *Nineteenth Century Fiction* 15 (1960): 207–19.

DeLaura, David. " 'The Ache of Modernism' in Hardy's Later Novels." *Journal of English Literary History* 34 (September 1967), 380–99.

Dickens, Charles. *Bleak House.* Boston: Houghton Mifflin, 1956.

——— *Great Expectations.* New York: Bobbs-Merrill, 1964.

——— *Little Dorrit.* New York: Odyssey Press, 1969.

Eagleton, Terry. "Thomas Hardy: Nature as Language." *Critical Quarterly* 13 (Summer 1971): 155–62.

Eggenschwiler, David. "Eustacia Vye, Queen of Night and Courtly Pretender." *Nineteenth Century Fiction* 25 (March 1971): 444–54.

Elam, Helen Regueiro. *The Limits of Imagination: Wordsworth, Yeats, Stevens.* Ithaca: Cornell University Press, 1976.

Eliot, T. S. *The Complete Poems and Plays.* Harcourt, Brace, 1952.

Fayen, George. "Thomas Hardy." In *Victorian Fiction: A Guide to Research,* edited by Lionel Stevenson. New York: The Modern Language Association of America, 1980.

——— "*The Woodlanders:* Inwardness and Memory." *Studies in English Literature* 1 (1961): 81–100.

Fernando, Lloyd. "Thomas Hardy's Rhetoric of Painting." *Review of English Literature* 6 (October 1965): 62–73.

Fischler, Alexander. "Theatrical Techniques in Thomas Hardy's Short Stories." *Studies in Short Fiction* 3 (Summer 1966): 435–45.

Friedman, Alan. *The Turn of the Novel.* Oxford: Oxford University Press, 1966.

Friedman, Alan Warren. *Forms of Modern British Fiction.* Austin: University of Texas Press, 1975.

Furbank, P. N. *Reflections on the Word 'Image'*. London: Secker and Warburg, 1970.
Gittings, Robert. *Thomas Hardy's Later Years*. Boston: Little, Brown, 1978.
—— *Young Thomas Hardy*. Boston: Little, Brown, 1975.
Gombrich, E. H. *Art and Illusion*. New York: Pantheon Books, 1960.
—— *The Image and the Eye*. Ithaca: Cornell University Press, 1982.
—— *Symbolic Images: Studies in the Art of the Renaissance*. London: Phaidon Press, 1972.
Goode, John. *Thomas Hardy: The Offensive Truth*. New York: Basil Blackwell, 1988.
Goodheart, Eugene. "Thomas Hardy and the Lyrical Novel." *Nineteenth Century Fiction* 12 (December 1957): 215–25.
Gregor, Ian. *The Great Web: The Form of Hardy's Major Fiction*. Totowa, N.J.: Rowman and Littlefield, 1974.
—— Introduction to *The Mayor of Cambridge*, by Thomas Hardy. New York: St. Martin's, 1974.
Grundy, Joan. *Hardy and the Sister Arts*. London: Macmillan, 1979.
Guerard, Albert J. *Hardy, A Collection of Critical Essays*. Englewood Cliffs, N.J.: Prentice-Hall, 1963.
—— *Thomas Hardy*. Cambridge: Harvard University Press, 1964.
Hardwick, Elizabeth. *Bartleby in Manhattan and Other Essays*. New York: Random House, 1983.
Hardy, Barbara. Introduction to *A Laodicean*, by Thomas Hardy. New York: St. Martin's, 1978.
Hardy, Evelyn, and F. B. Pinion. *One Rare Fine Woman: Thomas Hardy's Letters to Florence Henniker, 1893–1922*. Austin, Texas: University of Miami Press, 1972.
Hardy, Florence Emily. *The Life of Thomas Hardy*. Hamden, Ct: Archon, 1970.
Hardy, Thomas. *The Architectural Notebooks of Thomas Hardy*. Dorchester: Dorset Natural History and Archaeological Society, 1966.
—— *The Collected Letters of Thomas Hardy, 1840–1892*. Vol. 1. Edited by Richard Little Purdy and Michael Millgate. Oxford: Oxford University Press, 1978.
—— *The Collected Letters of Thomas Hardy, 1893–1901*. Vol. 2. Edited by Richard Little Purdy and Michael Millgate. Oxford: Oxford University Press, 1980.
—— *The Complete Poems*. Edited by James Gibson. New Wessex Edition. London: Macmillan, 1976.
—— *The Dynasts*. London: Macmillan, 1977.
—— *Far from the Madding Crowd*. New Wessex Edition. London: Macmillan, 1974.
—— *Jude the Obscure*. New Wessex Edition. London: Macmillan, 1974.
—— *A Laodicean*. New Wessex Edition. London: Macmillan, 1974.
—— *The Life and Works of Thomas Hardy*. Edited by Michael Millgate. Athens: University of Georgia Press, 1985.

———— *The Literary Notebooks of Thomas Hardy*. 2 vols. Edited by Lennart Björk. Gothenburg, 1974.
———— *The Mayor of Casterbridge*. New Wessex Edition. London: Macmillan, 1974.
———— *A Pair of Blue Eyes*. New Wessex Edition. London: Macmillan, 1974.
———— *The Personal Notebooks of Thomas Hardy*. Edited by Richard H. Taylor. New York: Columbia University Press, 1979.
———— *The Return of the Native*. New Wessex Edition. London: Macmillan, 1974.
———— *Tess of the d'Urbervilles*. New Wessex Edition. London: Macmillan, 1974.
———— *Thomas Hardy's Personal Writings*. Edited by Harold Orel. Lawrence: University of Kansas Press, 1966.
———— *Under the Greenwood Tree*. New Wessex Edition. London: Macmillan, 1974.
———— *The Woodlanders*. New Wessex Edition. London: Macmillan, 1974.
Harries, Karsten, "Metaphor and Transcendence." *Critical Inquiry* 5 (Autumn 1878): 73–90.
Heilman, Robert B. "Hardy's *Mayor* and the Problem of Invention." *Criticism* 5 (1963): 199–213.
———— "Hardy's Sue Bridehead." *Nineteenth Century Fiction* 20 (1966): 307–23.
Helsinger, Elizabeth K. *Ruskin and the Art of the Beholder*. Cambridge: Harvard University Press, 1982.
Herbert, Lucille. "Hardy's Views in *Tess of the d'Urbervilles*." *Journal of English Literary History* 37 (March 1970): 77–94.
Hewison, Robert. *John Ruskin: The Argument of the Eye*. Princeton: Princeton University Press, 1976.
Hirsch, D. E. *The Validity of Interpretation*. New Haven: Yale University Press, 1967.
Holloway, John. *The Victorian Sage*. London: Macmillan, 1953.
Horne, Lewis B. "The Darkening Sun of Tess Durbeyfield." *Texas Studies in Literature and Language* 13 (1971): 299–311.
Howe, Irving. *Thomas Hardy*. New York: Macmillan, 1967.
Hynes, Samuel. *The Pattern of Hardy's Poetry*. Chapel Hill: University of North Carolina Press, 1961.
James, Henry. *The Portrait of a Lady*. New York: Dell, 1961.
———— *The Wings of the Dove*. New York: Dell, 1958.
Jameson, Frederic. *The Prison-House of Language*. Princeton: Princeton University Press, 1972.
Janson, H. W. *History of Art*. New York: Harry N. Abrams, 1974.
Jones, Lawrence O. "Imitation and Expression in Thomas Hardy's Theory of Fiction." *Studies in the Novel* 7 (1975): 507–25.
Karl, Frederick R. "*The Mayor of Casterbridge:* A New Fiction Defined: 1960." *Modern Fiction Studies* 21 (1975): 405–28.
Kiely, Robert. "Vision and Viewpoint in *The Mayor of Casterbridge*." *Nineteenth Century Fiction* 23 (1968): 189–200.

Kline, Morris. *Mathematics: The Loss of Certainty.* Oxford: Oxford University Press, 1980.
Knoepflmacher, U. C., and G. B. Tennyson, eds. *Nature and the Victorian Imagination.* Berkeley: University of California Press, 1977.
Kucich, John. *Repression in Victorian Fiction.* Berkeley: University of California Press, 1987.
Kunitz, Stanley. *The Poems of Stanley Kunitz, 1928–1978.* Boston: Little, Brown, 1979.
LaFrance, Marston, ed. *Patterns of Commitment in Southern Literature.* Toronto: University of Toronto Press, 1967.
Langbaum, Robert. *The Poetry of Experience.* New York: Norton, 1957.
Lawrence, D. H. *Phoenix: The Posthumous Papers of D. H. Lawrence.* New York: Viking, 1963.
Lawson, Louis A., and J. Friedman. *The Added Dimension.* New York: Fordham University Press, 1966.
Leitch, Vincent B. "The Lateral Dance: The Deconstructive Criticism of J. Hillis Miller." *Critical Inquiry* 6 (Summer 1980): 593–607.
Lemon, Lee T., and Marion J. Reis. *Russian Formalist Criticism.* Lincoln: University of Nebraska Press, 1965.
Levine, George. *The Realistic Imagination.* Chicago: University of Chicago Press, 1981.
Lewis, C. Day. *The Poetic Image.* London: Oxford University Press, 1947.
Lodge, David. Introduction to *The Woodlanders,* by Thomas Hardy. New York: St. Martin's, 1977.
——— *The Modes of Modern Writing.* Ithaca: Cornell University Press, 1977.
——— "Thomas Hardy as a Cinematic Novelist." In *Thomas Hardy after Fifty Years,* edited by Lance St. John Butler. London: Macmillan, 1977.
McCarthy, Mary. "Harold Rosenberg: Ideas were the Generative Force of His Life." *New York Times,* 6 May 1979.
McDowell, Frederick P. W. "Hardy's 'Seemings or Personal Impressions'; The Symbolic Use of Image and Content in *Jude the Obscure.*" *Modern Fiction Studies* 6 (Autumn 1960): 233–50.
Macksey, Richard, and Eugenio Donato. *The Structuralist Controversy.* Baltimore: Johns Hopkins University Press, 1970.
Marsden, Kenneth. *The Poems of Thomas Hardy.* University of London: Athlone Press, 1969.
May, Charles. "*Far from the Madding Crowd* and *The Woodlanders:* Hardy's Grotesque Pastorals." *English Literature in Transition* 17 (1974): 147–58.
——— "Thomas Hardy and the Poetry of the Absurd." *Texas Studies in Literature and Language* 12 (1970): 63–73.
May, Derwent. Introduction to *The Return of the Native,* by Thomas Hardy. New York: St. Martin's, 1974.
Meisel, Perry. *The Absent Father: Virginia Woolf and Walter Pater.* New Haven: Yale University Press, 1980.
——— *Thomas Hardy: The Return of the Repressed.* New Haven: Yale University Press, 1972.

Midgal, Seymour. "History and Archetype in *The Mayor of Casterbridge*." *Studies and the Novel* 3 (1971): 284–92.

Miller, J. Hillis. *The Form of Victorian Fiction*. Notre Dame: University of Notre Dame Press, 1968.

——— *Poets of Reality*. Cambridge: Harvard University Press, 1965.

——— "Stevens' Rock and Criticism as Cure." *Georgia Review* 30, no. 1 (Spring 1976): 5–31.

——— "Stevens' Rock and Criticism as Cure, II." *Georgia Review* 30, no. 2 (Summer 1976): 330–48.

——— *Thomas Hardy: Distance and Desire*. Cambridge: Harvard University Press, 1970.

——— "Walter Pater: A Partial Portrait." *Daedalus* 105 (Winter 1976): 97–113.

Millgate, Michael. "Thomas Hardy." In *Victorian Fiction: A Second Guide to Research*, edited by George H. Ford. New York: Modern Language Association of America, 1978.

——— *Thomas Hardy: His Career as a Novelist*. New York: Random House, 1971.

Mitchell, W. J. T., ed. *Critical Inquiry 6: The Language of Images* (Spring 1980).

——— *Critical Inquiry 77: On Narrative* (Autumn 1980).

——— *Iconology: Image, Text, Ideology*. Chicago: University of Chicago Press, 1986.

Morgan, Rosemarie. *Women and Sexuality in the Novels of Thomas Hardy*. New York: Routledge, 1988.

Morrell, Roy. *Thomas Hardy: The Will and the Way*. Oxford: Oxford University Press, 1965.

Narramore, James. *The World Without a Self*. New Haven: Yale University Press, 1973.

Orel, Harold. *Thomas Hardy's Epic Drama: A Study of "The Dynasts."* New York: Greenwood, 1969.

Osborne, L. Mackenzie. "The 'Chronological Frontier' in Thomas Hardy's Novels." *Studies in the Novel* 4 (1972): 543–54.

Page, Norman. "Hardy's Pictorial Art in *The Mayor of Casterbridge*." *Etudes Anglaises* 25 (1972): 486–92.

———, ed. *Thomas Hardy: The Writer and His Background*. London: Bell and Hyman, 1980.

Panofsky, Erwin. *Studies in Iconology*. New York: Harper and Row, 1962.

Pater, Walter. *Essays on Literature and Art*. Totowa, N.J.: Rowman and Littlefield, 1973.

——— *Marius the Epicurean*. New York: Macmillan, 1909.

——— *The Renaissance*. New York: New American Library, 1959.

Paterson, John. The Making of *"The Return of the Native."* Berkeley: University of California Press, 1963.

——— "*The Mayor of Casterbridge* as Tragedy." *Victorian Studies* 3 (December 1959): 151–72.

——— "The 'Poetics' of *The Return of the Native*." *Modern Fiction Studies* 6 (Autumn 1960): 214–22.

Paulin, Tom. *Thomas Hardy: The Poetry of Perception.* London: Macmillan, 1975.
Pearce, Roy Harvey. *The Continuity of American Poetry.* Princeton: Princeton University Press, 1961.
Perkins, David. "Hardy and the Poetry of Isolation." In *Hardy, A Collection of Critical Essays,* edited by Albert J. Guerard. Englewood Cliffs, N.J.: Prentice-Hall, 1963.
Pinion, F. B. *A Hardy Companion: A Guide to the Works of Thomas Hardy and Their Background.* New York: St. Martin's, 1968.
—— Introduction to *Two on a Tower,* by Thomas Hardy. New York: St. Martin's, 1977.
—— *Thomas Hardy: Art and Thought.* London: Macmillan, 1977.
Purdy, Richard Little. *Thomas Hardy: A Bibliographical Study.* New York: Oxford University Press, 1954.
Rewald, John. *The History of Impressionism.* New York: Museum of Modern Art, 1961.
Richards, Mary C. "Thomas Hardy's Ironic Vision." *Nineteenth Century Fiction* 3 (March 1949): 265–79.
—— "Thomas Hardy's Ironic Vision." *Nineteenth Century Fiction* 4 (June 1949): 21–35.
Ricoeur, Paul. "The Metaphorical Process As Cognition, Imagination, and Feeling." *Critical Inquiry* 5 (Autumn 1978): 143–59.
Rorty, Richard. *Philosophy and the Mirror of Nature.* Princeton: Princeton University Press, 1979.
Rosenberg, Harold. *Saul Steinberg.* New York: Alfred A. Knopf in Association with the Whitney Museum of American Art, 1978.
Rosenberg, John D. *The Darkening Glass, A Portrait of Ruskin's Genius.* New York: Columbia University Press, 1961.
Ruskin, John. *The Elements of Drawing.* Vol. 4 of *The Works of John Ruskin.* New York: Merrill and Baker, n.d.
Ryan, Judith. "The Vanishing Subject: Empirical Psychology and the Modern Novel." *PMLA* 95 (October 1980): 857–69.
Sacks, Sheldon, ed. *On Metaphor.* Chicago: University of Chicago Press, 1979.
Schneider, Pierre. "All That Jazz," *New York Review of Books,* 11 April 1985, 28–31.
Scholes, Robert. "Language, Narrative, and Anti–Narrative." *Critical Inquiry* 7 (Autumn 1980): 204–12.
—— *Structuralism in Literature.* New Haven: Yale University Press, 1974.
Scholes, Robert, and Robert Kellogg. *The Nature of Narrative.* New York: Oxford University Press, 1966.
Schweik, Robert C. "Character and Fate in Hardy's *The Mayor of Casterbridge.*" *Nineteenth Century Fiction* 21 (1966): 249–62.
Scott, James E. "Spectacle and Symbol in Thomas Hardy's Fiction." *Philosophical Quarterly* 44 (1965): 527–44.
Smart, Alistair. "Pictorial Images in the Novels of Thomas Hardy." *Review of English Studies* 12 (1961): 262–80.

Smitten, Jeffrey R., and Ann Daghistany, eds. *Spatial Form in Narrative*. Ithaca: Cornell University Press, 1981.

Spiegel, Alan. *Fiction and the Camera Eye*. Charlottesville: University Press of Virginia, 1976.

Stevens, Wallace. *The Necessary Angel*. New York: Random House, 1942.

——— *The Palm at the End of the Mind*. New York: Random House, 1967.

Stewart, J. I. M. *Thomas Hardy: A Critical Biography*. New York: Dodd, Mead, 1971.

Sturrock, John, ed. *Structuralism and Since: From Levi-Strauss to Derrida*. New York: Oxford University Press, 1979.

Tanner, Tony. "Color and Movement in Hardy's *Tess of the d'Urbervilles*," In *Hardy, The Tragic Novels*, edited by R. P. Draper. London: Macmillan, 1975.

Truffaut, François. "François Truffaut's 'The Last Metro.' " *The New York Times*, 8 February 1981, Sec. 2, p. 21, col. 3.

Vande Kieft, Ruth. "Judgment in the Fiction of Flannery O'Connor." *Sewanee Review* 76 (1968): 337–56.

Van Ghent, Dorothy. *The English Novel: Form and Function*. New York: Harper and Brothers, 1953.

Vendler, Helen Hennessy. *On Extended Wings: Wallace Stevens' Longer Poems*. Cambridge: Harvard University Press, 1969.

Vigor, Penelope. *The Novels of Thomas Hardy: Illusion and Reality*. London: Athlone Press, 1974.

Wain, John. Introduction to *The Dynasts*, by Thomas Hardy. New York: St. Martin's, 1979.

Webster, Harvey Curtis. *On a Darkling Plain*. Chicago: University of Chicago Press, 1947.

Weschler, Lawrence. "Art World." *New Yorker*. 9 July 1984, 60–71.

Williams, Raymond. *The Country and the City*. New York: Oxford University Press, 1973.

Wimsatt, W. K. *The Verbal Icon*. Lexington: University of Kentucky Press, 1967.

Winner, Viola Hopkins. *Henry James and the Visual Arts*. Charlottesville: University Press of Virginia, 1970.

Witemeyer, Hugh. *George Eliot and the Visual Arts*. New Haven: Yale University Press, 1979.

Wittenberg, Judith Bryant. "Early Hardy Novels and the Fictional Age." *Novel* 16 (Winter 1983): 151–64.

Woolf, Virginia. *Collected Essays*. Vol. 1. Edited by Leonard Woolf. London: Hogarth Press, 1968.

——— *The Common Reader*. New York: Harcourt, Brace, and World, 1953.

——— *Mrs. Dalloway*. Middlesex, England: Penguin, 1969.

——— "The Novels of Thomas Hardy." In *Collected Essays*. Vol. 1. Edited by Leonard Woolf. London: Hogarth Press, 1968.

——— *To the Lighthouse*. New York: Harcourt, Brace, and World, 1955.

——— *A Writer's Diary*. London: Hogarth Press, 1969.

Wright, Walter F. *The Shaping of "The Dynasts."* Lincoln: University of Nebraska Press, 1967.

Zabel, Morton Dauwen. "Hardy in Defense of His Art: the Aesthetic of Incongruity." In *Hardy, A Collection of Critical Essays,* edited by Albert J. Guerard. Englewood Cliffs, N.J.: Prentice-Hall, 1963.

Zietlow, Paul. *Moments of Vision: The Poetry of Thomas Hardy.* Cambridge: Harvard University Press, 1974.

Index

Absurdist perspective, 6, 117, 121
"After the Journey," 139
"Anecdote of the Jar" (Stevens), 61
Arnheim, Rudolf, 30, 73, 104, 133, 147
Art, allusions to, 6–7, 42–43, 68–70, 80–81, 136–39
"At a Lunar Eclipse," 28, 137
"At a Watering-Place," 29
"At the Wicket-Gate," 102
"At Waking," 51–52, 117–18, 120

Bayley, John, 176, 184
Beckett, Samuel, 161
Beer, Gillian, 172–76
Benvenuto, Richard, 170
Between the Acts (Woolf), 40, 41
Blythe, Ronald, 135, 136
"Broken Appointment, The," 139
Brooks, Jean, 117
Brown, Douglas, 15
Buckler, William E., 12–13, 172

Christ, Carol T., 42
Cinematic method in literature, 6, 29, 31, 99, 138
Clifford, Emma, 101, 126, 142, 158–59
Closed endings, 112–15
Coleridge, Samuel Taylor, 35
Comi-tragedy or tragi-comedy, 117
"Commonplace Day, A," 121, 137

Contradictions, 26, 94, 110, 116, 177, 188–91
"Convergence of the Twain, The," 99, 120–21, 139

"Darkling Thrush, The," 100
Darwin, Charles, 172
Davie, Donald, 103, 147, 158
Dean, Susan, 125–26
Deconstructive criticism, 8–9, 93
DeLaura, David, 6, 183–84
Desperate Remedies, 14, 31
Dickens, Charles, 49
Disrupted images, 14–15, 90, 91–132
"Doom and She," 99
"Dream Is—Which?, The," 101–2
"During Wind and Rain," 189–91
Dynasts, The, 13, 96, 122–32, 138, 150, 173

Eagleton, Terry, 183
Eliot, T. S., 119
Empiricism, 13, 41–42, 43, 56, 94, 106, 112–15, 177, 188–89
Endings, 96, 112–15
Expressionism, 5–6, 14, 134–40, 152

Far from the Madding Crowd, 15, 16, 25, 36–37, 44–46, 55, 59, 63, 65–66, 69, 71, 73, 74, 79, 80–88, 89–90, 101, 108,

Far from the Madding Crowd (*Continued*) 114, 118, 119, 129, 134–35, 141, 144, 145, 177, 186
Fatalism, 96–97, 101, 159, 160–62
Fayen, George, 50
Fernando, Lloyd, 70–71
"Figure in the Scene, The," 61
Figures, large and startling, 115–23
Finer Optic, The (Christ), 42
Fischler, Alexander, 126
Framed images, 13–14, 55–90; disruptions of, 91–132
Furbank, P. N., 43, 92–93, 102

Genre formation, 96, 108–15
Gilbert, Sandra, 93–94
"God-Forgotten, The," 99
Gombrich, E. H., 30–31
Great Web, The (Gregor), 79–80
Gregor, Ian, 11, 79–80, 89, 176
Grotesque style, 96, 115–23, 134, 144
Grundy, Joan, 70–71, 80, 135, 158
Gubar, Susan, 93–94
Guerard, Albert, 6, 34, 106, 116

"Hap," 99
Hardwick, Elizabeth, 162, 169, 175
"Hardy and the Figure in the Scene" (Peck), 139
"Hardy's Anonymous Sincerity" (Pritchard), 139
Harries, Karsten, 43
Helsinger, Elizabeth K., 23–24
Heroines, destruction of, 88
Hockney, David, 104–5
Holloway, John, 15, 16, 159
Hynes, Samuel, 110, 116

"Idea of Order at Key West, The" (Stevens), 12
Images: disrupted, 14–15, 90, 91–132; framed, 55–90; as icons, 21–54; metamorphosis of, 157–87; relationships within, 133–53; visual structure and subjective vision conveyed by, 3–18
"In Church," 29, 65
"In Tenebris II," 95
"In the Cemetery," 29
Irony, 110, 122, 162

"January Night, A," 121
Jones, Lawrence O., 47
Jude the Obscure, 10, 28, 38–39, 41, 67, 69, 73, 97, 106, 120, 143–44, 145–46, 157, 158, 162, 165, 166–77, 178, 179, 186, 191

Keats, John, 53
Kiely, Robert, 10, 48, 61
Kinkead-Weekes, Mark, 105
"Kubla Kahn" (Coleridge), 35

Landscape, 56–63, 134, 147–53
Laodicean, A, 66–67
"Last Week in October," 101
Late Lyrics and Earlier, 95
Lawrence, D. H., 174, 175
Levine, George, 38, 94, 112, 116
Lewis, C. D., 43
Life of Thomas Hardy, 3, 4, 5, 7, 9–10, 11, 12, 17–18, 26, 32–34, 36, 43, 61, 63, 71, 86, 94, 107, 117, 130–31, 136, 137, 138
"Light Snow-Fall after Frost, A," 150
Lodge, David, 16, 29, 57, 66, 99
Love, theme of, 52–53, 175

Madwoman in the Attic, The (Gilbert and Gubar), 93–94
Marius the Epicurian: His Sensations and Ideas (Pater), 41, 106
Matisse, Henri, 136, 137
Mayor of Casterbridge, The, 10, 25, 28, 37, 48, 63, 67, 68, 69, 71–72, 74, 96, 98, 109–11, 114, 119–20, 141
Meisel, Perry, 168
Metaphors, 12, 13, 43–46, 51, 88–89
Migdal, Seymour, 110
Miller, J. Hillis, 8–9, 10, 16, 46–47, 49, 52, 53, 81, 159
Modern Painters I (Ruskin), 23
"Moments of Visions," 65
Mrs. Dalloway (Woolf), 39–40, 41–42

Narrative structure, 34, 43, 95
Narrative voice, 13, 27, 29, 40, 47–48; disruptive elements signified in, 96–108
Nature, 15, 59–63

"Nature's Questioning," 100–101
"Near Lanivet, 1872," 140
"Neutral Tones," 25–26, 59, 121, 137–38
"New Year's Eve," 99
Non-rationality, 4, 23, 117

O'Connor, Flannery, 117
Odeipus the King (Sophocles), 109, 161–62
Omniscient narrator, 47–48, 97–99, 100, 106–8
"On the Departure Platform," 52–53, 191
Opposition, 188–91
"Outside the Window," 29, 65

Page, Norman, 29, 98
Paintings, allusions to, 6–7 24, 42–43, 68–70, 80–81, 136–39
Pair of Blue Eyes, A, 58–59, 135–36
Panofsky, Erwin, 21–23, 91
Pastoral tradition, 15–16, 108
Pater, Walter, 39, 41–42, 106
Paterson, John, 109
Paulin, Tom, 189
"Pedigree, The," 9, 64–65
Pessimism, 6, 96–97, 101, 108, 126–27
"Phantom Horsewoman, The," 61–62, 131, 164, 165
Picasso, Pablo, 138
Place, 56–63, 134, 147–53, 158
"Place on the Map, The," 88–89
Plot resolution, 96, 112–15
"Poems of 1912–13," 139, 147–49
Poetic structuring, 32, 34–38, 95, 107
Point of view, 14, 17, 80. *See also* Narrative voice
Positivism, 189
Pound, Ezra, 36
Print, 140–47
Pritchard, William, 139
"Profitable Reading of Fiction, The," 35, 130

Rationality, antagonism toward, 4, 23, 117
Realism, 11, 34, 94, 95–96, 107–8, 115–16, 130
Realistic Imagination, The (Levine), 38, 94
"Re-Enactment, The," 121

Reflections on the Word 'Image' (Furbank), 43
Relativism, 106–7
Rembrandt, 69, 76
Renaissance, The (Pater), 41
Return of the Native, The, 26–27, 44, 50, 57–58, 60, 62, 63, 65, 69, 74, 75–79, 97, 108, 112–15, 151, 159, 175, 184, 188–89
Ricoeur, Paul, 44
Roads, 157, 158–63
Rosenberg, Harold, 10
Rural setting, 15, 59–63
Ruskin, John, 7, 23, 136

Satires of Circumstance in Fifteen Glimpses, 28–29, 120
"Science of Fiction, The," 35, 130
Seeing, 3–18, 73, 104–5, 110; vocabulary of, 24–31
Smart, Alistair, 66, 70
Social commentary, 134, 140–47
Spiegel, Alan, 31
Spying, 28–29, 64–68, 69, 81, 82
Steinberg, Saul, 10
Stevens, Wallace, 12, 53, 61
Stewart, J. I. M., 165
Storyteller, Hardy as, 32–38, 107
Studies in Iconology: Humanistic Themes in the Art of the Renaissance (Panofsky), 21
Subjectivity, 30, 71, 73, 90, 117, 149, 152; and visual structures, 3–18
Swigg, Richard, 102

Tanner, Tony, 7–8, 10, 16, 17, 49, 138–39, 158, 159–60
Tess of the d'Urbervilles, 7–8, 9, 10, 15–16, 24–25, 26, 28, 36, 37, 51, 59–60, 63, 64, 66, 69, 72, 74–75, 96, 97, 98, 116, 118–19, 141–43, 145, 157, 159–61, 165, 177–86, 191
Thomas Hardy (Guerard), 6
"Thomas Hardy's Rhetoric of Painting" (Fernando), 70–71
Thomas Hardy: The Poetry of Perception (Paulin), 189
Topography, 134, 147–53, 158
To the Lighthouse (Woolf), 40, 41
Tragedy, 109–11, 117

Tragi-comedy or comi-tragedy, 117
"Trampwoman's Tragedy, The," 103–4. 147, 165

Under the Greenwood Tree, 15, 71
"Under the Waterfall," 163–164

Van Ghent, Dorothy, 16, 159
Visual Thinking (Arnheim), 30
"Voice, The," 139, 164–65
Voyeurism, 28–29, 64–68, 69, 81–82

Watching, 28–29, 64–68, 69, 81, 82
Waves, The (Woolf), 40, 42

"Wessex Heights," 25, 121, 149–50
"When I set out for Lyonnesse," 123–24, 131
"Why Did I Sketch," 61
Will, 13, 46–54, 73, 79, 87, 124, 128, 162
Wimsatt, W. K., 21
Women's literature, 93–94
Woodlanders, The, 15, 16, 29, 50, 56–57, 58, 63, 64, 66, 69–70, 96, 98, 108–9
Woolf, Virginia, 31–32, 34–35, 39–41, 42, 106, 147, 170

Zabel, Morton, 5–6

About the Author

SHEILA BERGER teaches in the Department of English at the State University of New York at Albany, where she is also Director of the Master of Arts in Liberal Studies program. She holds a Ph.D. from New York University.

OHIO UNIVERSITY LIBRARY

Please return this book as soon as you have finished with it. In order to avoid a fine it must be returned by the latest date stamped below.

QUARTER LOAN

MAR 30 1992

MAR 30 1992

FEB 08 1991